= 2023 ANNUAL =

FourFourTwo

Welcome to the **FourFourTwo Annual**, packed full of the best features, interviews and exclusives from the world's greatest football magazine's past 12 months. We kick things off by reliving the incredible highs of England Women's glorious victory at Euro 2022 and look at how the win can be a platform for even more progress in the women's game. We also celebrate some of world football's deadliest marksmen, bringing you exclusive interviews with Erling Haaland, Harry Kane and Alessandro Del Piero, as well as fascinating profiles of South American superstars Gabriel Jesus and Darwin Nunez. We go back in time to discover Dynamo Kyiv's turbulent past, how Aston Villa upset German giants Bayern Munich to become European champions and relive Bobby Robson's time at Barça. We also delve into the world of football agents and look at what life is like for many players after their football days are over and how they're being supported. But that's only scratching the surface – we speak to England's 1966 World Cup hero Geoff Hurst, look back at the career of flawed genius Zinedine Zidane, celebrate 30 years of football's most loved video game, and much more. Enjoy!

= 2023 ANNUAL =
FourFourTwo

Future PLC Quay House, The Ambury, Bath, BA1 1UA

Bookazine Editor **Dan Peel**
Bookazine Designer **Thomas Parrett**
Editor **James Andrew**
Art Director **Anthony Moore**
Chief Sub Editor **Gregg Davies**
Staff Writer **Mark White**
Editor at Large **Andy Mitten**
Deputy Editor **Matthew Ketchell**
Senior Staff Writer **Chris Flanagan**
Staff Writer **Ed McCambridge**
Online Editor **Conor Pope**
Senior Art Editor **Andy Downes**
Head of Art & Design **Greg Whitaker**
Editorial Director **Jon White**

Cover images
Getty Images, Alamy

Photography
All copyrights and trademarks are recognised and respected

Advertising
Media packs are available on request
Commercial Director **Clare Dove**

International
Head of Print Licensing **Rachel Shaw**
licensing@futurenet.com
www.futurecontenthub.com

Circulation
Head of Newstrade **Tim Mathers**

Production
Head of Production **Mark Constance**
Production Project Manager **Matthew Eglinton**
Advertising Production Manager **Joanne Crosby**
Digital Editions Controller **Jason Hudson**
Production Managers **Keely Miller, Nola Cokely,
Vivienne Calvert, Fran Twentyman**

Printed in the UK

Distributed by Marketforce, 5 Churchill Place, Canary Wharf, London, E14 5HU
www.marketforce.co.uk Tel: 0203 787 9001

FourFourTwo Annual 2023 Volume 5 (SBZ4919)
© 2022 Future Publishing Limited

FUTURE
Connectors.
Creators.
Experience
Makers.

Future plc is a public company quoted on the London Stock Exchange (symbol: FUTR)
www.futureplc.com

Chief executive **Zillah Byng-Thorne**
Non-executive chairman **Richard Huntingford**
Chief financial officer **Penny Ladkin-Brand**

Tel +44 (0)1225 442 244

Part of the
FourFourTwo
bookazine series

Widely
Recycled

For press freedom
with responsibility

28

CONT

92

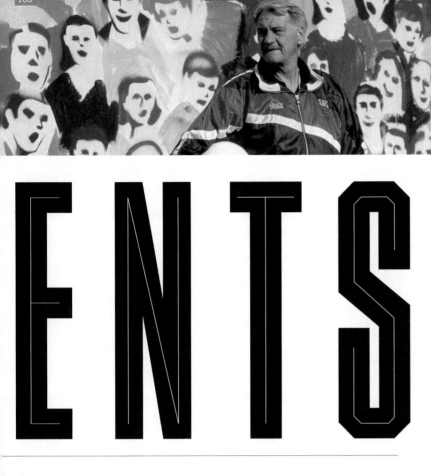

ENTS

46

138

Images All Getty Images except, Alamy (p40), PA (p126), Shutterstock (p138), Nick Eagle (p28)

100

86

56

40

ENGLAND 202[2]

HOW THE LIONESSES MADE HISTORY

England Women lifted their first major trophy at Euro 2022, beating Germany at a joyful Wembley – 31-cap Lionesses midfielder Izzy Christiansen covered the epic competition for BBC Radio 5 Live and talks *FFT* through an inspirational summer…

GROUP A
ENGLAND 1 AUSTRIA 0

"When the tournament got underway, you could sense that something special was in the air. There were 68,000 fans at Old Trafford – it felt like a Manchester United matchday, with the quantity of people around the city before kick-off, wearing shirts and singing. Something big was about to happen.

The match itself was very tense – the crowd were waiting for a goal. When it finally came, it was beautifully crafted by Fran Kirby, who was magnificent that night, and finished by Beth Mead. It lit up the whole stadium – the way fans celebrated was really special, and it started to capture the imagination of people around the country. It was a great way to start the tournament."

GROUP A
ENGLAND 8 NORWAY 0

"The team had received a bit of flak in the media after the opening match – I think a lot of people were slightly disappointed we'd only beaten Austria by a single goal, and said we weren't clinical enough. Well, what better way to answer that than by smacking eight past two-time Euros winners Norway, who we thought would be the toughest opponent in the group?

With respect, Norway were nowhere near where people thought they'd be at this tournament, in terms of their performance levels, but the squad was still filled with top players who turn out for teams in the best divisions around the world. Credit to England for taking them to pieces. They were ruthless."

GROUP A
ENGLAND 5
NORTHERN IRELAND 0

"It was a nothing game, as England had booked their place in the quarter-finals and Northern Ireland were out. But with the mentality of the Lionesses, there was never going to be any let up, given the attention to detail that the coaching staff have become known for. They wanted to win this one in style to keep the momentum.

Alessia Russo was sensational at this tournament. Like a lit match, she burst into life when she scored her first goal of this game. That was a decent finish, but her second... wow. The control on the spin, then the composure to slot it away. She's phenomenal. World class."

QUARTER-FINAL
ENGLAND 2 SPAIN 1

"I could talk for hours about this game. The level of quality from both sides and the level of entertainment was out of this stratosphere. England's ability to just stay in the game was inspirational – they were being passed off the park, and it's demoralising when you don't have the ball for long periods, but they dug in there and held on.

England were 1-0 down, on the rack, but Georgia Stanway took the game by the scruff of the neck. To score from 25 yards like she did was amazing – on the run, in that context, against a top team and goalkeeper. The crowd responded to that moment – the euphoria was palpable. That was the moment people started to believe it might be our year."

"ENGLAND DUG IN AND HELD ON – THAT WAS THE MOMENT PEOPLE STARTED TO BELIEVE IT MIGHT JUST BE OUR YEAR"

SEMI-FINAL
ENGLAND 4 SWEDEN 0

"Sweden had been tipped as favourites for the Euros, and they had a chance in the opening minute when Mary Earps made a great save. If that had gone in the game could have been so different, but England went 1-0 up through Mead and it was like somebody had a needle and popped Sweden's balloon. They had no response, and the Lionesses were better than them in every single department after that.

Russo's backheel to make it 3-0 was just another ridiculous finish – one of the best goals of the tournament. The audacity, the guts to go for that... then the technique to actually pull it off. It was a wonderful goal to complement a fierce performance from England."

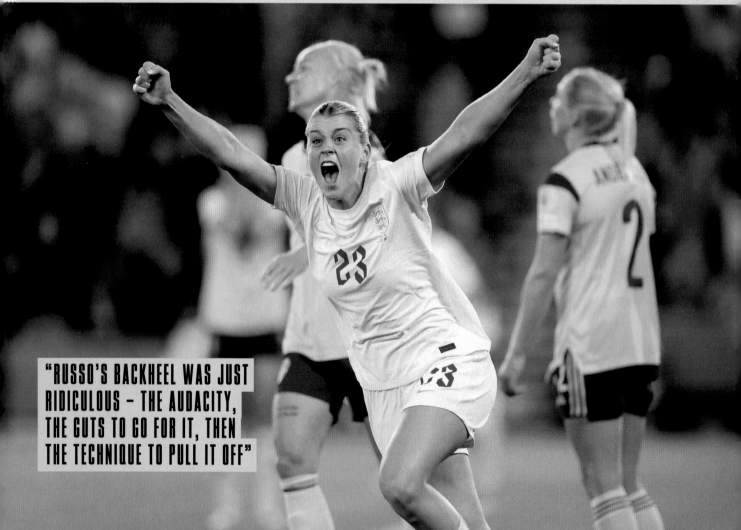

"RUSSO'S BACKHEEL WAS JUST RIDICULOUS – THE AUDACITY, THE GUTS TO GO FOR IT, THEN THE TECHNIQUE TO PULL IT OFF"

FINAL
ENGLAND 2 GERMANY 1

"The way I described this game is like it was a bird sitting on a branch. The bird was perched there, and it could have gone either way – either falling off and tumbling down, or starting to fly. There were times when England had to cling on while Germany threw everything at them, but Keira Walsh's composure to thread an unbelievable pass through to Ella Toone, then Ella's ability to lift the ball over the keeper on the run to make it 1-0... that was jaw-dropping – a goal worthy of winning any tournament.

The Germans' never-say-die attitude produced a wonderful equaliser, and you could sense the tide swinging the other way. That bird was back on the branch, but Chloe Kelly had come on and she was like a woman possessed, scrapping for every ball, trying to whip the crowd up whenever it went out for a throw or corner. She meant business, and no one deserved that winning goal more. It won't go down as her favourite in terms of craft, but it'll be the best she'll ever score because it won the Euros for England. She was an injury doubt ahead of the tournament, but she fought back.

The celebrations afterwards still give me goosebumps now – I'd never seen anything like it. I can't even begin to describe how amazing the atmosphere inside Wembley was. The DJ deserves a medal... what a set! It was the most incredible climax to the competition. The Lionesses didn't just win through skill but through sheer resilience, belief and hard work."

Izzy Christiansen will provide regular punditry as part of BBC Radio 5 Live's Premier League coverage this season

UEFA WOMEN'S EURO 2022

"THIS REALLY FELT LIKE A BREAKTHROUGH. LET'S BUILD ON THAT LEGACY"

Jacqui Oatley has been reporting on the women's game since England hosted the Euros in 2005 – after the elation of this summer, she hopes the Lionesses' triumph can be a platform for even more progress

A single moment can alter everything – it can change perceptions, break new frontiers and attract a whole new generation of fans. Alessia Russo's semi-final backheel against Sweden was that kind of moment.

I watched that incredible goal with my daughter, and suddenly had the feeling of being in a car dropping over the crest of a hill. My stomach turned over. I just thought, 'Wow, something special is happening here'. Nobody mentioned 'women's football' when

> "ENGLAND BROUGHT FOOTBALL HOME. NOW IT'S UP TO US TO KEEP THE LEGACY BURNING"

that goal went in – it was just football. The barriers were down.

Euro 2022 provided a whole summer of extraordinary moments like that. England supporters had the privilege of seeing the Lionesses lift the trophy on July 31, but fans from every nation were treated to a tournament of high-quality displays, intense competition and scintillating action. With Wembley packed to the rafters for the final, and a reported 17 million people watching on television across the country, it was clear that people of all ages, genders and backgrounds were proud to call this England team theirs.

To be totally honest, I've always felt that women's football would get to this stage some day. Don't get me wrong, there have been plenty of times when I've seen just how far behind the game has lagged, and how it's been derided for not being good enough. But it was

obvious to me that perceptions would eventually change once players turned professional, as many are now. That's not to say women weren't talented in the past, but how could they have been expected to maximise their potential while holding down jobs on the side?

This summer, more so than ever before, women have dazzled. We saw talents like Lauren Hemp, just 22 years old, flourishing on the biggest stage after honing her craft on the training pitch at Manchester City. People who might normally criticise the technique, quality or goalkeeping have been impressed – from Beth Mead's lethal finishing to Mary Earps' rock-solid stops. Euro 2022 has felt like a genuine breakthrough. But then, we've been here before...

After we hosted the tournament in 2005, reached the final in 2009 and packed stadiums for women's games throughout London's 2012 Olympics, organisers spoke of turning a corner – of legacies being laid and the women's game becoming a force. Each of those occasions proved to be false dawns, as attendances for women's matches dropped once the buzz wore off. That must be avoided now.

There are many ways we can do this. Pressure has to be put on the FA to encourage girls across the country to play football, whether that's kicking a ball around in the playground at school, or signing up for local teams. The Women's Super League needs to start yelling from the rooftops, letting people know where and when their fixtures are taking place, and how to buy tickets. Players, too, have to use their growing platforms to champion the sport they love and encourage the next generation.

Meanwhile, clubs themselves must start funding their women's teams properly – as many in America's NWSL have done for decades. The types of facilities offered to men's teams here in the UK need to be provided to the women as well. Clubs like Arsenal have been doing that for a long time. Others, huge sides included, still don't do anywhere near enough.

I pray that parents use this massive opportunity to take their children to women's games, whether in the WSL or lower down. Not only will they see that standards are higher than ever, but they'll also find that tickets are far cheaper than men's matches, and the atmospheres are inevitably safer and more child-friendly than at Premier League grounds.

Everyone needs to play their part to ensure this wonderful summer isn't wasted. Sarina Wiegman's Lionesses brought football home. Now it's up to all of us to keep that legacy burning. ◌

JESUS WILL S

AVE YOU NOW

Dropping out of the top four, not helped by their No.9 curse, Arsenal needed a redeemer. Their new Brazilian forward has offered some divine inspiration

Words Andrew Murray

Mikel Arteta stood before his morose squad and let them have it. Four days after a 3-0 defeat at Spurs had gifted Champions League football to their north London rivals, Arsenal had just lost 2-0 to Newcastle, duly wrapping their present to Tottenham and adding a neat little bow.

"They were 10,000 times better than us in everything!" spat Arteta in that St James' Park dressing room on May 16. "We didn't earn the right to play; we didn't win a f**king duel, or a second ball. We were f**king *horrible* with the ball."

Heading to face the TV cameras, Arteta knew something had to change. "Today," he went on, "it's hard to defend you guys. Hard."

What the Spaniard wanted was a winner; someone with a single-minded spark to add intensity and fight to a team that, despite improving, had capitulated when it mattered most. Arteta wanted Gabriel Jesus. The same Gabriel Jesus who had just posted the worst all-competitions goals return of his five full Manchester City seasons? Well, yes... and no.

Desperate to beat Chelsea and Spurs to Jesus' signature, Arteta dispatched director of football Edu, who'd known the 25-year-old since his mid-teens. "Gabriel, I'm here to try to sign you," Edu told his fellow Brazilian. "But not the Gabriel from this season – the Gabriel from years ago. This year, you haven't played the way I know you. You've lost your shine."

Jesus looked at his compatriot and nodded. "You're right."

Gabriel Jesus and Edu are from opposite sides of Sao Paulo's footballing tracks. Whereas the latter is from a middle-class Portuguese-Italian family that emigrated from Europe, Jesus is a child of the street ▶

who grew up in the Jardim Peri favela, honing his craft on the city's dustbowl amateur pitches before graduating from the academy of boyhood club Palmeiras. He was 15 years old when he first came to Edu's attention, and the former Arsenal midfielder was immediately struck by the youngster's determination to succeed.

Jesus' career began in prison. When he was eight, his first club, Pequeninos do Meio Ambiente, played on a scrap of poorly maintained land just inside the grounds of Romao Gomes jail. He would turn out for Pequeninos every Saturday and Sunday morning, then jump in a neighbour's car to be driven with childhood friends Higor and Fabio (both now part of his entourage) to Uniao do Peri, another amateur club he would play for in the afternoons.

Showing a go-getting attitude he'd learned from his mother, Vera Lucia, who worked three jobs to make ends meet, a 13-year-old Jesus wanted better for himself and asked the family's matriarch to find him a new club. "I can't help with that," she said. "You know I work night and day. You have to chase it."

Vera Lucia's son did just that. Jesus joined Anhanguera, a local semi-pro outfit with better facilities and links with Palmeiras. Two years later, the young forward signed for the club he supported. Not for the first time, his dogged desire to succeed had triumphed.

Breaking goalscoring records for Palmeiras' age-group teams put Jesus on Edu's radar (the pair would link up again in the Brazilian national team, where Edu was the general manager). After making his Palmeiras debut aged 17, Jesus helped to transform a listing club – who'd recently had to bounce back up from Serie B, amid one of the worst periods in their history – into a side that had won the domestic title and Copa do Brasil by the time he departed for English shores in January 2017. Palmeiras fans adored him.

Tim Stillman, an Arsenal supporter who writes for fan site *Arseblog* and specialises in Brazilian football, tells *FFT*: "It's so hard to predict how talented kids will adapt, because there are so many variables, but occasionally you see someone and immediately think, 'Yeah, he's going to make it'. Gabriel Jesus is one of those. I've been following him since his debut. I knew he'd be playing for a big European club by the end of his teen years, absolutely smashing it."

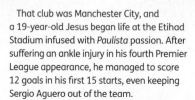

Above Jesus answered the call from north London **Below** Poor Lucas Perez was one of the Gunners' less illustrious No.9s

That club was Manchester City, and a 19-year-old Jesus began life at the Etihad Stadium infused with *Paulista* passion. After suffering an ankle injury in his fourth Premier League appearance, he managed to score 12 goals in his first 15 starts, even keeping Sergio Aguero out of the team.

Yet Jesus' progress stalled. Despite City's record-breaking goal returns, the Brazilian never scored more than 14 in a single league campaign, and last term he averaged barely one shot on target per 90 minutes as Pep Guardiola increasingly preferred a false nine with Jesus stuck out on the right wing. Even after he plundered four goals in City's 5-1 demolition of Watford in April, Jesus seemed destined for an exit, as Guardiola admitted: "Maybe he decides, 'I want more minutes, I want to leave'."

This summer, Arsenal used their Samba connections to snaffle Jesus for a bargain at £45 million. What the Gunners lacked in Champions League football, they made up for in a project to promise – and, in Edu and Arteta, two people Jesus trusted. Sure, he'd won eight major honours with Manchester City – four of them under the guidance of Guardiola's then-assistant, Arteta – but Jesus wanted to be much more than a squad player, even if it meant leaving perhaps the finest team in the history of English football.

"Guardiola has been extremely generous in selling two top-class players, in Jesus and Oleksandr Zinchenko, to a Premier League rival," former Arsenal frontman Alan Smith tells *FFT*. "Arsenal may not be a title rival but Jesus can still score two against City later in the season. The relationship with Arteta has really benefited Arsenal. His modus operandi is to have hungry players, and Jesus certainly seems to have that hunger."

Arsenal's director of football was no less important. "Edu's chat was vital in getting the Jesus deal over the line," says Stillman. "Having two people who Gabi knows well and trusts, at a critical stage of his career... well, if Arsenal couldn't get that deal done, they should pack up and go home.

"There was untapped value in Gabi Jesus, because he was very good at City but he had been 'Pepped', as one of six good attackers who played far from every game. Someone *needed* to buy this kid, put him up front and make him the main man. Club and player bumped into each other at the perfect time."

Jesus instantly flourished at Arsenal. Busy enough in the opening-day beating of Crystal Palace, he then scored twice and added two assists in a 4-2 defeat of Leicester, playing as a roving No.9. Against the Foxes he had 15 touches in the penalty area, the most by any

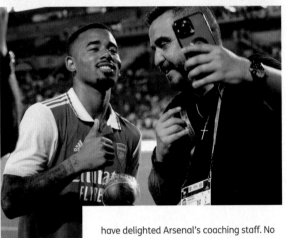

"HE DIDN'T FEEL LOVED AT CITY AND IF HE HAS ONE WEAKNESS, IT'S THAT HE IS TOO SENSITIVE"

Ramsdale. "He fights for every ball. A 50-50, even a 70-30: he'll turn it in his favour. He's so happy, but he's got a nasty streak. He has to win. That's feeding into our team now."

Jesus' mentality shift has had such an effect on the squad that Arteta has already made him a vice-captain. "We have a new confidence – a spark – and that winning mentality that he has," reasoned the Spanish tactician. "He's still young, but experienced, and he's a really good role model for the other boys. He's so mobile, so intuitive, and always sharp and proactive in any moment or phase in the game."

It all sounds very like Thierry Henry. It's perhaps a *little* early to compare him to Arsenal's all-time leading goalscorer, but Jesus is another distressed asset for Arsenal to mould and polish. Henry, Dennis Bergkamp and Patrick Vieira all became Gunners greats but each arrived after struggling in Italy.

"I think of them as broken eggs," explains Stillman. "That's always what Arsenal at their best have had to do. Aubameyang and Lacazette weren't that: they came with big reputations and wouldn't be moulded. If you bring Aubameyang to your club, he's going to do Aubameyang things. He's not going to do anything else."

A successful former Arsenal No.9 himself, Smith is ecstatic that his somewhat cursed old shirt – later worn by such Premier League luminaries as Lucas Perez, Julio Baptista and Park Chu-young – has a vibrant new home. "He has a point to prove; it brings pressure and responsibility, but he's thriving on it," says Smith. "My old No.9 has been a funny one: a few players have had it who haven't been that type of player, like Lukas Podolski and maybe Eduardo, but it's nice to see someone given it who wants to embrace that role and be the focal point in the box when the ball comes in."

Jesus' predatory instincts and willingness to sacrifice himself for the team have quickly resonated among the Arsenal fanbase.

"I don't think he ever felt loved at City and if there's one weakness with him, it's that he is too sensitive," says *Arseblog*'s Stillman. "One of the reasons he used to miss lots of chances, particularly at City with Aguero in front of him, was the pressure of having to score, thinking: 'Even if I score four, I might not play next week'. He needs to feel the love.

"With Brazil, the mistake Jesus made was trying to engage with 200 million people who decided he was a failure because he didn't score at the World Cup. He tried to explain his position to a non-receptive audience. The connection between Arsenal and the fans keeps growing. He'll keep feeling the love."

Return Arsenal to the Champions League for the first time in seven years and he'll feel even more affection. "The target has to be top four and winning a trophy, getting that consistency over the course of a season," says Smith. "When you arrive at a club, the first thing you want to do is win over the fans, and Arsenal have a totally different optimism now. Everyone loves to be loved, don't they?"

A love that could change destinies – Jesus and Arsenal are a match made in heaven. ◦

Gunners player in the past seven seasons, while his heatmap resembled a seven-year-old's particularly chaotic fever dream, darting in myriad directions. Alexandre Lacazette's heatmap in the same fixture last season was basically a straight line through the middle of the pitch.

A week later, Jesus bullied Bournemouth centre-back Marcos Senesi into submission before sashaying through the Cherries' defence to lay on Martin Odegaard's opener in a 3-0 win. "It displayed everything you want in a centre-forward: that strength, that touch and the ability to beat a man, but also knowing when to release the ball," Smith tells *FFT*. "It was such a fantastic passage of play – you'd go a long way this season before you see a better few seconds from a centre-forward in terms of his hold-up play, chance creation and intelligence.

"His enthusiasm, movement, pace and appetite to prove himself as a genuine No.9

Top Arteta wonders if Pep should stick this guy up front
Above left Several years down the line, Mikel got his man
Above Jesus quickly became a popular figure at Arsenal

have delighted Arsenal's coaching staff. No disrespect to Lacazette or [Pierre-Emerick] Aubameyang, but he gives more."

Stillman believes the Gunners now have the multi-functional player they've often lacked. "Jesus adds a fluidity of movement to a front line that already has [Bukayo] Saka, [Gabriel] Martinelli and [Emile] Smith Rowe," he says. "You can already see just how much better Martinelli looks alongside that type of striker. I always thought it'd transform how Arsenal play, but this is like walking somewhere and suddenly someone gives you roller-skates."

Playing through the middle was essential. After the 2018 World Cup, when he started as Brazil's No.9 instead of Roberto Firmino to create space for Neymar's self-indulgence on the left, Jesus doubted whether a central berth was right for him. But the Selecao's proliferation of widemen forced a rethink. Now he feels ready to try again.

"After the World Cup, I thought I couldn't play as a No.9," he said recently. "I started to play on the wing more at City and for Brazil. I thought that for a while, but now I believe in myself much more. I'm smiling again when I'm playing football. I'm very blessed, as I can play across the front three, but I'm a No.9 – I'm there to finish our chances."

Is he ever. Jesus may excel all over the pitch but he comes alive in the box – each of his first 60 Premier League goals were scored from inside it. "He's ruthless and he knows what it's like to win – you see it every day in training," revealed Gunners keeper Aaron

THEY'RE OUT OF THE WOODS NOW

Nottingham Forest's 23-year ordeal began with their star man on strike before finally ending in ecstasy this summer. Now, as they prepare for a return to the big time, *FFT* charts two decades of agony with those who endured it. Aaaaand breathe...

Words Chris Flanagan

Wes Morgan had a stunned look on his face – and he wasn't the only one. Kris Commons, Jack Lester and James Perch; David Johnson, the father of Brennan; Gareth Taylor, staring at the floor and wishing it would swallow him up.

Nottingham Forest had just lost 3-0 at Yeovil in 2005, keeping them mid-table in League One. Now, two fans were stood before them in the tiny dressing room at Huish Park, berating them for their display. Gary Megson, Forest's manager, was stood to one side, letting them get on with it. It was he who'd invited them into the dressing room in the first place. Nothing else he'd attempted was working. This was a desperate last resort, from the Phil Brown school of desperate last resorts; a play to get a response – *any* kind of response – from his players.

Instead, they seemed more bewildered than ever. "They just looked shell-shocked, like, 'Who is this and why are they speaking to us?'," says Jon Enever, the supporter who did most of the talking in the dressing room that afternoon. "Danny Cullip stood up to say something back, but my mate was about 6ft 5in and told him, 'Sit down and show some respect, he's speaking'. Cullip sat back down – they just didn't know what to do. Wes Morgan was sat to my right. I could sense he was thinking, 'It's come to *this*...'"

Months earlier, Forest had become the first former European champions ever to suffer relegation to the third tier. The glory days of Brian Clough had long gone. That season, they'd go out of the FA Cup 3-0 to Chester, lose to Macclesfield in the League Cup, and get dumped from the LDV Vans by Woking.

Having dropped out of the Premier League in 1999, Forest were destined to spend 23 distressing years outside the top flight. Each of David Platt, Joe Kinnear, Billy Davies, Steve McClaren, Alex McLeish, Stuart Pearce, Aitor Karanka, Martin O'Neill and Chris Hughton came and went, among others. Amid chaos on and off the field, none of them could take the club back to the big time. But then came Steve Cooper – and everything changed...

"CHANGE ALL THE MANAGERS FOR CATS"

Every person who becomes Forest boss is stepping into the shoes of *the* man who'd gone before – the man who managed them between 1975 and 1993, serving up one league title, two European Cups and a host of appearances in domestic finals.

"Under Clough, we had success without spending loads," long-serving ex-goalkeeper Mark Crossley tells *FFT*. "I made my debut in 1988 and we were regularly in the top six – eighth was classed as a mediocre season. We went to Wembley for the FA Cup final, three League Cup finals, the Simod Cup, the Zenith Data Systems Cup, even the Mercantile bloody Credit Classic or whatever that thing was called (the Football League's centenary tournament). But when the Premier League

"PIERRE HAD HIS REASONS BUT PLAYERS DIDN'T AGREE. THERE WAS ANGER WITHIN THE SQUAD"

started and the big money arrived, we began to lose some of our better players."

Forest went down in the Premier League's inaugural campaign – Clough's final season – but bounced straight back, finishing third upon their return in 1994-95. It's still a joint-Premier League record for a promoted club, matching what Kevin Keegan's Newcastle had done a year earlier.

Within two years, though, Stan Collymore had been sold to Liverpool and Forest were relegated again. Another immediate return owed much to the 29 goals of Pierre van Hooijdonk, but the Dutchman's relationship with boss Dave Bassett was uneasy.

"We were doing f**k all in training," Van Hooijdonk later shrugged to *FFT*, refusing to give Bassett credit. "People say we became champions, but so what? If you changed all the managers in the league for cats, at the end of the season there will still be one champion and three will get relegated. Does that mean the cat who is champion is fantastic and the three who got relegated are s**t? It's about players as well."

That summer, Forest were weakened by the departures of Kevin Campbell and Colin Cooper, prompting a miffed Van Hooijdonk to go on strike – he claimed the club had reneged on an agreement to let him leave as well. Without him, the team took only nine points from their opening 11 matches. "Pierre had his reasons but I didn't agree with it," says Crossley, part of the squad for

Clockwise from above The great green jumper gets one final airing in '93; Van Hooijdonk was adored before he turned his back on Forest; "Just run me through the cats thing one more time?"

a decade by then. "The players didn't agree that they were strong enough reasons to go on strike – he was by far our best player, our hope, our top goalscorer, and when a team loses that, there was anger. He came back three months later but it was a bit late."

When Van Hooijdonk scored against rivals Derby in his second game back, most of his team-mates chose not to celebrate with him. Forest never escaped the drop zone for the rest of the season. Ron Atkinson replaced Bassett in January but accidentally sat in the away dugout before his first game against Arsenal, only realising his mistake once he noticed the Gunners' subs alongside him.

"I loved Ron, especially when he did that," chuckles Crossley. "He came into the dressing room afterwards and said, 'I couldn't believe we were getting relegated when I had so many good players sat around me on the bench'. That summed him up as a character, but we were too far adrift for him to save us."

Three weeks later, Manchester United won 8-1 at the City Ground – Ole Gunnar Solskjaer came on as a sub with 19 minutes to go and scored four. Relegation was confirmed with three games left, and Atkinson retired at the end of the season. Forest finished bottom.

"I still thought we'd bounce straight back again," says Crossley. "At the least, I'd have expected the club to get back within three years – I didn't expect 23. But David Platt came in, it was his first managerial role in England, he signed some Italians and it just didn't work."

Gianluca Petrachi, Salvatore Matrecano and Moreno Mannini were all unable to help Forest launch a promotion bid, in what was Platt's one and only job as a club manager in England – he'd previously had an ill-fated six-match spell in charge of Sampdoria. Ian Wright and a teenage John Terry joined on loan, but Forest finished 14th, then 11th;

Platt departed, and was replaced by youth coach Paul Hart.

Debts mounted without Premier League football, worsened by the collapse of ITV Digital's deal. Forest's wage bill was slashed and the entire squad were put up for sale – Jermaine Jenas was among those who moved on – although Hart improbably lifted them into the play-offs a year later, where they lost to Sheffield United.

Repeating the feat proved impossible – Forest dropped into the relegation zone in 2003-04, and Hart was sacked. Joe Kinnear moved them away from danger, but the club faced threats of winding-up proceedings from the city council and plunged back into relegation trouble the next season. Kinnear resigned after a grim 3-0 loss at Derby, then Michael Dawson and Andy Reid were sold to Spurs in January. A young Morgan took on extra responsibility under new boss Megson, but a 6-0 hammering at Ipswich preceded their inevitable drop into League One.

"Forest going down from the Championship did seem unthinkable, but when you look at the chain of events it was on the cards," says Thomas Newton, from *1865: The Nottingham Forest Podcast*. "Kinnear had got the place going again, but he thought that we'd spend money – he said we were going to get Dennis Bergkamp and it was never going to happen. We knew we were going down by December. We couldn't score and we couldn't defend.

"Then Megson came in – he'd been at the club in the '80s but never played a game, because Clough said he couldn't trap a bag

Below Platt had no appetite to try again after his dodgy stint

of cement. It was a match made in hell – how he wanted to play football was against everything our supporters had been brought up on under Clough."

GLOVERS TIFF

If being a gigantic fish in a small pond provided hope of a turnaround in League One, it didn't turn out that way. As well as that League Cup defeat to fourth-tier Macclesfield, Forest lost five of their first seven league games – the first three losses to Walsall, Swindon and Scunthorpe – as relationships strained between Megson and some of his squad. Defeat at Southend and their LDV Vans Trophy reverse to Woking followed, during a period when Conference teams were allowed to take part in it. Four days later came the trip to Yeovil.

"There was a novelty factor in League One, the opportunity to visit new grounds, but it quickly wore off," recalls Enever, who ventured south to Huish Park with a friend, having followed the club since 1980 when Forest were European Cup holders. "Teams raised their game for us – when we played Yeovil, it was massive for them because they'd come out of non-league and were playing the former European champions.

"Forest sold out for every away game in League One, so we could only get tickets in the main stand. In the first half, we were awful – I don't know whether some players thought the game was beneath them, but the whole performance was inept. Gareth

Taylor got sent off and we were 2-0 down – when we walked back to our seats for the start of the second half, because of how small the ground was, I ended up right next to Gary Megson, face to face.

"Without thinking, I said to him, 'That was awful – we've lost every challenge, they've outfought us, the whole ground can see it'. He said, 'That's not dissimilar to what I've just said to them. Come and tell them at full-time – with five minutes left, the two of you come and sit with me in the dugout'.

"I didn't think it would actually happen but we went to the front, the stewards stopped us and Megson said, 'No, no, they're with me'. Afterwards, we waited outside the changing room while he spoke to the players – nerves were kicking in, thinking, 'What are we going to say?' He just told us, 'My only plea is don't personalise whatever you say – a changing room is a volatile environment, I need to be careful how I manage this'.

"Then we went in and he said, 'Right, these two have travelled a long way, and they want to have a word'. The dressing room was tiny. We were standing, they were sitting, and I said, 'Look, all we ever want to see is you giving 100 per cent. People have paid money to come to watch you, and to be frank, you lost all of the first 15 challenges in the game – there doesn't look to be the commitment we'd expect'. They looked startled. My friend said a bit, then that was it.

"Megson showed us out and said, 'You were really articulate, I'm grateful for you doing that – just please don't disclose any of this ▶

to the press'. We didn't, but by Monday it was everywhere – it was talkSPORT's main story, Sky were ringing up, even magazines from Australia. Gary Megson's PA called and said that he wanted to speak to me – I said, 'I promise you, I haven't spoken to anyone'. He said, 'No, no – we had a chat on Sunday and decided to leak it, to get a reaction from the players this week'.

"It's just bizarre when you look back on it all. They won the next match at home to Bradford but Megson got sacked that season – I think the relationship between him and the players was just broken."

Drawing 1-1 at home to Weymouth in the FA Cup First Round did him no favours, before Forest fell 3-0 at Chester in the second. "They were better than us – it was embarrassing," says podcaster Newton. Megson's last game was a 3-0 loss at Oldham in February which left Forest 13th in the table. They immediately went 10 matches unbeaten under caretaker duo Frank Barlow and Ian McParland – 10 days after Megson's departure, they smashed Swindon 7-1 at home.

Promotion appeared to be on the horizon a season later when Forest's former stopper Colin Calderwood guided them seven points clear at the top by November, but then they slipped to fourth and catastrophically lost to old foes Yeovil in the play-off semis – Forest even won 2-0 at Huish Park, before crashing to a 5-2 defeat at the City Ground.

Thankfully, it was third time lucky – the East Midlands outfit went up automatically in 2008, climbing into second on the final day with victory at home to – yep, Yeovil, their Glovers demons finally banished. With a maturing Morgan in defence, Forest kept 24 clean sheets.

Below "Oi, ball boy – fancy taking over training this week?"; Forest's play-off woe became too familiar

"YOU CAN'T SACK HIM, IT'S CHRISTMAS…"

Two years later, Billy Davies had replaced Calderwood and Forest were on the verge of a return to the Premier League – they'd finished third in the Championship table, in a campaign where they bludgeoned local rivals Leicester 5-1.

All looked promising until Blackpool beat them in the play-off semi-finals, en route to promotion. Another play-off semi defeat followed a year later, this time to Brendan Rodgers' Swansea, who were also bound for the Premier League.

At that point, Davies' uneasy relationship with chairman Nigel Doughty cracked after a dispute with Forest's transfer acquisitions committee, containing ex-Spurs chief David Pleat. Davies was ousted for Steve McClaren, recently an Eredivisie winner with FC Twente – but the former England boss lasted just 10 league games before resigning after a home defeat to Birmingham, where fans protested about a perceived lack of funding. Doughty stepped down as chairman, then died of a heart attack months later.

Fawaz Al Hasawi was president of Kuwaiti champions Qadsia SC, and bought the club from Doughty's estate in July 2012.

"Al Hasawi turned up to massive fanfare – when you get bought by someone from the Middle East, you think he's going to plough loads of money in," says Newton. "It started OK in terms of spending, but he was out of his depth. He meant well, his heart was in the right place, but he was very naive. He might have been fine in Kuwait where the scrutiny's not as high, but he didn't have a clue how to run an English football club."

A couple of months before the takeover, Gary Brazil had joined as a youth coach. He's stayed ever since, becoming academy boss in 2014 and experiencing three spells as first-team caretaker. Asked what the club was like in that first year, his response is a chuckle as he searches for a diplomatic answer. "Not like it is now," he tells *FFT*. "There was room for improvement. There was always a big desire to reach the Premier League – it wasn't for the want of putting money in. It was finding a way to get there."

Patience wasn't one of Al Hasawi's strong points: straight after the takeover, incumbent Steve Cotterill had his summer targets green-lit by the new regime, only to be sacked a day later – then asked if he could still compile a report on the playing squad anyway. His replacement Sean O'Driscoll lasted just five months – dismissed after a win over Leeds on December 26, with reports that Al Hasawi had to be talked out of delivering the news on Christmas Day. Next, Alex McLeish left by mutual consent in early February, after one win from seven and a failed deadline-day move for George Boyd – Forest bizarrely pulled out citing an "inconclusive eye test".

Billy Davies was brought back, but a string of key figures left the club and a number of journalists were banned. "He came back and said he'd got unfinished business, but Billy could have argued with his own shadow – he had a blackout with the media and it was

AFTER COTTERILL GOT SACKED, AL HASAWI STILL ASKED HIM TO COMPILE A REPORT ON FOREST'S SQUAD

just incredibly strange," continues Newton. "The club turned into North Korea."

On the final day of the campaign, Davies unusually opted to hold his post-match press conference before the actual game.

Aided by Al Hasawi's investment, Forest were challenging for the play-offs in their next season, but a six-match winless streak was followed by a 5-0 defeat at Derby, and outspoken Billy got the boot for a second time. A divided dressing room – partly due to the arrival of big earners – had to be pulled back together by Gary Brazil.

"It was a privilege to be the caretaker, but that was toughest of the three spells – the changing room wasn't in a good place," he admits. "It was trying to pick senior players up. I gave the team one game, we lost, then I shook the squad around a bit, just trying to create a more positive environment – players who really wanted to have a go."

Club legend Stuart Pearce rocked up that summer, but even Psycho got sacked seven months later with Forest again in mid-table, after Jamaal Lascelles and Karl Darlow had been flogged without his knowledge. Dougie Freedman was next in, lasting a whole year despite almost impossible conditions, with wage delays beginning to materialise.

"He couldn't spend anything because we had an embargo for breaking Financial Fair Play rules, but Freedman brought in good players," says Newton. "We thought that something was wrong, though – at press conferences he looked shattered. Fawaz would summon him to a meeting in London at 11pm because it's their culture [in Kuwait], then he'd have to drive back to Nottingham and take training the next morning."

Inevitably fired after a poor run, Freedman received a phone call from Al Hasawi a week later, asking if he could provide some advice on possible recruits. "You've just sacked me," the Scot replied incredulously.

The City Ground's capacity was briefly reduced to zero by the council, amid issues over a safety certificate, then former Real Sociedad boss Philippe Montanier got the chop after seven months in January 2017, with the club battling relegation and star signing Nicklas Bendtner proving ineffective – his most notable contribution had been an own goal against Derby.

Discontent towards Al Hasawi had grown sizeably, with a Supporters' Trust launched and demonstration held. "We marched from the city centre to the City Ground, and had a protest in the car park," says Newton, one of the Trust's founders. "There was concern that the club might go bust, because money was being spent but there was no return on the field, and crowds were dwindling. There were only 17,000 at matches – people were fed up with false promises and we made Watford look patient with managers.

"We wanted the Trust to be a critical friend and it's still there – it's been good because it made Fawaz realise the fans didn't want him. He fell on his sword."

JUST LIKE WATCHING BRAZIL

Al Hasawi began talks with Olympiacos chief Evangelos Marinakis over a deal to sell the club – but first, Forest had to avoid another slide into League One. Brazil was installed as caretaker again, adding Robert Page to his ▶

Below Pearce wasn't the only Forest great to suffer in charge

FALLEN KINGS

Forest became the first ex-European champions to drop into the third tier – but others have suffered after glory

MILAN
The Rossoneri were twice European Cup champions when they were demoted for match-fixing in 1980, despite coming third. They returned to Serie A within a year, then got relegated again (this time for being rubbish), then won Serie B again – aided by goals from Joe Jordan.

MANCHESTER UNITED
Six years after tasting European Cup glory in 1968, United went down but bounced back at their first try, winning the Second Division title under Tommy Docherty. The Red Devils' average crowd in 1974-75 (47,781) was still the highest in the land.

MARSEILLE
L'OM were Ligue 1 runners-up in 1994 but demoted after scandalous revelations of match-fixing from the previous season came to light – a year where they'd lifted the Champions League trophy. Marseille swiftly won the second tier title and even got to keep their place in the UEFA Cup.

ASTON VILLA
The Villans bagged the European Cup in 1982 – five years later, they were rock bottom of the First Division but returned to the top tier at the first attempt. It took the Midlanders three seasons to recover after another drop in 2016 – they finished as low as 13th in the Championship.

JUVENTUS
Yet more scandal – the Old Lady, twice continental kings, were ready for another crack at European glory in 2006, only to be stripped of their Serie A title and also relegated for their role in *Calciopoli*. They won Serie B ahead of fellow giants Napoli.

HAMBURG
The 1983 European Cup conquerors had never been relegated before succumbing in 2018 – four years later they're still in the second tier, having lost a play-off this May to a Hertha Berlin side led by former Rothosen gaffer Felix Magath. *Scheisse.*

coaching staff before being made interim manager for the season.

That was until early March, when a defeat at Burton led to Brazil stepping down again. Mark Warburton arrived as permanent boss. "They decided that they wanted Mark long term, which was right – it was never one for me," says Brazil. "Fortunately, we managed to stay in the league – it was tight and went to the last game at home to Ipswich. That match was massive – Jordan Smith made an outstanding save at 0-0, and if we hadn't scored the first goal, we'd have been in some real trouble. Going down would have been a tough situation for the club."

Eleven days after victory confirmed safety on goal difference, Marinakis took over to end a reign that had seen the club's league position decline in each of Al Hasawi's five seasons: 8th, 11th, 14th, 16th, then 21st.

Their new Greek owner didn't get off to the most amazing start, either: Warburton was gone by the end of December, replaced by Aitor Karanka, as Forest finished 17th. During the managerial transition, however, caretaker Brazil led Forest to victory over Arsenal in the FA Cup Third Round, in front of 27,000 at the City Ground. "We started with five lads from the academy – I remember telling them this

COOPER'S SWANSEA OVERHAULED FOREST FOR A PLAY-OFF SPOT IN 2020, WITH A FIVE-GOAL SWING

was the type of occasion the club should be involved in every week," explains Brazil.

Forest returned to the top half of the Championship in 2018-19, but it still wasn't enough to prevent Karanka from quitting in January – nor former European Cup winner Martin O'Neill being jettisoned in June after a ninth-place finish. Sabri Lamouchi was announced as his replacement exactly 18 minutes later, and seemed to be guiding the Reds back to the play-offs in 2020 – Forest looked nailed on to make the top six with just 24 minutes of the season left, when Swansea needed a five-goal swing to overhaul them. Typically, Steve Cooper's Swans notched three late on at Reading; Forest leaked three at home to Stoke. Four matches into their next campaign, the East Midlanders had lost all four. Lamouchi was given the elbow.

Above "Aww, c'mere you..."

In 2021-22, another poor start looked set to ruin their season again – Chris Hughton was fired after one point from seven games, with the club rooted to the foot of the table.

"I went to a couple of those games at the start, because I'm a supporter as well, and I thought that team was getting relegated," says Mark Crossley. "Let's be honest: it was a club going nowhere."

Absolutely nothing that had happened over the past decade suggested Forest were about to return to the Premier League. "We'd waited 18 months to get back into a stadium after COVID, but the atmosphere was toxic," admits Newton. "We played Bournemouth first up – they had 10 men but we were so defensive and lost. Then Hughton got sacked after losing to Middlesbrough. We were bad."

Last summer, though, Forest hired a new chief executive from Barnsley, Dane Murphy – aged only 35 – after the Tykes had made the top six. His first key decision was to bring in Cooper, who'd left Swansea shortly after beating Barnsley in the play-off semis. He was Forest's 20th managerial appointment since relegation in 1999 – but under the guidance of a man who had previously led England to Under-17 World Cup triumph, the team were immediately transformed.

QUE SERA, SERA...

The play-off final was Forest's first trip to Wembley since 1992 – now only eight of the 92 await a visit to the rebuilt stadium

Team	Last Wembley fixture
Ipswich	2000
Newcastle	2000
Colchester	1998
Bournemouth	1998
Blackburn	1992
Accrington	Never
Crawley	Never
Hartlepool	Never

"EVEN BETTER THAN GUARDIOLA"

Forest fell agonisingly short in their unlikely bid for automatic promotion, losing against Bournemouth in their penultimate fixture, but Brice Samba's penalty shootout heroics delivered them a play-off semi-final victory over Sheffield United, before Huddersfield were defeated at Wembley.

"For the second leg of the semi-final, I was with my son, sat with the Forest fans," says Crossley. "Seeing all the penalty saves was the best £27 I've ever spent! I couldn't go to Wembley for the play-off final because I had a charity function I'd planned six months earlier, but I kept nipping out to watch it. I was the only person jumping up and down in Doncaster! Promotion was a miracle."

In London, plenty more were jumping with him. Having played at Wembley seven times between 1988 and 1992, this was Forest's first visit for 30 years.

"My first ever game was Brian Clough's last home game, in 1993," says Newton. "I'd never seen Forest play at Wembley – the season we bombed out of the Premier League was my last year at primary school, and now I'm 34. We've had 23 years of torture, but when that final whistle blew against Huddersfield, people had tears in their eyes for everything we've endured. Relegations. False promises. To be in the promised land after 23 years... I'm welling up even now. It was so emotional.

"Steve Cooper instilled so much belief in the players, and he just gets it. He's been a match made in heaven. Some of our other managers couldn't be doing with the history of the club, but he embraced it – the old European Cup team meet up once a week, and he goes with them for a coffee. Pound for pound, he was the best boss in England last season, even better than Pep Guardiola. I haven't known a manager to be loved this much since Clough."

For Gary Brazil, seeing his former academy graduates help Forest back to the top flight gave him even more reasons to smile, in a campaign when the club also reached the FA Youth Cup final. Brennan Johnson, Joe Worrall and Ryan Yates all started the play-off final at Wembley, with Alex Mighten on the bench – the club have also raised £57m in recent years for a host of other former youth team stars, among them Matty Cash and Ben Brereton. "It's like preparing your own children for university," he says. "I was chuffed to bits for them at Wembley – I got down to the pitch afterwards. Just to see the boys you've watched from under-nines – now Joe Worrall was leading the first team back to the Premier League.

"When Jack Lester was coaching with us, I remember an under-18s game when he stood in the changing room and told the players that they'd have the opportunity to put this club back into the Premier League one day. After the play-off final, I spoke to Jack and said, 'You were right, mate'.

"It's up to those players to prove they can play there now, but the FA Cup games against Premier League opposition showed that they could handle it. They won't go in with fear. They'll be thinking, 'I can play in this league'."

When Forest travelled to Newcastle for their opening game on August 6, they were going for four successive Premier League wins – curiously, they won the last three games of their relegation season in 1999. They lost 2-0, but just the occasion itself was reason to celebrate.

Seventeen years after walking into the dressing room at Huish Park, at the lowest point of Forest's history, Jon Enever is looking forward to the season immensely. Now a successful businessman who had a spell helping out as a director at neighbours Notts County, he's even got to know one of the Reds players he berated in 2005 – the dad of current star Brennan Johnson. "I'm mates with David Johnson now – I played football against him not that long after the Yeovil game and he broke two of my ribs," chuckles Enever. "He didn't do it on purpose – we laughed about it afterwards and he said, 'You asked for that in the changing room!'"

For the first time in decades, watching Forest has transported this lifelong fan back to childhood and the legendary Clough era.

"The last season has just been the stuff of dreams," he says. "It hasn't only been the results, it's the way that the team plays. The atmosphere has felt like what it used to feel like. You're excited to watch them again."

If he'd been invited into the dressing room after the full-time whistle at Wembley, what would Enever have said this time?

"Well done, and thank you," he says with a smile. This time, they're the only words he would have needed. ⊙

"There'd been a number of false dawns, but the atmosphere at the training ground took such a positive tone – Steve changed the feel around the place," reveals Brazil. "It's been as settled as I've ever known the first-team environment – not just the 11 who play on a Saturday, but everyone. You can get boys who aren't in the team with a bottom lip, but that hasn't been the case because of how Steve deals with players. He talks to people, he engages with the person ahead of the footballer – he really gets to know them all. It sounds obvious but he does it very well. He makes really good tactical decisions, too."

With exactly the same squad, Cooper lost only one of his first 15 league games, coaxing outstanding performances from Brennan Johnson, Djed Spence and many more. Centre-back Steve Cook arrived in January after being frozen out at rivals Bournemouth, as Forest matched their attractive football with defensive resilience: following Cooper's arrival on September 21, they conceded just 28 goals in 38 games and collected 76 points – a higher tally than champions Fulham. Arsenal were defeated again in the FA Cup, then Leicester larruped 4-1 in the next round.

"WAZZA SAID THAT ONE DAY I'D BREAK HIS RECORD – AND I'VE STILL GOT MANY MORE YEARS IN ME"

International defenders, beware: Harry Kane
is going nowhere for quite some time yet.
Spurs' talisman is on the verge of breaking
Wayne Rooney's England goals record – and
happily prepared to make life hard for anyone
who attempts to topple him, as he tells *FFT*...

Words Chris Flanagan **Portraits** Nick Eagle

Sometimes, the simplest of things can trigger a childhood memory. For Harry Kane on this midweek afternoon, it's just a single red stripe. The 28-year-old is standing in front of *FourFourTwo*, surveying the collection of retro England shirts we've brought along for today's photoshoot, when one particular jersey leaps out to him. "That one," he says, instantly linking it with a moment he's never forgotten. "From when we beat Germany 5-1."

Back then, Kane was an impressionable young pupil at Larkswood Primary Academy in Chingford, when he perched in front of the television one September evening and witnessed a match that inspired him for years to come. "It was an incredible game," he says. "What was that, 2001? I was eight years old and you just remember something that stands out like that. Michael Owen's hat-trick, Steven Gerrard's goal, Emile Heskey with the other one. Just amazing."

As he watched England's victory unfold, that wide-eyed eight-year-old had no idea what future lay ahead of him. A World Cup Golden Boot, a famous moment of his own against Germany at Euro 2020, and already more goals for England than Owen scored in the whole of his distinguished career. At the time of our interview, Kane sat on 49 goals from just 69 games for the Three Lions – it's a matter of when, not if, he matches Wayne Rooney's record of 53 goals. It's not impossible it could even happen in the next few weeks.

If you'd told Kane all of that back in 2001, his mind would have been blown. "Back then I wouldn't have even thought about it!" he laughs, admitting that reality has already gone far beyond that young boy's wildest dreams. "It's really special to be on 49 England goals. It's been an amazing journey so far."

HERE IN 79 SECONDS

For Kane, that England journey has been amazing from the very start – since a goal with his first touch for the Three Lions, at that. Some take years to bag for their country; Kane needed seconds. Looking back, it was a pretty obvious sign that he was destined for greatness.

There's a smile on the striker's face as he thinks back to that senior debut against Lithuania in March 2015 – so rapidly has he galloped towards the England goalscoring record since then that it doesn't even seem that long ago. "Yeah, I know," he chuckles. "Every season goes by so quickly, we play so many games – we pretty much play or train for 49 weeks of the year, one after the other, so you don't really get time to process it all."

As we chat today at TOCA Social, inside London's O2 complex, he gets a brief moment just to sit and reflect on that special evening in his career. "An amazing day, an amazing game," he says. "I had all of my family there – my brother, mum and dad, my wife. I had extended family there as well – everyone was just so excited to see if I'd play, if I'd get on and make my debut. Thankfully, I did."

Oh, he certainly did. England were 3-0 up in a Euro 2016 qualifier at Wembley when Roy Hodgson summoned Spurs' new sensation, already buoyed by 29 goals in a breakthrough campaign at club level. Fittingly, he came on for Rooney, the nation's established striking star making way for his successor. The memory of it all is still vivid for Kane.

"I was waiting to come on – it felt like I was waiting there for about 10 minutes, the ball wouldn't go out of play!" he laughs. "I was there for three or four minutes, then I finally came on for Wazza and got an amazing reception – the fans gave me a great cheer. Then it was just about 'can I score? Can I help the team?'"

Within two minutes, the answers were yes and yes, as Kane took up the perfect position to nod home a back-post header – the goalkeeper got his hands on the ball but wasn't quite able to scramble it out of the net. Again, fittingly, the left-wing cross came from Raheem Sterling – the first glimpse of what has since been hailed as one of the most potent double acts in England history.

"To score a goal in 79 seconds, I think the number was, it was just everything I'd dreamed of," he says. "Playing for England at Wembley, scoring on your debut, it all just came true in that moment. I still remember it so clearly, that ball going over the line, sneaking in there at the back post."

"That's definitely in my top three most special moments – to score, to have all my family there... it just couldn't have gone any better. It will always be a great achievement in my career, because it's not easy to play for your country. It really kick-started things and settled me into international football."

Although Kane hasn't quite been able to sustain that prodigious strike rate of a goal every 79 seconds – he'd have found the net 4,061 times by now if he had – he's never looked back from a debut moment that proved to everyone, not least himself, that he was capable of transferring his burgeoning club form to the international stage.

He's shone with incredible consistency ever since – consistency that makes it easy to forget that even after his first goal against Lithuania, there were still a considerable number of people across England who pondered whether he might be a one-season wonder.

His phenomenal emergence at Tottenham had been such a surprise – from a series of fairly unremarkable loan spells with Leyton Orient, Millwall, Leicester and Norwich, to one of the most lethal goalscorers in the Premier League – that some questioned if he could possibly maintain it. Opposition supporters even chanted 'one-season wonder' at him during club games. Knowing what we know now, that memory seems almost absurd.

"I know, yeah..." laughs Kane, revealing how he used those chants to push him on to greater success. "I mean, fans are fans, you can see the rivalries between clubs, and people try to sing songs and say what they like. But in a way, you take it as a compliment. They're chanting about you because you're probably one of the top players on the other ▶

Right and below
Making his debut;
then making an
immediate impact

"IF I'VE SCORED 49 IN
MY FIRST SEVEN YEARS,
THEN WHY CAN'T I DO
SIMILAR IN THE NEXT
SIX OR SEVEN YEARS?"

Shirt 1990 England
home shirt supplied by
Classic Football Shirts

team, so you use it as a bit of motivation. If they're singing about you, you must be doing something right for your team. I was fully focused early in my career. I was someone who wanted to be consistent over many, many years."

With more than 300 goals to his name for club and country now, it's probably fair to say that he's made his point to the one-season wonder brigade. "Yeah, for sure, absolutely," he chuckles. "And I'm only 28 now – I've still got loads of time to keep improving, so that's what I'll try to do."

That he wasn't a teenage superstar, having had to wait until he was 21 for his breakthrough season, Kane developed a work ethic that was required to claw his way to the top – the kind he's never relinquished and has been key to his consistency. "I think so," he admits. "When you're playing week in, week out, sometimes people forget the journey

"I REMEMBER WATCHING WORLD CUPS, GOING MENTAL. KNOWING I GAVE THAT FEELING BACK TO PEOPLE GIVES ME GOOSEBUMPS"

Top to bottom
Captain Kane lines up against Scotland; last-minute joy to topple Tunisia; Harry's header to see off the Germans sends Wembley nuts

you've been on. It wasn't a straightforward journey for me: I had to go on loan, I had to be patient, I had to wait for my opportunity.

"I've always been someone who's studied every moment in training, every game, to try to get better, and that's helped to get me to where I am today. I know what I was like trying to take someone else's spot when I was young, and I know there are young players who will be looking at me to try to do the same. So I have to make sure I'm not letting my foot off the gas, to play for England for as long as possible."

"I GOT A BIT EMOTIONAL"

Within a couple of years of making his England debut, not only was Kane a regular in the line-up, he was also the captain. Aged just 23, the forward was handed his armband by Gareth Southgate for the first time when England travelled to Hampden Park to face Scotland in World Cup qualifying.

"To lead the boys out for the first time was a proud moment – and to score in the last minute was nice, too..." he smiles, after such an understatement. England had trailed 2-1 to a pair of Leigh Griffiths free-kicks, about to lose to their neighbours for the first time since 1999, when the Three Lions' new skipper popped up at the far post to volley home in the 93rd minute, silencing Hampden.

Up until then, Kane had registered five goals in 17 appearances for England – a relatively modest tally by his standards. His first major

tournament had ended in disappointment at Euro 2016, meanwhile, when he was unable to find the net. After being handed the captaincy – albeit initially on a rotational basis with Jordan Henderson – he hit 14 goals in 10 appearances, a glut that continued all the way into the World Cup itself.

He still regards the opening game of the tournament, against Tunisia in Volgograd, as another of his top three career highlights. Having been surprisingly asked to take corner-kicks at Euro 2016, this time he was lurking in the six-yard box, making the most of his predatory instincts to score from two of them; the latter gave the Three Lions a dramatic victory in stoppage time.

"I loved that game," he tells *FFT*, thinking back. "The World Cup is so special and it was such a big game. To score in a World Cup at all was incredible, but to get the winner in the 91st minute... I still remember watching it down the pub and going mental when we scored – it gives me goosebumps knowing that I gave everybody that feeling back."

In the very next game came a hat-trick in a 6-1 win over Panama – only the third time an England player had scored a treble in a World Cup match, after Gary Lineker against Poland in 1986 and some chap called Geoff Hurst in a little-talked-about fixture against West Germany in 1966. A penalty followed against Colombia in the last 16, to leave Kane on six goals from just three appearances, having been rested for the final group game against Belgium. Already, he'd done enough to secure the World Cup Golden Boot, joining an illustrious list of names from throughout history including Ronaldo, Gerd Muller, Eusebio and

DO ONE, RON

At 28 years and 10 months old, Kane's age at the time of our interview, even CR7 couldn't match his international goal tally

50	49	47	46	27	22
LIONEL MESSI	HARRY KANE	CRISTIANO RONALDO	ROBERT LEWANDOWSKI	KARIM BENZEMA	ZLATAN IBRAHIMOVIC

Lineker himself, England's only previous winner of the award. "When you think of the players who've played in World Cups, and the players who were playing in that World Cup in 2018, to get the Golden Boot in my first was incredible," he reflects. "It holds a special place in my heart." Not least because it helped England to reach a first World Cup semi-final since 1990.

If the 2018 World Cup delivered many memorable moments for the Three Lions, Euro 2020 produced even more of them. The striker was coming under increasing scrutiny midway through last summer – such is his outstanding strike rate for club and country, all it took was three games without a goal in the group stage for a nation to start asking, 'What's up with Harry Kane?'

The answer was nothing. Nothing at all. No one should have been surprised when he sprang into life with four goals in the next three matches, hauling England into a first final since '66, and ending up one behind top scorers Cristiano Ronaldo and Patrik Schick.

It's the victory over Germany in the last 16 that he describes as the other top-three moment from his England career so far, given the scenes around Wembley when his header sealed the win. "There was a lot of pressure on that match, a lot of anticipation – being at home and playing against a very good Germany side," he explains. "To come through that and score, to show that we're here and we can do it in the big tournaments against the big teams, that was a very special moment. Anyone who was at the game or watched it on TV will know. The crowd were going crazy, and *Sweet Caroline* after the game... it gave me goosebumps.

"It's emotional thinking about the game even now – I remember getting a bit emotional in the interview afterwards, just hearing the fans singing. It was a tough time for the world, for our country after COVID, and to see everyone out there enjoying it was amazing. When the second goal went in... even when the first one went in, you just saw bodies flying all over the place all around the stadium, everyone going absolutely nuts.

"Then you see the videos afterwards of people in the pubs, people on the streets. Just knowing that you're bringing the country together is a really special feeling. Major tournaments do that. Whenever you're at one, you have that opportunity."

Eight days after that Germany joy, Kane was stood at the opposite end of Wembley, taking the biggest kick of his life. In the first half of extra time against Denmark, England won a penalty to put them on the brink of a historic major tournament final. Up stepped their star striker – no pressure, Harry...

"Obviously I'm someone who takes penalties a lot, and I practise them a lot," he reveals. "So when I get a penalty, of course it's nerve-wracking, but once I put the ball down, I go into my routine. I do the same thing every game, every time I have a penalty, so I go into my own zone. It was a tough game, it was extra time, so the body was tired and I didn't hit it how I wanted to. That sometimes happens."

As the ball moved towards the bottom corner of the goal, so too did goalkeeper Kasper Schmeichel. Did he experience a split-second feeling of horror, as he realised Schmeichel was going to save it? "I don't think there was enough time!" he chuckles. "It all happens ▶

so quickly – as soon as you look up and he's saved it, the reaction was a striker's one. You're always looking for the rebounds, or to score from deflections. To see it bounce back out to me was a nice feeling – it just fell to me and I was able to tuck it home. Those are the fine margins in football. That one went my way."

THERE'S A MUSEUM FOR THAT

After scoring the goal that steered England to a first final in 55 years, Kane converted his spot-kick rather more emphatically in the shootout against Italy, only for things to go awry for Southgate's side.

It's left him hungry for more when the World Cup comes around again, this winter. "Getting to a semi-final, getting to a final – we want to win, that's the ultimate goal," he insists. "We need to try to use the momentum we're building and see if we can do something special this year."

If Kane were to lift the World Cup as England captain in December, it would be a fitting moment for a player who has already achieved so much individually. Those achievements are being marked in a new exhibition dedicated to Kane at the Museum Of London, which began on May 21 and runs until December. A wide range of his memorabilia is on display, including shirts, awards and his MBE, which he received in 2019, not long after his role in England's run to the World Cup semis.

"WE WANT TO WIN, THAT'S THE ULTIMATE GOAL. WE NEED TO USE THE MOMENTUM WE'VE BUILT AND TRY TO DO SOMETHING SPECIAL"

Today as we chat at the O2, hundreds of schoolchildren have been milling around, ready for a Young Voices concert in the main arena. It's the next generation that Kane hopes to inspire with his exhibition.

"The museum wanted a Londoner to encourage boys and girls, and it's a fantastic way of doing that by having all my memorabilia there – my trophies, my Golden Boots," he says. "It's a place where people can go and see what I've achieved, and the hard work and dedication it took along the way. It wasn't just straight to the top, I went on loan first, and it will have all of that there in the museum.

"There's my MBE, too: that's one that I kind of... I don't forget about it, but because it's not football-related you almost do. Receiving an MBE? You never dream about stuff like that. You dream about scoring, about being a captain, but to get that was a real surprise at the time. I went down to the palace with my wife and family, and we shared that moment – just nice recognition for bringing the country together, which is what we did after the World Cup.

"I've got three children now and I think it's important to inspire the younger generation, to help them understand what it might take to be a footballer – the ups and downs."

Kane is well aware that his position as England's captain and star striker makes him a role model for others – something he's always taken very seriously. If his approach to the game has long earned him respect on the field, he's also become more vocal regarding off-field matters in recent times – speaking out for equality, both over the issue of taking the knee, and also when team-mates have been the victims of racial abuse during matches.

During a pandemic that hit lower-league teams hard, he also helped out his first loan club Leyton Orient with an unusual sponsorship deal; Kane donated money and arranged for a range of good causes to be emblazoned across the east London outfit's shirt, including the NHS, the Mind mental health charity, the Tommy Club for war veterans and the Haven House children's hospice.

"When you're young, all you think about is making it as a footballer and playing football, which is right," he explains to *FFT*. "But when you

Clockwise from top Euro 2020 Final hurt has left Kane hungry for success; showing off his World Cup Golden Boot; "If you don't sign for the Villa, I'll have this MBE back..."

do make it, you understand that there are other responsibilities that come along the way. You have people scrutinising your every move, people are listening to you, and you need to try to use your voice for as much good as possible. Of course you're not going to change everything, but anything you can help with, that's what I try to do.

"When I was growing up, I always looked at footballers – not just what they were doing on the pitch, but off the pitch too. That's what makes a good role model. As a person, it's really important for me to show that image." ▶

SPEEDY DOES IT

Only two players have ever got off the mark quicker for England

19 SEC

BILL NICHOLSON

Before he became Tottenham's greatest manager of all time, Nicholson scored 19 seconds after kick-off on his England debut against Portugal in 1951. Alas, injury problems meant it proved his one and only outing on the international stage.

30 SEC

JOHN COCK

No sniggering, please. The first Cornishman to play for England bagged his first goal within half a minute, against Ireland in 1919. Like Nicholson, his Three Lions career didn't last very long – he played once more, scored once more, then that was that.

"CONTE BRINGS REAL PASSION AND ENERGY – YOU WANT TO WORK HARD AND RUN FOR HIM. I THINK MY GAME'S IMPROVING UNDER HIM"

"IT WASN'T THE START I WANTED..."

Kane's presence as a figurehead has probably had at least a small part to play in the improved relations between the England squad, the general public and media in recent years. Results are undoubtedly a factor in that – not only has the striker delivered consistently on an individual basis, but he's brought the Three Lions closer to glory than at any point in the last half-century.

His goalscoring feats propelled Spurs to another level, too: a first ever Champions League final and a second-place finish in the Premier League – their highest position since 1963. Kane has won the league's Golden Boot on three occasions – on the day we speak, his tally for the club stands at 244 in just 382 games.

He emphatically returned to form in the second half of 2021-22, after Antonio Conte's arrival, and has already earned legendary status at the club. "Again it goes so quick – I can't believe I've been playing in the Premier League now for seven years or so," he says, assessing his time in the Tottenham first team. "I've still got stuff to improve on, we've still got goals we want to achieve, but Antonio is a really good manager and I'm really enjoying working with him.

"He brings a real passion, an energy, an enthusiasm to training and games, and makes you want to work. You want to work hard for him, you want to run for him. He's won titles everywhere he's gone, so you respect him a lot, and I'm enjoying it. I've worked with some brilliant managers and he's another. I feel like my game's improving under him. Hopefully it continues."

Kane talks to *FFT* having already struck 34 goals for Tottenham and England during the campaign – not bad considering that the first half of the season was regarded as arguably his most difficult at club level since breaking through in 2014.

He bagged seven England goals in the space of four November days – three against Albania and four in San Marino – which took his tally to 16 goals in 16 games in 2021, beating the previous national record for a calendar year which stood at 12. He also notched seven in cup competitions for Spurs, but his second league goal of the season only came on December 19 – an almost unthinkable statistic – after the club suffered a poor start under Nuno Espirito Santo and Kane had an unsettled summer in which his future was more uncertain than ever.

With Jose Mourinho gone and Tottenham finishing a disappointing seventh last term, Manchester City looked set to lure him to the Etihad Stadium, only for chairman Daniel Levy to reject their bids. Kane has insisted that what happened behind the scenes must remain between him and the club, and he doesn't want to go into details now, but he does concede that the last 12 months haven't gone perfectly for him. ▶

THE LIONS LADDER

Kane will become the 10th man to claim England's outright goals record

WILLIAM KENYON-SLANEY
2 GOALS

The Three Lions' first ever international finished goalless against Scotland – Kenyon-Slaney bagged a brace in the return fixture in 1873. Later, the former Eton student was elected as a Conservative MP.

CHARLES BAMBRIDGE
11 GOALS

The son of Queen Victoria's snapper, Bambridge reached six goals after netting in a 13-0 victory over Ireland in 1882, only for Aston Villa's Howard Vaughton to level with him. Bambridge then hit five more to regain the outright record.

TINSLEY LINDLEY
14 GOALS

An amateur who wore walking shoes instead of boots as he felt they made him faster, the Nottingham Forest forward was in a tie for the accolade when he and Fred Dewhurst matched Bambridge's tally, then claimed it all for himself.

STEVE BLOOMER
28 GOALS

Only Jimmy Greaves has hit more goals in England's top tier than Bloomer's 314 – he broke the Three Lions scoring record in 1898, then doubled it. Derby's anthem is named after him, sung by Jim Smith and actor Robert Lindsay.

VIVIAN WOODWARD
29 GOALS

The Chelsea forward scored twice against Wales in 1911 to pip Bloomer by one goal. His career was ended by injuries sustained in World War One, but he held the goal record for 45 years until Nat Lofthouse matched his tally in 1956.

Shirt 1980 England home shirt supplied by ScoreDraw.com

TOM FINNEY
30 GOALS

The Preston legend was the Three Lions' outright leading scorer for just one match – his goal against Northern Ireland nudged him past Woodward and Lofthouse in 1958, but the Bolton icon pulled level less than three weeks later.

BOBBY CHARLTON
33 GOALS

Charlton seized the England goal record for the first time when he surpassed Finney and Lofthouse in 1963, then upped it to 33 the following summer when he provided the Three Lions' eighth strike in a 10-0 tonking of the USA.

JIMMY GREAVES
44 GOALS

It was Greaves not Charlton who went into the 1966 World Cup as England's record scorer – four goals against Norway took him to 43 shortly before the finals, but he didn't find the net once it had started, adding just one more in 1967.

BOBBY CHARLTON
49 GOALS

Charlton overtook Greaves in '68, then became the second player to grab the goal and cap records at the same time, after Bloomer. Charlton was the holder of the goal record for over 500 games – England have only ever played 1,028.

WAYNE ROONEY
53 GOALS

The Liverpudlian surpassed Charlton as Manchester United's record scorer in 2017 – two years earlier, he'd done the same at international level. His final England goal was a penalty in the infamous Euro 2016 defeat to Iceland.

"Obviously it's been up and down," he admits. "It wasn't the start of the season that I wanted, of course. I'm my own biggest critic, I know when I'm playing well, I know when I'm not, and I know when I can do better. It was disappointing – England and the other competitions were going OK but the Premier League wasn't quite falling for me. As a team we weren't doing well, so there was a mixture of stuff going on.

"But I'm proud of the way I've turned it around and got back to some decent numbers in the league. It's all part of the journey – I'm always looking to be consistent, but there will be times when things don't go your way and you have to find a way of turning it in your favour. I feel like I've done that, but I'll look back – after every season I assess the good, the bad, the things I can improve on. I'll do the same this year."

Every time he's found the net for Spurs, Kane has inched ever closer to Jimmy Greaves' club record of 266 goals, which looks within reach in 2022-23. "Jimmy was an amazing player for club and country – he scored an incredible amount of goals in a short amount of games," says Kane. "It's something to try to achieve. I've still got a few more to go, but of course it'd be great to be Spurs' all-time record scorer."

WAYNE'S WORLD? PAH...

Before then, he'll surely hit a half-century of England goals, then equal Rooney's international record of 53. "Fifty will be a nice number – it's a step closer to breaking the record, and we have four games in June so hopefully I'll be able to nick a few and get some wins," says Kane. All four summer fixtures are in the Nations League – away to Hungary and Germany, then home to Italy and Hungary. Reverse ties against the Azzurri and Germany follow in September before the World Cup.

Kane has already matched Bobby Charlton's tally of 49 goals, and topped Gary Lineker's 48. "To be among those names and hopefully one day go past them is really special," he says. "I was playing when Wayne broke the record [right]. We beat Switzerland 2-0 – I scored, then he scored a penalty. As players, we knew he had the chance to break the record and we were excited for him. It's pretty strange now to have been on the pitch, and scored, on the same day – Wazza was great and helped me as soon as I went into the England team as the captain, giving me advice. He said that one day I'd break his record."

For that reason, when Rooney received a gold plaque from the FA to mark his record-breaking international career, he requested that Kane be the man who awarded it to him. "He asked me to do it with Gareth – I presented it to him and he said, 'I'll be giving this back to you in a few years'," chuckles Kane. "I saw him again after the Euros last summer – he was there at the final. He's in management now and in a totally different mindset, but we had a little catch-up and he said well done for what I've been doing."

Rooney was 12 years into his England career when he claimed the goalscoring record. Kane is seven years on from his debut, potentially

"IT'S DIFFICULT TO FOCUS ON RECORDS – FOR NOW IT'S, 'CAN I IMPROVE, CAN I GET BETTER?'"

ENGLAND: A KIT STORY

With the aid of Score Draw and Classic Football Shirts, Kane donned a number of retro England kits during our photoshoot

1982 AWAY

England ran out in this red number for their first game of the 1982 World Cup – Bryan Robson needed 27 seconds to open the scoring in a 3-1 victory over France in Bilbao.

1982 HOME

Arguably the most stylish home shirt in England history, though Kevin Keegan doesn't have fond memories of it – his miss against Spain sealed the Three Lions' World Cup exit.

1990 HOME

Gary Lineker struck four goals sporting this jersey at Italia 90 – one against Ireland in the group stage, then two against Cameroon and another in the semis against West Germany.

1990 THIRD

England didn't actually need the third kit at the 1990 World Cup, but it was iconic all the same – New Order's Bernard Sumner wore it in the famous *World In Motion* music video.

2002 H

England's
World Cup
a year ear
wore it fo
Greece, af
netted a

only halfway through his career, which explains why he's struggling to fully get his head around the fact that he's already set to achieve something that will form a significant part of his legacy.

It was those seven goals against Albania and San Marino – the first back-to-back hat-tricks by an England player since Tommy Taylor in 1957 – that moved him to within touching distance. From a distant 12 behind Rooney, sixth in the all-time chart, he'd overtaken Owen and Greaves in a flash, and was suddenly within five of the record. His own penalty against Switzerland in March nudged him another goal closer.

"It's difficult for me to focus on records – they're amazing and I'm extremely proud of them, but it's always just on to the next thing, the next game and the next achievement," he says. "I'm sure when I'm retired in 10 years or so, I'll look back and take it all in, but for now it's, 'Can I improve, can I get better?'

"The ultimate goal for us as a team is to win games, to win major tournaments. But I know after the two games against Albania and San Marino, everyone was talking about it a lot more because I was a lot closer than I was – seven goals in two games obviously helped to boost my numbers. I'm still young, though: I'm only 28, so I still feel like I've got plenty of time in my England career to go. I've got plenty of aims on the horizon and a big year ahead – another major tournament this winter. It all comes around so fast, it's going to be here before we know it and I'm really excited for that. I've just got to keep improving, keep working, and hopefully I can score a few more."

How many, is the question. Kane could reach a number that remains unsurpassed for decades – he's not a player who has relied on searing speed, so could have greater longevity than many, his predecessor Rooney included. Kane's boyhood hero Teddy Sheringham proved increasingly adept at dropping into a slightly deeper position as the years went on, extending his England career until the age of 36, and Kane has displayed signs of a similar trait in his link-up with Sterling at international level and Son Heung-min at Spurs.

So, good luck to the next bloke trying to beat him? "I'd never put a limit or a number on how many goals," he says. "Obviously, it's game by game. It's a cliché, but I feel like I've got many more years in me for England, so if I've scored 49 in my first seven years, then there's no reason why I can't do similar in the next six or seven."

That would put him close to 100 goals, a mark that only Cristiano Ronaldo and Iran's Ali Daei have ever surpassed in the men's game. Is even that incredible number possible? "Let's see what happens," he chuckles cautiously, understandably not wanting to declare a three-figure target. "Let's just take it game by game..."

It's a mantra that has served him well in his England career so far: 69 games, 49 goals. As we reach the end of our chat and photoshoot, Kane bids farewell by politely shaking the hand of every member of the *FFT* team, then makes his exit. He passes a group of kids on the way out. "Yo, that's Harry Kane!" one excitedly exclaims, stunned that he's just seen one of the most famous people in England, on a random Wednesday afternoon at the O2.

There's barely a single corner of the country that he could visit now and not be seen as a national hero. Soon, he'll be England's greatest goalscorer of all time. ⊙

DEATH, GLORY AND DYNAMO KYIV

The Ukrainian giants inspired *Escape To Victory*
and overcame Chernobyl – before their players
had to flee once more. This is their heroic story

Words Chris Flanagan

The final of the European Cup Winners' Cup was just six days away, when the disaster happened. Just 70 miles north of Kyiv, a huge reactor at the Chernobyl Nuclear Power Plant had exploded, filling the night sky with radioactive particles. Nowhere in the vicinity was safe – not even Ukraine's biggest city.

As the Soviet Union hurried into damage limitation mode, 100,000 children were evacuated for their own safety. Among them was a nine-year-old Dynamo Kyiv junior by the name of Andriy Shevchenko, whisked 500 miles by bus to sanctuary by the Sea of Azov, on Ukraine's south coast.

First, Shevchenko's club faced one of the biggest matches of their history, at Lyon's Stade de Gerland against Atletico Madrid. While chaos reigned back home, Dynamo put on a masterclass, dismantling Los Colchoneros in a 3-0 triumph. Goalscorer Oleh Blokhin was already a Ballon d'Or winner; months later, strike partner Ihor Belanov would lift the award as well.

Valeriy Lobanovskyi's Dynamo Kyiv were hailed as the finest team in the history of Eastern Europe. Not for the first time, Ukraine's most successful club had battled adversity on the path to greatness.

THE DEATH MATCH

Escape To Victory wasn't just a fictional account of prisoners of war taking on the Germans in a football match during the Second World War – the 1981 movie was inspired by a real story, with a much less Hollywood-friendly ending.

Founded by the new Soviet Union's Dynamo sports society in 1927, Dynamo Kyiv had been in existence for little more than a decade when war broke out. After Kyiv replaced Kharkiv as the capital of the Ukrainian Soviet Socialist Republic in 1934, the new club had become Ukraine's only representative in the first ever season of the Soviet Top League in 1936, finishing second behind Dynamo Moscow.

Their emergence came during highly troubled times under Joseph Stalin, however: almost four million people died across Ukraine in 1932 and

1933 because of The Great Famine, sparked by the Soviet Union's decision to enforce collectivisation of agriculture under their tyrannical leader. Some Dynamo players fled Kyiv; another pair were arrested and sent to work "for the good of the country" for two years in a penal colony after trying to exchange pieces of cloth for food. When the squad went unpaid, team captain Konstantin Shchegotsky attempted to escape and play for Dynamo Dnipropetrovsk, but was forcibly returned to the club, then later jailed for 15 months. Two players were shot dead as part of Stalin's Great Purge, because of suspicions that they might be spies.

The team had slipped to eighth place in the Soviet Top League when football was abruptly halted in June 1941, after Germany invaded the USSR. Kyiv fell to the Nazis by September, following a battle that lasted more than a month when German troops encircled the city. Ukraine's new capital suffered widespread damage, before an even greater horror – the massacre of nearly 34,000 Jews in just two days at Babi Yar, a ravine within the city. Several of the Dynamo squad had joined the army and quickly ended up in prisoner of war camps.

Dynamo Kyiv went into hibernation as the Nazi occupiers dissolved all Soviet organisations and clubs – but they didn't prevent new teams from being established. So, when a group of former Dynamo players started work at a bread factory, in an attempt to guarantee a vital food supply for their families, they founded the team FC Start, which also incorporated three ex-players from Lokomotiv Kyiv.

The team began playing matches in June 1942, taking on another new Ukrainian club FC Rukh, who'd originally tried and failed to recruit the same players. FC Start won 7-2, before posting victories over clubs from the Hungarian and Romanian militaries – allies with the Nazis during the war. A 7-1 shellacking of a Nazi artillery team soon followed, as did a 6-0 thrashing of a side made up of German railway workers.

"This victory can't be recognised as an achievement," said the *New Ukrainian Word*, a pro-German newspaper published during the occupation. "The German team consists of individual strong players but can't be called a team – there's a lack of training, without which no team can do anything. Start consists of players from

Clockwise from below Dynamo reached the semis of the Champions League; the 'Death Match' poster; Loba the pioneer; Blokhin sinks Atleti

the former Dynamo team – you should demand much more from them than what they gave in this match."

On August 6, FC Start faced Flakelf, a side made up of Luftwaffe anti-aircraft gunners. FC Start prevailed 5-1 – the Nazis responded by arranging a rematch three days later, drafting in some of the finest footballers they could find for a fixture in front of 2,000 people at the city's Zenit Stadium. Describing the Flakelf team as 'reinforced', the dual language poster for the match billed it as 'Futbol Revansh' or 'Fussball Revanche' – football revenge.

The Germans took the lead, but their new line-up still wasn't enough – FC Start came roaring back to win 5-3, inflicting a defeat that the Nazis hadn't anticipated. Players drank vodka to celebrate that night, then thrashed FC Rukh again a week later – this time 8-0. On August 18, though, the Gestapo turned up at the bread factory and arrested six of the team. A couple more were detained two days later.

Throughout the 80 years since, conflicting reports have arisen about the reason for the arrests. The official Soviet narrative described it as retribution for their second victory against Flakelf; others have called FC Rukh's manager a collaborator, claiming he reported them to the Nazis in anger after his side's loss.

The Dynamo sports society had links to the USSR's secret police, and the players were believed to have been arrested because of suspicions that they could launch sabotage acts within Kyiv. None of the team's former Lokomotiv Kyiv players were apprehended. Two of FC Start's players soon died – one as a result of torture during his interrogation, another shot as he tried to escape. Eight more of the footballers, all

formerly of Dynamo Kyiv, were subsequently transferred to the Syrets concentration camp, next to Babi Yar.

On February 24, 1943, six months after their arrest, Olexi Klimenko, Ivan Kuzmenko and popular goalkeeper Nikolai Trusevich were among a group of prisoners executed by the Nazis and thrown into Babi Yar's mass grave. Other players had been working just outside the camp at a shoe repair factory that day, and fled when they heard the news.

Kyiv was liberated nine months later – Soviet propaganda connected the deaths with the Flakelf fixture, which became known as 'The Death Match', although unsurprisingly, the truth was far more complicated. In 2005, a Ukrainian investigation found no direct links between the result of the game and the executions.

Regardless, no one at Dynamo Kyiv has ever forgotten the players who perished. All received posthumous medals for courage from the USSR, with the surviving footballers also given awards for battle merit. The war was over, and the club had to be rebuilt after tragedy.

THE EASTERN EUROPEAN FERGIE

Dynamo initially found life hard when the Soviet Top League resumed – winning just one of their 22 fixtures in 1945, then finishing bottom a year later. Thankfully, they were exempted from relegation following their wartime trauma, and were slowly able to regroup.

By 1961, they became the first club from outside Moscow to secure the Soviet title, assisted by 10 goals from 22-year-old winger Valeriy Lobanovskyi, who specialised in scoring direct from corners.

Under new boss Viktor Maslov – pioneer of the 4-4-2 formation and the revolutionary tactic of pressing – the team swept to three straight titles between 1966 and 1968. Dynamo defeated reigning champions Celtic in their very first European Cup fixture, but opted to pull out of the competition in 1968-69 after the USSR invaded Czechoslovakia, and UEFA responded by pairing all of the Eastern Bloc clubs against each other in the first round.

In 1973, a 34-year-old Lobanovskyi was appointed joint-manager alongside his former Dynamo team-mate Oleh Bazylevych, and the club's finest era began. Lobanovskyi had retired as a player aged 29, ▶

DYNAMO HAVE NEVER FORGOTTEN THE PLAYERS WHO PERISHED – ALL GOT POSTHUMOUS MEDALS FOR COURAGE

then spent four years in charge of Dnipro, guiding the team into the Soviet top flight and an impressive sixth position in their first season.

Destined for greatness of Sir Alex Ferguson proportions in Eastern Europe, Lobanovskyi trained his Dynamo players to be capable of playing in any position on the field, while the managerial duo also implemented an early version of sports science to tremendous effect, showing foresight that allowed them to steal a march on their rivals.

Before winning league titles in each of their first two full campaigns under Lobanovskyi, Dynamo beat Zaria Voroshilovgrad (modern-day Zorya Luhansk) in the Soviet Cup final, gaining entry into the 1974-75 European Cup Winners' Cup. PSV Eindhoven were despatched 3-0 in the semi-final first leg in front of a gargantuan 100,000 Kyiv crowd – Ferencvaros similarly proved no match in the final, succumbing 3-0 in Basel as Dynamo became the first Soviet winners of a European trophy. When the USSR fell in 1991, only one other club had achieved such an honour – Dinamo Tbilisi in the 1981 Cup Winners' Cup, after winning 4-1 at West Ham in the quarters.

En route to glory, Dynamo Kyiv had triumphed in eight out of nine matches – a win percentage not surpassed by any European trophy winner until Bayern Munich bagged 11 victories out of 11 on their way to the 2020 Champions League crown. There would also be individual glory for Oleh Blokhin, who netted a fine third goal in the final against Ferencvaros, then hit all three in a 3-0 aggregate triumph over Bayern Munich in the European Super Cup. The 23-year-old forward romped to the Ballon d'Or months later, winning the vote by a landslide ahead of Franz Beckenbauer and Johan Cruyff.

Lobanovskyi and Bazylevych shared the World Sports Coach of the Year award, before the latter stepped down in 1976. Lobanovskyi went on to capture three more league titles and reached a European Cup semi-final, then left in 1982 to coach the USSR.

Within two years he was back, though, recruiting Ihor Belanov from Chornomorets Odesa to form a formidable strike partnership with Blokhin. What followed was another charge to a European trophy – in the 1985-86 Cup Winners' Cup, Dynamo won all four of their home matches by at least three goals, pulverising poor Rapid Vienna 9-2 on aggregate in the quarter-finals and easing to victory over Dukla Prague in the semis.

Then came Chernobyl, days before the final. Despite the unfolding nuclear disaster, Lobanovskyi managed to keep his players focused as they trounced Atletico Madrid 3-0 in Lyon. The Soviet regime had provided as little information as possible about the meltdown, but the squad had still been swamped by questions about it from foreign journalists prior to the game.

Dynamo had given an important gift to Ukraine, during one of its toughest moments, and their performance earned praise from media across Europe who'd been dazzled by their slick attacking play. "The superiority of the Dynamo Kyiv players was obvious," gushed Spanish paper *AS*. "They demonstrated exceptional speed, amazing change of rhythm, and created numerous chances. The scoreline could have been much bigger." Belanov edged out World Cup Golden Boot winner Gary Lineker to that year's Ballon d'Or.

SHEVA-LUTION

Dynamo would win the Soviet Top League three more times under Lobanovskyi before the USSR collapsed, with their record total of 13 titles one ahead of fierce rivals Spartak Moscow – a feud that came to represent Ukraine versus Russia, and came to an abrupt end when the former declared independence in 1991.

Lobanovskyi had stepped aside as boss once again in 1990 after accepting a lucrative offer to manage the UAE national team, then Dynamo briefly slipped into financial crisis after independence. By the time he returned for a third spell seven years later, the club had recovered and assumed total dominance over Ukraine's new top division, winning four consecutive crowns with a new forward line of Andriy Shevchenko and Serhiy Rebrov showing real potential.

The club had struggled to make an impact in Europe – but their iconic coach solved that, steering them to the quarter-finals of the Champions League in 1997-98 thanks to two of the most famous

WHEN SHEVA THWARTED PUTIN

Ukraine only faced Russia in two competitive matches before games between the countries were banned – and the head-to-head ended in disappointment for Vladimir Putin.

The pair were drawn together in the same qualifying group for Euro 2000 – Ukraine triumphed 3-2 in Kyiv, as Russia lost their first three matches. They recovered with a string of wins, however, to set up a Moscow decider in their last encounter. Having beaten

world champions France in Paris, victory over Ukraine at the Luzhniki Stadium would put Russia top of the group, eliminating their neighbours and sending France into a play-off.

Putin was among 80,000 in the Luzhniki's first sell-out crowd for 15 years – Russia's new Prime Minister was shown punching the air when Valeri Karpin fired the hosts in front with just 15 minutes

left. All looked pretty good for Putin – until Andriy Shevchenko looped an 88th-minute free-kick into the area and goalkeeper Aleksandr Filimonov implausibly dropped the ball into his own net. Russia were out.

France won the group, en route to eventual Euro 2000 triumph, with Ukraine making the play-offs. The tournament remains the only Euros that Russia have missed since the fall of the

USSR. "I feel like quitting football forever," manager Oleg Romantsev said in the aftermath.

"The only consolation would be to see Ukraine losing in the play-offs – let us die together, as eternal rivals," hissed the *Moskovskiye Vedomosti* newspaper. Ukraine lost to Slovenia and have never played Russia since. UEFA banned fixtures between the two nations at both international and club level following the hostilities of 2014.

CRIMEA: LEAGUE OF ISOLATION

Until 2014, two members of Ukraine's Premier League played in Crimea – but the peninsula has spent the last eight years separated from the wider football world.

Tavriya Simferopol were Ukraine's first ever domestic champions in 1992, and took on Bayer Leverkusen in the Europa League in 2010. But Russia's annexation of Crimea in 2014 saw both Tavriya and their neighbours Sevastopol kicked out of Ukraine's top flight.

A new version of Tavriya Simferopol was established in the southern Ukrainian city of Kherson, joining the amateur leagues and working their way back up to the third tier.

In Crimea, Tavriya's successor club became TSK Simferopol, who applied to join the Russian league alongside another new team, FC SKChF Sevastopol. Both of them were admitted to the third tier before the Ukrainian FA complained and UEFA barred the move – instead, a standalone Crimean Premier League was launched and has contained eight sides in recent seasons.

Sevastopol have dominated, winning the title on three occasions to Simferopol's one. The league has remained cut off from any access to European competition.

"WE WOKE UP TO THE SOUND OF BOMBS EXPLODING. THE NIGHTMARE HAD BEGUN"

Above A flag of Lobanovskiy's face is proudly flown in Kyiv in happier times

victories in their history. In the group stage, Dynamo had won at PSV and drawn with Newcastle when a Barcelona side containing Rivaldo and Luis Figo visited Kyiv. They didn't see what was coming: Rebrov smashed home an early goal from a ludicrous angle, as the Catalans were crushed 3-0 at a cacophonous Olympic Stadium. Two weeks on, Dynamo headed to the Camp Nou for the return fixture – disbelieving away supporters waved Ukrainian flags in joy as Shevchenko scored a first-half hat-trick, Rebrov bagged another and Lobanovskyi's side sensationally won 4-0.

Dynamo topped the group – they were halted in the last eight by eventual finalists Juventus, but were at it again a year later by taking four points off Arsenal to triumph in their group once more. This time they overcame Real Madrid in the quarters, before going 3-1 up in the semi-final first leg against Bayern Munich. The Germans eventually hit back, denying Dynamo a return to Barcelona to face Manchester United in the final of Sheringham, Solskjaer and all that.

That summer, Shevchenko sealed a switch to Milan, and the great days of Dynamo Kyiv drew to a close. They won the Ukrainian title undefeated in 1999-2000, but their impact in Europe waned, Rebrov signed for Tottenham and Lobanovskyi's health deteriorated. Having initially been unable to travel to Champions League away games because of blood pressure problems that made flying impossible, he suffered a stroke and collapsed during a match against Metalurh Zaporizhzhia in May 2002 and died in hospital six days later, aged 63. He'd won 13 league titles as Dynamo manager, the same number as Ferguson at Manchester United.

A month after his death, Shakhtar Donetsk celebrated their maiden Ukrainian crown, pipping Dynamo on the final day. The balance of

power started to shift. Between 2001 and 2020, Shakhtar lifted 13 titles to Dynamo's six, aided by big investment from billionaire Rinat Akhmetov and an influx of talented Brazilians under the guidance of Mircea Lucescu. Domestic football was now being dominated not by the club from the capital with a largely Ukrainian nationalist fanbase, but by one from a city with an almost 50/50 population split between ethnic Ukrainians and Russians – at least until 2014, when war in the Donbas forced Shakhtar to shift bases to Lviv, Kharkiv and then Kyiv.

Dynamo's 2020-21 perch-returning plan was a controversial one: ignoring protests to appoint former Shakhtar boss Lucescu. "I hope the fans will reconsider – it takes courage to do what I did," Lucescu told *FFT* after crossing the divide. It worked rather better than Rafa Benitez at Everton: Dynamo won the league by 11 points last term.

This season they were neck and neck with Shakhtar by the annual mid-season break – the squad had only just arrived back in Ukraine after a winter training camp in Turkey when football was halted by Russia's invasion. Uruguayan midfielder Carlos de Pena and Brazilian forward Vitinho joined Shakhtar's Kyiv-based foreign stars in fleeing the country, after Russia's all-out assault on the city began.

"We woke up to the sound of planes and bombs exploding – the peace ended and the nightmare began," De Pena said on Instagram. "Out in the street, I saw the desperation of the people. Together with Vitinho, we went to a hotel to take refuge with other Brazilian players – we spent the night on an underground floor. The explosions felt close, civilians began to die and fear grew.

"We decided to take a train to the border with Romania, despite the risk of suffering some problems on the way to the station. After 17 hours, we arrived at a city on the border, where we took a bus until we crossed into Moldova. I was very scared – I cried several times."

Polish defender Tomasz Kedziora evacuated westwards towards his homeland. Just like during the Second World War, Dynamo players had been forced to flee for their lives in the city that connects east and west, with all the problems that perennial power struggle brings.

In 95 years of existence, Dynamo Kyiv have been through so much. Sometimes, football has been the last thing on their minds. ◉

THE FIRST GALACTICO

...ster City have had many great players during Pep Guardiola's reign, but none have arrived with quite th...
...atus as Erling Haaland. His task? To help them finally win the Champions League, as he explains to *FFT*

Words Leo Moynihan
Additional reporting Benjamin McFadyean

A

Sunday afternoon in May 2012. An 11-year-old boy sits in his living room watching the team he supports play a game that should, for the first time in 44 years, see them crowned the glorious champions of England. For now though, with the game nearing its end, there is gloom. The boy fidgets, leaning back on the sofa, looking to his father's eyes for reassurance that doesn't come.

It's a scene replicated all over Greater Manchester and beyond. Decked in sky blue, sons, daughters, fathers and mothers, sit staring, hoping, dining out on fingernails. Our scene is in Norway. We're into injury time and on the television, Manchester City trail Queens Park Rangers 2-1 at the Etihad Stadium. Title rivals Manchester United have won 1-0 at Sunderland. City must score two goals. The boy is Erling Haaland, his father is Alfie, a former City player, a man with much to know and say about the club's past, but who now has no words of encouragement for its present. The clock is ticking.

"I remember that day so well," says Erling Haaland, as he sits in front of FourFourTwo. "Like it was yesterday. It was crazy. The day had been all about winning. This was our moment, this was the day the club became league champions. I remember we settled down to watch, my dad was just as excited as me, but things went crazy. City are losing to 10-man QPR. We're massive favourites, and we're losing. United have already won. It's despair. But then, after 91 minutes I think it was, Edin Dzeko scores. There's hope, but there's so little time."

Haaland's eyes, like any City supporter being asked to transport themselves back to that afternoon, light up as the conversation takes him into the 93rd minute of the match. "The winning goal felt so strange," he recalls. "Mario Balotelli on the ground, but somehow getting the ball to Sergio Aguero. The striker shuts his eyes and hits it, then it's madness. Me and my dad, we're up off our seats, we're running around the living room screaming. The top comes off, and it's spinning around the head. Special. What a moment."

ARRIVAL OF THE INEVITABLE

Ten years have passed, and there have been many more special moments at Manchester City. Five Premier League titles have followed; domestic cups, great teams, great players and the most lauded coach this generation has known have all made their way through the Etihad's gates. Sky blue joy is common, and on a July afternoon this summer, when the club unveiled their new goal-getter to a raucous, already smitten support outside their ground, it felt like another gargantuan moment in City's recent history.

Wonderful footballers have arrived at the club over the last 15 years, but this one feels different. Erling Haaland feels different. He certainly looks different. Six foot five inches tall, lean, powerful. Haaland, arguably the most sought after player on the planet, was unveiled as if he himself was a trophy.

Perhaps for the first time, Manchester City had gone out and got the elite, rather than a player who would later become the elite. As thousands of fans gathered to get a look at their new, white-blonde haired superstar, with flames and razzmatazz all around, this felt new. It also felt inevitable.

City's £51 million signing, still only 22 years of age, meets FFT at the club's training base a couple of hundred yards away, chatting on an impressive, full-size indoor 4G pitch. Even here, Haaland fills the room. The striker has time to spare before a pre-season session – in tracksuit bottoms, hoodie and pristine white trainers, he's courteous and perfectly relaxed

> **PERHAPS FOR THE FIRST TIME, CITY HAVE GONE OUT AND GOT THE ELITE, RATHER THAN A PLAYER WHO BECOMES THE ELITE**

in his new surroundings. Despite widespread interest from a host of Europe's biggest clubs, including Real Madrid, Manchester United and Chelsea, was there an inevitability that he'd one day turn up at the club he roared on as a boy?

"That's a good question," he says. "I'm not sure about that. Of course, there was a lot of speculation, there were a lot of rumours, and as a footballer, a footballer playing well, you have to live with it. There was plenty of talk, but I couldn't control any of that. If I thought about the rumours, my head would explode and it wouldn't help me on the pitch.

"It's on the pitch that I have to be at my best, I have to perform. To do that, I have to be relaxed. That's important to me. Rumours are part of football, I get that, but they're out of my control. If I can't do anything about it, then I ignore it.

Above and left
City pulled out all the stops to welcome their new superstar

"But with City, I don't know, you're right, there was something there from the start. I like the club very much, I always have of course. I know a lot about the place from my dad's time here. But also, just as importantly, I like how they've played since Pep Guardiola arrived. From that point of view it was a club and team I always had my eye on. Inevitable, I don't know, but yes, there has always been an interest from me to be here."

There are some who believe that Haaland's career has been mapped out – that each step, from club to club, has been planned to aid his improvement. Nothing has been done rashly. At Bryne, his boyhood club in Norway, he was offered a trial at Hoffenheim, but his dad and other advisors recommended he stay in his homeland, and he joined Molde.

From there, a move to an established big club in Europe (it was suggested Leeds made

a concrete offer) may have materialised had impatience prevailed, but instead it was Red Bull Salzburg in Austria where the frontman further flourished. Then, despite links with United and Madrid, Haaland's next step was Germany and Borussia Dortmund, a place where a player's nourishment is as vibrant as their yellow shirts.

Of course goals followed with frightening regularity, but so did a maturity, a willingness to play for the team and not just the goal chart. The biggest of clubs were all looking, and once again, a simple decision to move on was met with considered calm.

Time spent, lessons learned, craft further mastered and the next rung of the ladder ascended. "It's part of the job now," explains Haaland. "You move on, and I like being out of my comfort zone – that's something I've done a few times and, yes, I enjoy it. It's so nice to be at Manchester City, to be working. It's nice to get to know new people, to get used to a new country. I've been the new boy several times now – it's something I enjoy."

New boy maybe, but this time there is that familiarity, one that comes from his main advisor and mentor, his dad. Alfie Haaland's Manchester City career may have only lasted 47 appearances over three years, but there's a cult around the former midfielder. Famous run-ins with Roy Keane always help, but so did watching a match in West Ham's away end as a fan, or encountering a group of City supporters at a petrol station after a 4-0 loss ▶

on his debut at Charlton in 2000 and paying for their fuel, so aware was he of his and the team's inept performance.

Younger City fans are excited by a true star from their *FIFA* games, while others will feel the warmth from an old friend. Has that link helped with the move? "I don't think my dad's history here will directly help me to settle in or to score goals," insists Haaland, who was born a month after his father moved to Maine Road from Leeds. "It's nice to have that link, though. You know, I remember being young and knowing that my father did something special at a club, and he went on to become my role model, so my dad has always been very important. I grew up knowing he'd been a professional, and I wanted to do the same. That's a great thing. It's triggered me."

"THERE'S SOMETHING SPECIAL ABOUT THIS"

It's also triggered an immediate bond with his new employers, that has not needed goals or stunning form to take shape. "I like the vibe here already," he says. "The dressing room feels great. What strikes you is how hungry everyone is. I like the way people are around the place and I've already received so much support from the people in the city and beyond, so it makes things a bit easier."

Having come from Dortmund where the player-fan relationship is an intrinsic part of the club's DNA, Haaland is in no doubt about both working with and for the supporters. "I love that close bond with the fans," he says. "It's important. We are all just normal human beings – it's about treating everyone the same and knowing that the people who come to watch us, and the people who will support me every week no matter what, are just like me. That's how you get a bond, and you keep that in the back of your mind. I'm no different to them. I play, they support. We are the same. I know I'm lucky to be able to play, and I'll try to thank the fans by scoring and getting them success."

We are the same. Words supporters long for – the link between player and punter here is already unquestionably strong. "There's something special about this," says City fan David Mooney, fittingly named for his role on the *Blue Moon* podcast. "From a footballing

HISTORY MAKER

Haaland was 11th in the 2021 Ballon d'Or. In the award's 66-year existence, only two Norwegians had previously been nominated

RUNE BRATSETH
The sweeper came 20th in the 1992 Ballon d'Or after helping Werder Bremen to European Cup Winners' Cup glory against Monaco. A year later, his club won the Bundesliga, Norway reached the World Cup ahead of England and Bratseth rose another five places in the poll.

BENT SKAMMELSRUD
Rosenborg's captain picked up a single vote in the 1997 Ballon d'Or, putting him level with Rivaldo in joint 33rd, after the Norwegian side reached the Champions League last eight. The 31-year-old midfielder soon joined Bayer Leverkusen, but the move didn't work out.

point of view, I don't think any of the signings City have made before this – and I'd include Yaya Toure, Kevin De Bruyne, David Silva and Sergio Aguero - were sought-after superstars. One tabloid called De Bruyne a £57m Chelsea reject. Those players had to come and prove themselves, whereas Haaland, who of course has to prove something, is the first one you'd call some kind of Galactico, who you could imagine Real Madrid selling out the Bernabeu for, just for his unveiling. The supporters have taken to him immediately and maybe it's the sentimental football fan in me, but with his dad's influence, I was always pretty relaxed about the deal. I presumed he'd be coming to us this summer."

Haaland further endeared himself at his unveiling when he suggested that he found it difficult to even say the words 'Manchester United', and that he's longing for the local derby in October (a 6-3 City win in which he scored a hat-trick). "It's just so easy to love him when he speaks like that," says Mooney.

Haaland himself grins mischievously when he's reminded of that statement – with his great pal playing in red, there may be great scope to play the noisy neighbour. "Jadon Sancho and I had a great connection on and off the pitch at Dortmund," he continues. "He plays for the other lot now though, so maybe we'll have to meet in secret!

"Look, it's all about banter and I enjoy that. I've already met some United supporters here in the city, and we're always joking with each other. It's about not taking everything too seriously. There are a lot of United fans in my home town in Norway, so I've always had to have a go at them. I'm used to this and I love it. Don't take things too seriously. I want to be able to talk a bit like the fans, otherwise it gets a bit boring, doesn't it?"

For all the attention on goals and success, there's a fun side to Haaland, a fondness for friendship and the players' currency of banter. Going way back to his childhood with Byrne, Haaland's coaches advocated manners, the importance of relationships within the game and being friendly to team-mates. From that education, Haaland has a calmness about him, a knowing stillness.

His home town in the scenic south-west of Norway has a population of 12,000 people; a rural, coastal setting. The marksman still visits a family farmhouse – he may be able to park the private jet in a nearby airstrip, but mucking in with the pigs and the potatoes is enough to have the stench of modern football taken from your clothes. Today, he also likes to meditate. "It's important to me," he says. "I like to relax and clear my head."

The Manchester City that Haaland Jr has joined is of course a far cry from the one his father departed back in 2003. "It's huge," he says. "The facilities around us, the staff, all the people around the club, it's an enormous organisation. It's a very professional club – it does everything in a good way to help their players, which I really like." ▸

Below Alfie's stint at City has helped fans immediately identify with Erling

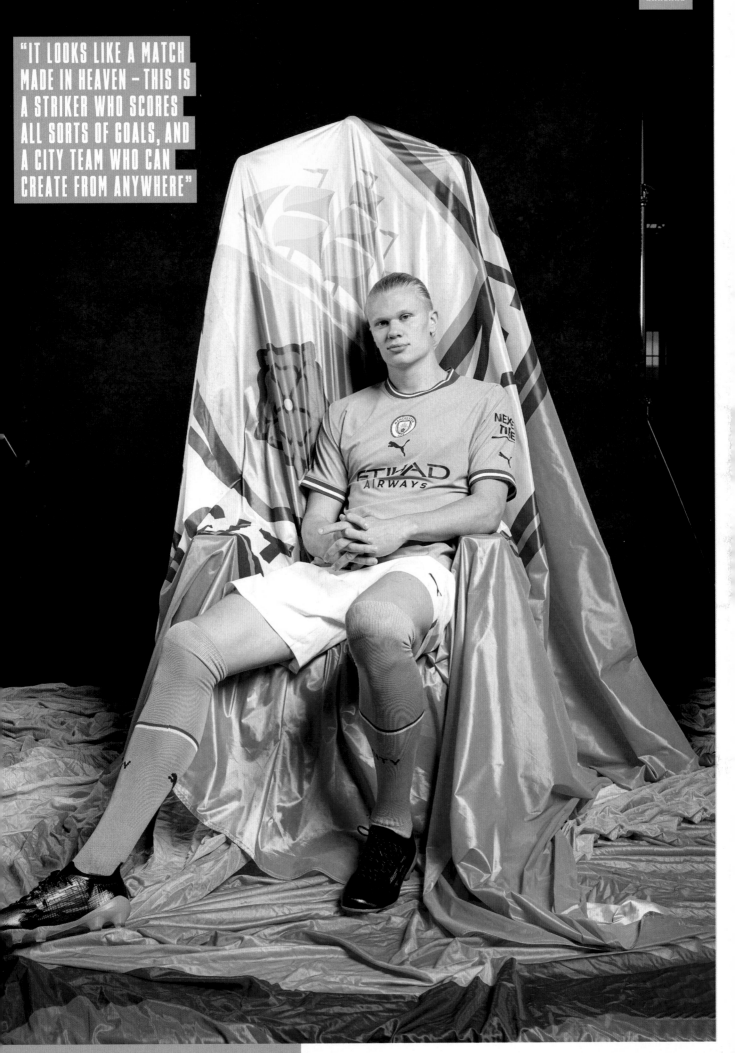

"IT LOOKS LIKE A MATCH MADE IN HEAVEN – THIS IS A STRIKER WHO SCORES ALL SORTS OF GOALS, AND A CITY TEAM WHO CAN CREATE FROM ANYWHERE"

"I'M CONVINCED HE'LL LEARN SO MUCH FROM PEP – SOON HE'LL BE A COMPLETE STRIKER"

The incredible facilities that surround us as we talk, the players he now calls team-mates, the global recognition and a gluttonous want for silverware, are all what make the modern Manchester City such a new and desired place to work. But there's also Pep Guardiola, and Haaland's eyes dance when his latest manager is mentioned.

"Well, he didn't have to sell the club to me, that's for sure," says Haaland. "He didn't have to sell anything. For starters, he's a special trainer and that was so important to me. We all know what he has done for his clubs, but also for players and for the game in general. That's something I want to be part of. I think we can have a lot of fun together."

NO MORE FALSE NINES

Observers taking an interest in Haaland from a young age have looked to terms such as the 'perfect striker'. You can easily see why. The physicality, the athleticism, the hunger for goals all point to as much, but Haaland will have none of it. He's come to learn? "Yes, of course," he states. "I don't know what will happen, but it must always be about learning, about developing. You can never stop looking for new ways to become better. Look at Karim Benzema at Real Madrid. He's 34 now, and suddenly he's developed into an even better player over the last couple of years – that's insanely good. I want to always do that."

Comparisons with Benzema are inevitable. The French talisman has gone against type recently, not quite reinventing the No.9 role, but along with Haaland they've made the

number and its central position real again. False nines beware. "I was watching the Premier League a lot before I arrived here, and I think over the past few years the big No.9 has become more and more rare, but that's why it's even better to be one now!" smiles Haaland. "It's the final position and I always wanted to be a striker because of that. I love my position."

Fans love his position, too. For all of modern football's nuance, supporters adore an out-and-out goalscorer. False nines may be hard to mark, but they can be hard to idolise too.

"That's right," explains Mooney. "Let's be honest, the reason us City fans loved Aguero is because he scored so many goals. There's something about having a No.9 up front who is supremely good, and to have somebody who bullies the opposition and scores a ton of goals – it excites people. City are a weird team because we score loads of goals, but we all think we don't score enough. Now we have someone who'll play a lot of the game in the 18-yard box, which we haven't had for two years. We've spent that time seeing De Bruyne drive the ball across goal and saying, 'Oh, there's no one there'. Now there's going to be, and he's one of the most sought-after players in Europe. We're thrilled."

Clockwise from above "It wasn't quite like this back in dad's day"; Pep wants Haaland to be his terminator; the striker's debut in England ended with defeat in the Community Shield

Haaland is too, and he's eager to show his versatility. "In the modern game, of course there's lots of play, play, play and that's fine, I like it, I can contribute to that," he says. "But I also love a wideman going down the wing, crossing the ball in and me scoring. It can be that easy sometimes. I think the No.9 today needs to be able to do both and enjoy doing both – hopefully I will."

The play, play, play line here is crucial. You won't witness much more of it than in a Pep Guardiola outfit, and since Haaland's arrival, there has been much analysis about how both player, manager and team will adapt to each other. "I don't listen to all of that," says Haaland. "When I'm here I train, I work hard, then I go home and switch off. I have to. My head is very important – it needs to be in the right place so I can play at my best, so all the outside noise about systems is nothing to me. I work with the coach, I work with the team, for the team. That's it."

The thing is though, Manchester City scored 99 goals en route to the Premier League title last season, and their 150 in all competitions wasn't bettered by any team in Europe's top five leagues. Yet onlookers never stopped remarking that something was missing, and Guardiola himself suggested (after the 2-2 draw against Liverpool in April, but he may well have been discussing their profligate Champions League campaign) that his team had a tendency to "leave teams alive".

So will Haaland's goals act as the deathly cyanide capsule that makes trophy hunting easier? He will do the work on the training pitch, but others see where that work might

be put to best use. Ex-Denmark international Niclas Jensen played alongside Alfie Haaland at Manchester City before joining Fulham – having kept a close eye on his team-mate's son, he acknowledges where there is room for improvement.

"Erling is a very clever player," says Jensen, now running the Nordic Sky talent agency in Copenhagen. "But his first touch, and playing in small spaces, are areas he can improve on. I'm convinced he'll learn so much from Pep, so soon he'll be a complete striker. The other way around, too – I'm sure the team will learn to use his strengths as well."

Another former team-mate of Alfie is Nicky Weaver, the former City goalkeeper whose penalty heroics in the 1999 Second Division Play-off Final memorably changed the club's fortunes, arguably helping them get to where they are today. Weaver describes Haaland's arrival as a "no brainer" and sees absolutely no reason to fret about systems and tactics.

"Top players just adapt," he says. "He'll play nearly every game, certainly the big games, and you'd be very surprised if he didn't score at least 20 goals. To me it looks like a match made in heaven, as this is a striker who scores all sorts of goals – he can poach, he's great in the air, he's a top finisher – and this is a City ▶

THE MISSING PIECE

City hope Haaland can deliver them the Champions League – these stars won it in their first year at a heavyweight club

CARLOS TEVEZ

Manchester United were Premier League winners in 2007, but lost to Milan in the Champions League last four. Then Tevez rocked up from West Ham and alongside Wayne Rooney and Cristiano Ronaldo, the trio secured European glory in 2008.

GARETH BALE

Real Madrid had waited over a decade for La Decima – again Ronaldo couldn't do it without a bit of help, provided by Bale's arrival in 2013. Within 12 months, the Welshman had netted in a Champions League final victory over rivals Atletico.

LUIS SUAREZ

As Paris Saint-Germain again showed last term, Lionel Messi and Neymar isn't necessarily a combination that will win you the Champions League. MSN certainly was, after Suarez signed for Barcelona in 2014, then smashed seven goals en route to lifting Ol' Big Ears that season.

ALISSON

Loris Karius' blunders proved costly for Liverpool in the 2018 Champions League Final – they soon signed Alisson to solve their goalkeeping problem. The Brazilian kept the Reds alive with a big save against Napoli, then helped them go all the way.

side who can create from everywhere. People think of them as this intricate team, which they can be, but they love to get crosses in. They fizz them in, and the likes of De Bruyne and Phil Foden must be relishing having that focal point, especially when games are tight."

"HE CALLED ME A WHORE"

At the highest level, there's simply too much quality at the centre of defences for games not to get tight.

Eighteen months ago, Haaland named his best three centre-backs in the world at that time: Sergio Ramos, Virgil van Dijk, Kalidou Koulibaly. This season, he'll face two of them in the Premier League. You wonder who'll be most drawn to putting more hours in the gym, but Haaland's tussles with Liverpool's Van Dijk and Chelsea's Koulibaly could go a long way to defining the outcome of those matches. With Van Dijk especially – a man

he'd met before in the Champions League for Red Bull Salzburg – could this be a rivalry within a rivalry?

"I'm not sure about that," insists Haaland. "It's not me versus Virgil. It's not one against one. It's 11 versus 11. I know he and I will be up against each other, but I'll also be against Alisson and the rest of their defence. This is modern, top-class football – it's about more than good individuals. We have to be great as a team, working together. It's important not to look at individual battles too much."

When pressed on Van Dijk though, there is a devilishness to his otherwise professional answer. "It's always nice to face the best and that's what Van Dijk is," he says. "I've played against him a few times, and he's a really good guy as well as an exceptional footballer. I like to play against him because he may be the best in the world." Then comes the smile. "But I have scored at Anfield and for Norway against the Netherlands…"

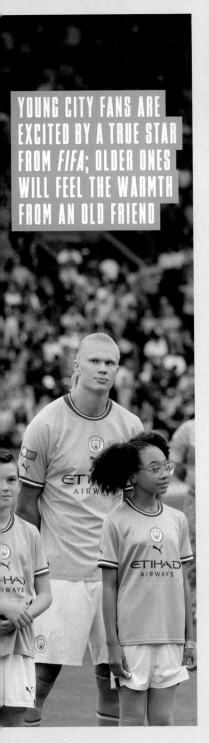

YOUNG CITY FANS ARE EXCITED BY A TRUE STAR FROM *FIFA*; OLDER ONES WILL FEEL THE WARMTH FROM AN OLD FRIEND

is fine and we're friends in the end. It's good to have a bit of that on the pitch, I enjoy it. Afterwards we're all the same, and we can all be mates."

You sense there will be a few friendly run-ins with opponents along the way, personal rivalries will come and go, but Haaland won't get sucked into anything long term and he certainly won't let a desire for awards like the Golden Boot and Ballon d'Or blur the lines. "Individual awards will come if you perform with the team," he says. "The focus is all with the team. Play good with the team and see what comes after."

But he must set goal targets for the season? "If I had them I wouldn't tell you, but I don't," says Haaland. "What's important is that while I want to score as many goals as I can, if I'm in on goal but, say, Riyad Mahrez is in a much better position, I'll be passing to him. That is normal for me."

Will things remain normal though? For the club, and their fans, they're hoping this is the signing, the big one that keeps them not only at the top of English football, but gives them that first taste of Champions League glory. It's a competition that Haaland has already fallen for. When he was at Salzburg, he drove around in his car playing the competition's anthem. "I love the Champions League," he says. "I love the anthem, I love the occasion, and I hope to help the team, the fans and, yes, the coach win it with Manchester City."

Those reporting on games may have to face up to a new normal, too. Haaland has been fascinating to speak to in this interview, on a relaxed afternoon before the season starts, but he's developed a reputation over recent years for amusingly quick and curt responses, especially to those holding a microphone to his mouth straight after a match.

"Ask a stupid question, you'll get a stupid answer," he's said previously, and the English press will have to be on their toes as much as any centre-back. "I wonder if the British media are looking forward to me?" chuckles Haaland. "It's going to be interesting. We'll see how it is." Talking of the media, there's every chance he'll run into his dad's nemesis Roy Keane along the way. That little smile returns to Haaland's face. "We'll see."

The one person who you sense will take all of this in his stride is Erling Haaland. Being the big thing in the gargantuan Premier League could buckle a few knees, and any fame that his considered career trajectory has afforded him thus far is about to expand considerably. It's not as if he can just blend into the crowd. "It's true, I'm not a normal looking man on the street," he says. "I'm tall, have long hair, blonde; everyone sees me, so that is different, but I'm not complaining about it at all. My dad knows the game, he knows lots of things about being a footballer and he's helped me, but I take all the fame stuff in my stride. If I ever changed, I have enough people, not just my dad, to tell me. The people in my home town are really important to me, and I'll always remember where I've come from. I'll never change. I'll never change who I am, or how I behave."

City fans wouldn't want it any other way. ○

It would be difficult to add further spice to the recent hotpot served up between City and Liverpool, but maybe this is the signing to do just that. Haaland has loved watching previous clashes between the heavyweights, and can't wait to be part of the blue tribe for those Premier League clashes.

"From the outside looking in, it was so high level," he says. "I've watched many games between the teams, and I think the level has probably been the best in the world. They were pushing each other to the absolute limit, winning, winning, winning, until the very last game when either of them could have won the title. I mean, after 60 minutes, if Liverpool score against Wolves, they might well have taken the title. That's special. It's great to be involved in it now. I'm very excited."

A total of 86 goals in just 89 appearances for Dortmund; 28 goals in just 22 Champions League games; 21 goals in just 23 caps for his country; an incredible 20 goals in his first

Clockwise from left Eyes on the prize; Van Dijk is the man to beat; Haaland's move appeals to City fans of all ages; West Ham failed to nullify him on matchday one

13 games for City. Haaland's mesmerising desire to introduce the ball to the net is frightening, but with that rise the talisman is aware that he's now in the line of fire, that people will be gunning for him, and not all of them will be wearing football boots.

In June, Real Madrid owner Florentino Perez suggested that Haaland would have only made the substitutes' bench had he chosen the Bernabeu over the Etihad this summer. Haaland once again grins. In an international against Sweden the same month, the striker claimed that opponent Alexander Milosevic had threatened to break his legs and called him a whore. The Norwegian went on to bag a brace and found the time to clarify that he was, in fact, not a whore.

"It happens in football," concedes Haaland. "I like to have a laugh myself, but I don't think too much about outside talk. I can't. It means I'm not focusing and not at my best. It's good to have some fun, though. Talking

"WEAH WAS LIKE A CHILD DISCOVERING A CHOCOLATE AT EASTER – I'VE NEVER SEEN ANYONE EXPLODE ONTO THE SCENE LIKE HIM"

GLORIOUS GEORGE

In 1995, George Weah did something no African footballer had ever done before in winning the Ballon d'Or – and hasn't again in the 27 years hence. But how did a former weed-smoking striker conquer the world... without really scoring that many goals? Allow *FFT* to explain...

Words Huw Davies

Can a Ballon d'Or winner be underrated? Blame Cristiano Ronaldo and Lionel Messi for freakishly skewing records and expectations. Messi's award-winning 2012 featured 91 goals for club and country, including 59 league goals. Fifty-nine.

In 1995, George Weah scored only seven. To the overly invested Ronaldo stans and 'Messi GOAT' accounts on Twitter, that may seem laughable for a striker also named the world's best player that year – just as three European league titles and five domestic cups makes for a comparatively lean career CV. Nor was Weah a YouTube footballer: he made great goals look simple and his most famous strike, that instantly recognisable ▶

box-to-box dribble for Milan against Verona, underwhelms some critics because he's half-tackled on halfway before regaining control.

However, we owe more respect to the man known as King George (or Mr President, these days) in his native Liberia, and Paris Saint-George in, er, Paris. Weah's goals were varied, vital and brilliantly timed. He thrived against the fiercest opponents. His personal honours board features not just the Ballon d'Or and FIFA World Player of the Year – where only Brazil icon Ronaldo denied him back-to-back wins – but African Footballer of the Century, as befitting its only 20th-century Ballon d'Or recipient. If three African Footballer of the Year awards – one at Monaco, one at PSG and one at Milan – sounds slightly insufficient, it's because he was competing with fellow legend Abedi Pele in his Champions League-winning pomp and voted into second place on four occasions.

Weah wasn't *about* goals. That's why the Ballon d'Or went to him and not Alan Shearer or Jurgen Klinsmann. Weah's all-round game made him a modern great. He pioneered the lone striker role without playing as one. When he wasn't pressing or scoring headers, he was creating space by dragging defenders away from the penalty box, whereupon he'd set up a team-mate or simply knock the ball past his marker and chase it. What's a defender to do against an intelligent, technically excellent striker who's also quick, strong and tireless?

Zoom out from Weah's goal against Verona and you'll see it all: his work outside the box, his first touch like the weaving of golden silk, his desire to collect a wayward opposition corner in the game's closing moments and score 14 seconds later.

"I looked in front of me, spotted five players and thought I could go through them all," he told *FFT* in 1998. Weah was a child again; the pitch was his career laid out before him.

THE SURPRISE SUPERSTAR

By today's standards, Weah was relatively old when he departed Africa. The continent's

> "I DIDN'T KNOW WHETHER MY PARENTS WERE DEAD OR ALIVE – EUROPEANS DON'T APPRECIATE WHAT AFRICANS GO THROUGH"

21st-century football luminaries relocated to Europe almost exclusively in their teens, often for France (Didier Drogba, Sadio Mané, Michael Essien, Emmanuel Adebayor and El Hadji Diouf) but alternatively Switzerland (Mohamed Salah), Belgium (Yaya Toure), the Netherlands (Nwankwo Kanu), Germany (Jay-Jay Okocha) or Spain (Samuel Eto'o). In contrast, Weah was nearly 22 when he debuted for Monaco in 1988.

His upbringing in Monrovia had been both ordinary and extraordinary. Raised by his grandparents in one of the Liberian capital's slums, Weah gambled, smoked marijuana, worked as a switchboard operator and played football to distract from gambling, smoking marijuana and working as a switchboard operator. But the Pele fan also visited Brazil as part of his sporting development thanks to Samuel Doe, president of Liberia, supporter of the national team and a personal friend. Useful, no doubt.

Weah won titles with such magnificently monikered clubs as Young Survivors, Mighty Barrolle and Invincible Eleven before moving to Cameroon's Tonnerre Yaounde, which is where, when and why Cameroon manager Claude Le Roy recommended him to Arsene Wenger at the Stade Louis II. "George Weah was a real surprise," admitted Wenger. "For me, it was like a child discovering a chocolate bunny in his garden over Easter. I've never seen anyone explode onto the scene quite like George did."

A long fuse burned first, as Wenger got Weah up to speed with fitness training and

Clockwise from above right On target with PSG; League Cup joy in '95; en route to a Champions League golden boot; "Who loves Wenger most?"

extra work on the striker's movement – but then came that explosion. The Frenchman had treated his £12,000 signing like a son, in Weah's words, housing him and saying he could be the world's best player ("I thought he was talking stupid"). The protégé repaid his mentor and father figure by scoring 14 league goals, one every 120 minutes, plus a couple in the European Cup. Monaco's final fixture featured some soon-to-be Classic Weah, with a solo run from halfway and powerful flicked header from just inside the penalty area making for a hilariously good brace against Nantes.

Later in 1989, Liberia entered a long and bloody civil war. Weah was living in New York, where he'd met his future wife, and flew to and from Monaco each week by Concorde – but physical distance could hardly provide emotional distance. "I didn't know whether my parents were dead or alive," Weah told *FFT* in 1996. "People didn't understand my torment. Europeans find it hard to appreciate what Africans go through when we think about home. As far as they're concerned, we are paid to do a job and we just have to do it."

Boy, did he do it. With Weah, Monaco went deep into the European Cup, reached a Cup Winners' Cup final and sealed the Coupe de France. In 1992, PSG pounced, as they would for Kylian Mbappe 25 years later, though he would cost a little more than £6.5 million.

In his first season in the capital, Weah won the Coupe de France and would have lifted a league title, too, but for his own employers. When match-fixing Marseille were stripped of their 1992-93 domestic crown, runners-up PSG were offered the honour instead, only for club owners CANAL+ to refuse it because they feared that outraged Provence viewers would cancel their subscriptions.

CANAL+ also turned down l'OM's berth in the Champions League, but that did at least allow Les Parisiens to upset Real Madrid at the Bernabeu in the Cup Winners' Cup, Weah scoring the only goal. The pain of losing their semi-final to Arsenal was soothed by success back home, as PSG became champions of

France for the second time in their history. No need for charity this time: they positively cantered to the title, losing only one game after August, powered by the goals of David Ginola and Weah.

Weah always boasted a better strike rate in Europe than in league football, and his continental showings stood out despite his four PSG trophies all coming at home (he left shortly before their 1996 Cup Winners' Cup triumph, which remarkably represents half of all European honours ever won by French clubs). In three campaigns, Weah scored in the back yards of Barcelona, Juventus and Napoli, as well as home and away against Bayern Munich and Real Madrid, including

a UEFA Cup quarter-final triumph in 1992-93. PSG beat Real Madrid 4-1 to overturn a 3-1 first-leg deficit, before losing to Juve through three goals from Roberto Baggio, who'd form a great partnership alongside Weah at Milan.

Inevitably, with Weah the competition's top scorer, PSG found themselves in a Champions League semi-final. It was 1995, and it would be the Liberian's annus mirabilis.

AFRICA'S BALLON D'OR

For a player whose game wasn't defined by goals, Weah executed every kind of stellar finish. In one-on-ones, he'd preface his dink, poke or finesse with a subtle pause, as if to steady himself, wrong-foot the keeper and assure the ball that it'd soon be safely home. From range, he'd launch blistering surface-to-net missiles, their fierce power emanating from the beauty of a clean strike. He headed the ball with accuracy and implausible force, and he combined tenacity with close control to wriggle out of tight spaces: one mesmeric goal saw Weah surrounded by four Auxerre defenders, only to vibe his way through, get to his feet and nonchalantly flick the ball beyond the keeper.

PSG's 1994-95 Champions League season served as Weah's de-facto video CV. They won all six group-stage games and he found the net in five of them, including a late winner at Bayern's Olympiastadion that showed his sublime skill. Following good hold-up play on a shoddy surface, the striker played a one-two and derisively dragged the ball sideways past a prone Thomas Helmer as he hopelessly tried to grab Weah's ankle, then darted past Jorginho's tackle, jinked inside Mehmet Scholl and unleashed a rocket past Oliver Kahn. It was unstoppable. *He* was unstoppable. Two weeks later, Weah netted a ridiculous double against Spartak Moscow. His first goal was another Thor's Hammer, thrown in from 25 yards; the second, a dribble that floored the same defender twice.

A quarter-final against Johan Cruyff's Barça would provide a sterner test. Theoretically, anyway. In front of 115,000 fans at the Camp Nou, Weah had Albert Ferrer on toast and equalised from a free-kick he'd won by giving the hapless right-back twisted blood. In the second leg, Weah didn't score – he just ran Ronald Koeman ragged, hit the bar, pressed the Catalans' defence, created a number of opportunities and made the space for Vincent Guerin to drive home PSG's winner.

Milan liked what they saw even as they beat PSG in the semi-final. After Weah lifted the inaugural Coupe de la Ligue and a third Coupe de France, the Rossoneri took him to Serie A, land of unbreachable defences. The 28-year-old scored just seven minutes into his debut at Padova, before assisting the winner with a sublimed chipped pass to play a one-two with – wait for it – a rampaging Franco Baresi. Weah's son, George Jr, was celebrating his eighth birthday (future USA forward Timothy would be born in Brooklyn five years later), so consider that kid's thunder stolen.

The new signing was immediately Milan's clutch player. Eight weeks in, Fabio Capello's ▶

WEAH: LEADER, LEGEND... LANDLORD

Liberia's manager Peter Butler – the itinerant Halifax native, once of West Ham, Southend, Cambridge and more – lives in a house owned by the great...

It's impossible to escape George Weah in the nation of his birth. Just ask Peter Butler, the Halifax-born ex-journeyman midfielder who is currently in charge of the Liberian national team.

Butler resides in a house owned by the country's current president and, though the pair don't exactly sit down together and discuss tactics over a glass of red, the 55-year-old tells *FFT* that Weah is an omnipresent figure in Liberian life.

"It's every kid's dream to emulate him," he explains to *FFT*. "George Weah was a football icon in Africa and massively respected. We could do with him now, to be honest – our current top scorer has five international goals! I've been getting lads from overseas who are eligible to play for Liberia – players in their early 20s and could have 10 years ahead of them.

"Trying to emulate someone like George is a tough task, however. I occasionally see him in person but his face is all over the country. You can't avoid the fact that he's the most recognisable man in Liberia. He's still probably the most recognisable footballer in the whole of Africa."

Butler, who was a midfielder for Notts County when Weah was embarrassing opposition defenders and winning the Ballon d'Or with Milan, took on the job back in 2019, shortly before the onset of a pandemic that has done little to help improve the fortunes of either Liberia's national team or the country at large.

Liberia's hopes of making it to a first ever World Cup finals ended in November, when Butler's team came third in their qualifying group behind Cape Verde and Nigeria. Their two victories were against Central African Republic, who finished bottom. Despite that disappointment, Butler says it's his job to lay a foundation to help move Liberian football forwards.

"My job wasn't to qualify [for the Africa Cup of Nations or the World Cup] – it was to make a positive impact," he says. "We just don't have the finances – the country doesn't spend loads on football because they don't have that kind of money.

"There are bigger issues to try to tackle. We're trying to create an identity. Could European football do a bit more to help Liberia? Undoubtedly. Europe has pretty much bled the continent dry for its talent and not given a whole lot back in return.

"You can only achieve success in Africa if you've got money and backing. It's so hard for countries like us to compete."

Liberia gave the world Weah, but even as president he can only take them so far.

charges topped Serie A with 17 points and 13 goals. Weah had scored or assisted 10 of them. Matchday two: a left-footed cross on the turn against Udinese for Baggio to bag the winner. Matchday three: two fine goals that transformed defeat into victory away at Roma. Matchday four: two unselfish assists in beating Atalanta 3-0. And then, with the Rossoneri facing reigning champions Juve at a raucous San Siro while someone dressed

as the devil sprayed the dugouts purple (no, us neither), Weah won a free-kick by juggling a bouncing ball beyond the reach of five opponents, and Marco Simone converted it. The two soon combined again for 2-0, Weah brushing off Pietro Vierchowod – named by Gary Lineker as the hardest defender he ever faced – and tucking the ball smartly past Angelo Peruzzi. Milan won 2-1.

It continued. A late winner at title-chasing Lazio here, a smart assist for an equaliser in the Milan derby there... when the Rossoneri needed a goal, Weah found it. On December 23, 1995, the striker had a hand in both goals as Milan drew 2-2 with Fiorentina, who were second. The next day, he won the Ballon d'Or.

That award was commonly known as the European Footballer of the Year, and with good reason: non-European players weren't eligible. That all changed in 1995. Weah was one of six African nominees among the 50 players shortlisted, ranging from Finidi George of Champions League-winning Ajax to Japhet N'Doram, Nantes' Chadian striker, and his win

Left and below
"Catch me if you can!"; Weah and Baggio proved a potent strike duo at San Siro

was hugely significant. The Liberian called it "mission accomplished... I'd proved African players could do it at the highest level".

Serie A was the world's best league and Weah had tamed it. He was dictating games; winning games. Milan scooped the 1995-96 Scudetto, leading uninterrupted from the first week to the last as Weah ended his debut campaign with 11 goals and 14 assists in 26 league appearances. In a 4-0 thumping of Vicenza he was responsible for all four goals, scoring none. No wonder Thierry Henry, he of the joint-most assists in a single Premier League season, identified Weah as one of his three inspirations, alongside Romario and Ronaldo. Henry said these talismen could "pick the ball up anywhere and score", which is why the aforementioned late clincher at Lazio – and you can watch the whole match online with commentary from the legendary Peter Brackley – encapsulated the George Weah that exists in our mind's eye.

Receiving a pass far closer to the halfway line than the Lazio 18-yard-box behind him, Weah escaped a desperate hack on the turn and saw Cristiano Bergodi and Alessandro Nesta in his way. He simply flicked the ball between them, ran after it and, with his next touch, punted past keeper Francesco Mancini with insulting insouciance. Game over.

A marriage of confidence and composure bore glorious offspring: it made Weah great, and great fun to watch. You didn't *do* that to 1990s Italian defences. If the score was 0-0 after 87 minutes in a clash between first and third, that's because it was meant to finish 0-0. Good job, everybody, a decent point for us both. Hang on, who's this guy? What's he doing? How *dare* he?

HELLO, MR PRESIDENT

Weah didn't play many Champions League matches for Milan. In November 1996, the reigning World and European Player of the Year received a six-match suspension for headbutting Porto defender Jorge Costa in the tunnel after full-time, breaking his nose.

Costa had accidentally-on-purpose stood on Weah's hand in their previous meeting, necessitating 16 stitches, and then made a staggeringly high tackle this night. Weah said the defender had also made repeated racist remarks, but had no witnesses. Costa

GOALS: OVERRATED, MATE

Weah scooped the 1995 Ballon d'Or by a relatively comfortable margin, beating Jurgen Klinsmann to top spot with 144 points to the Bayern Munich striker's 108.

Third was Ajax's Champions League winner Jari Litmanen on 67, 10 ahead of Alessandro Del Piero. And trailing in joint-32nd, alongside Ian Wright with one point? Alan Shearer, scorer of 37 goals in all competitions as Blackburn

won the 1994-95 Premier League title, and another 20 before the year was up.

If ever there was a sign of how the Ballon d'Or has shifted in the modern era, this was it. Rovers' main man had fired the Lancastrians to a surprise title victory and liberally bludgeoned goals throughout the year, yet was basically a nobody beyond Britain's borders. Back in a pre-internet 1995, European and international exploits were vital.

Suddenly, Shearer flew up to third in 1996 on 107 points, behind Ronaldo and Matthias Sammer. Blackburn had tried to defend their title but finished seventh, while England were knocked out of Euro 96 in the semi-finals... but crucially, their leading marksman had bagged the Golden Boot and secured a world-record transfer to Newcastle. Evidently, it's quite helpful when folks know your name...

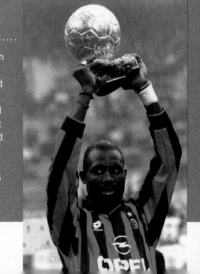

"I DIDN'T LEAVE MILAN, AND SACRIFICE £1.4M, TO BE TOLD TO SHUT UP AND F**K OFF"

sued for damages and defamation, but it was wildly out of character for Weah – so much so, FIFA gave him their Fair Play Award weeks later. Context can be instructive: just a few days before headbutting Costa, UEFA president Lennart Johansson had recollected a meeting with South African administrators and declared, "It's dark when they sit down together... 'I thought, 'If this lot get in a bad mood, it won't be funny'." This prompted a UEFA suit to explain his "joking manner" and Johansson to give the immortal apologia, "I cannot recall using the term 'blackie' but on the other hand I can't exclude it."

Weah's hefty ban, and Milan's contrivance to finish 11th and 10th between Scudetti, meant he didn't appear in the Champions League again until November 1999, against Galatasaray. He scored, of course, but that would be his final outing in Europe.

Unwanted by Milan boss Alberto Zaccheroni and barred from joining rivals Roma, Weah went on loan to Chelsea and turbocharged his tradition of fast starts by scoring a debut winner against Tottenham. He threw himself into English culture, quickly making friends, contributing to Chelsea's execrable FA Cup final song and wearing the trophy lid on his head after playing all bar two minutes of the Blues' Wembley win over Aston Villa.

His next spell, at Manchester City, was less successful. Even at 33 he represented a coup, City having been in the third tier two seasons previous. Immediately injuring Manchester United's Denis Irwin in his own testimonial

Clockwise from top
"No Lara, this is how to shoot"; lifting the FA Cup with Chelsea; George became the president of Liberia

must have pleased a few fans, but after 10 weeks Weah was gone, collecting £500,000 in severance on top of £250,000 in wages. "I sacrificed £1.4m from Milan to come here," read an extraordinary statement. "I didn't leave that for someone to tell me to shut up and f**k off." He moved to Marseille, while City were relegated.

Following a stint in Abu Dhabi, Weah retired and took the obvious next step: running his country. This time, success wasn't instant. Running for the presidency in 2005 brought defeat and claims of political naïveté – he'd lost to Ellen Johnson Sirleaf, an economist who studied at Harvard, worked for the World Bank and later won a Nobel Peace Prize – so Weah earned a high-school diploma in 2006, aged 40, then collected a Bachelor's degree in business management and a Master's in public administration. He lost again in 2011, but was finally elected to the senate in 2014 and, despite rarely attending parliament and neither introducing nor co-sponsoring any legislation, became president in 2018.

President Weah is popular among Liberia's young electorate – especially after offering free university tuition – but has faced criticism for prioritising his own former neighbourhood, delivering on a meagre eight per cent of his manifesto promises in the first three years of his tenure, and for generally being a bit, well, 'celeb'. He has also released four songs since becoming president, returned to the national team in his 50s for a friendly against Nigeria in order to retire his No.14 shirt, and takes part in regular kickabouts where no one dares tackle him (or, possibly, just can't).

Still, it's not the first time he has controlled Liberia's destiny. "I single-handedly sponsor the national team without any government assistance," Weah told *FFT* in 1996. "I buy the playing gear, return international airfare for European-based players, and pay match bonuses." Team-mates could also stay in his Monrovia hotel before matches.

With respect to Messrs Litmanen and Best, there's plainly no contest: Weah and Liberia represent football's widest chasm in ability. He was the world's best player. They were far from the world's best side. Later in his career, Liberia reached their highest FIFA ranking of 66th – their average placing without him is 130th. Their Africa Cup of Nations record reads zero qualifications before Weah came along; two when he was playing and zero since, despite the tournament's expansion.

The World Cup was elusive. Their Italia 90 bid kicked off with young Weah scoring in his country's first qualifying victory a few days after making his Monaco debut, but in a pool that featured 12 games and 13 goals, Liberia finished behind Egypt, who would then join the English, Irish and Dutch in the bleakest group stage in competition history. After that, Liberia were defeated by civil war for USA 94 and, more prosaically, by Tunisia ahead of France 98. They were set to reach the 2002 edition but, sidetracked by rare success in their concurrent AFCON qualifying campaign, faltered late on and ended one point behind the star-studded Nigeria generation of Kanu, Okocha, Yobo & Co.

In the aptly-named Lone Stars' only other fruitful campaign, Weah funded, organised and played in all seven meaningful fixtures, despite a busy European schedule. The year? 1995. Truly, there was nothing he couldn't do. ◌

MORE ON FOURFOURTWO.COM

• What really happened to Ali Dia, 'Weah's cousin'? On the trail of the Premier League's worst player *(by Richard Edwards)*

• 14 of the best ever Premier League loan signings *(by Greg Lea)*

• Why Arsene Wenger's legacy will forever endure in Africa *(by Aanu Adeoye)*

"I FELL IN LOVE WITH THE FACT YOU
COULD TELL YOU WERE IN A WORLD –
A LIVING, BREATHING WORLD. IT WAS
A ROLE-PLAYING GAME FOR FOOTBALL"

30 YEARS OF DISTRACTION

It's created legends, ruined entire weeks and prompted the most infamous split in gaming history. *Championship Manager* arrived to snotty reviews from the press in 1992 – then became the most loved football video game ever. *FFT* hears how from those who made it...

Words Mark White

The multiverse theory dictates that every choice we make creates a parallel universe. If so, there's a reality in which *Championship Manager* never existed. In its place: the music of '90s band Elevate.

Former A&R manager Miles Jacobson and the game's co-creator, Paul Collyer, first met when Miles, who had worked with the likes of Blur, Fatboy Slim and Feeder, saw something in Paul's "difficult" London band and offered them a deal. With this single sliding door, the programmer could've dropped *CM* in a haze of Britpop. "Elevate had potential," says Miles. "But every time someone told them that one of their songs was good, they'd rewrite it."

"One of the stupidest things I ever did was say no to Miles over the music thing," reflects Paul, smiling. "Still, it was never going to make any money, so we did the right thing."

It would hardly be the last time Miles heard from Paul Collyer – or from his brother, Oliver.

Now, in 2022, it's 30 years since the release of *Championship Manager*, when Miles – now the studio director of Sports Interactive, the company behind *Football Manager* – was one of the first converts. Written in a Shropshire bedroom by Paul and Oliver ('Ov' to his mates), it was developed only because they "hadn't discovered girls yet", as Miles jokes. It was a labour of love in between life, music and university – the latter finally abandoned by both – by a pair who just wanted to create something they'd enjoy playing themselves.

Three decades and millions of users later, it's fair to say that others enjoyed it, too. This is the story of a cultural phenomenon...

"WHO CARES WHAT *PC FORMAT* THINK?"

"We thought other games were all a bit limited," Paul tells *FFT*, of *CM*'s inspiration. ▶

"You could drop yourself into other games and be the centre of that universe – other teams wouldn't have real players or real names. But we wanted to create a football world and throw the user into it."

Miles (right) brings up another significant limitation: "At that time, a lot of the games would reset at the end of the season. You'd get promoted and your players would have completely different skill levels the next year.

"People forget how basic things were back in those days – the idea of a living, breathing world was a massive difference. I, like many others, fell in love with the fact that you could tell you were in a world. It was a role-playing game for football."

Paul and Oliver first had their vision for *CM* around the mid-80s. Addictive Games' *Football Manager*, originally released back in 1982, was an early beast of the genre that became extinct even before *CM* started using real player names; *Kick and Run* was another forerunner, appearing in arcades as the bootlegged Mexico 86.

The Collyers played both and thought they could do better. Their attempt was a project they coded on the side of schoolwork and during holidays. They offered it to publishers as *Championship Manager* just as the premier competitions in both English and European football were rebranding as the Premier League and Champions League respectively. Electronic Arts turned them down, claiming the game didn't have enough live action – understandable, perhaps, given they were working on the *FIFA* series which would come out in time for Christmas 1993.

But Putney-based Domark took a chance on the pair, which meant that *CM* would get its release on September 1, 1992, a fortnight after Brian Deane's inaugural Premier League goal for Sheffield United. Early reaction to the game was mixed. EA were right: there wasn't a lot of exciting graphics. The Collyers, however, weren't making something for gamers. "We got a score of 30 per cent in *PC Format* and Oliver was very upset by that," recalls Paul. "I was like, 'F**k it, who cares what *PC Format* think?'"

"We've got some of those reviews on the wall at the office," says Miles with a grin. "It didn't matter what the press said, really – the game spread on the playground. It was people swapping disks; one person would buy it, pirate it for other people, then those people would start to get into it as well. The audience built organically – it was something we dubbed 'word of mouse'."

Miles knew that very well from the music industry: it took only one person to buy a CD and share it for a fanbase to grow. It didn't hurt the publishers too badly, either: buying a game made by two brothers in a bedroom turned out to be cheap enough for Domark to break even. There was enough promise to make a second game – and importantly, a community was beginning to grow.

It was around then that Miles was asked by the Collyer brothers to assist as a business manager. He agreed – and from there, things really started to take off. The in-game detail was about to become groundbreaking.

"My very first game in the series was *CM2* in 1995," says Dave Black, an author of two *Championship Manager* books, who still runs the dedicated fan site cm9798.co.uk. "I was immediately sucked in by the amount of detail available in terms of player abilities alone. I was hooked, even though I was really bad at it. Then the series evolved, with European leagues. As a huge fan of *Football Italia* on Channel 4, it was a dream come true to manage the likes of Ronaldo without trying to coax them to St James' Park."

By this point, the Collyers (right) had moved to London. Written in a Cricklewood flat (next door to future Mayor of London Ken Livingstone, oddly), *CM2* boasted improved graphics, photos in background screens and the tones of budding BBC mic man Clive Tyldesley on commentary. Stats, tactics, transfers and contracts were heavily updated as well. It was too jam-packed with features to even run on certain formats.

"I had to buy a PC on hire purchase just to test *CM2*," remembers Miles. "I went over to Dixons in Camden. It's still the only thing I've ever bought on hire purchase."

"Amiga couldn't run the bloody thing," adds Paul. "Domark got some poor person to do an Amiga version of it and you couldn't do anything. I remember them showing me and asking, 'We don't understand why, when you turn it on, nothing happens for an hour – what's going on?'"

"GET ME DIONYSIS CHIOTIS!"

Weirdly, the more niche that *CM* became – there was still no attempt to appeal to traditional gamers, it being unavailable on

the dominant Atari ST and Amiga platforms – the more its developers noticed something deeper. Back then, access to discovering new players was largely limited to international tournaments, *Football Italia* and snippets in humble pages such as these. This wasn't just a computer game. In a pre-Google age, *CM* was becoming a year-round scouting tool; a plaything for football anoraks.

"Most of my memorable signings came on *CM 97/98*," superfan Black recalls fondly. "When Alan Shearer picked up a long-term

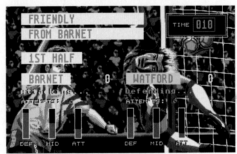

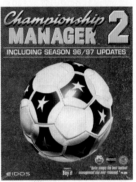

injury, I took a punt on Ibrahima Bakayoko from Montpellier, who definitely would have gone on to surpass any of the records Shearer achieved, had I played that long. You can imagine how stupid I felt after telling everyone that he would turn Everton into title contenders.

"It has stood the test of time because of the amount of cult players. They hold such fond memories for fans."

It wasn't just the cult players, either. Dave lists Robert Pires, Jose Chilavert and a young £7 million Rio Ferdinand as signings he'd bring in on his first-ever *CM* game – players who would become household names. Fans became obsessed with knowing the next big stars of real life... Ibrahima Bakayoko aside.

Paul Collyer says that part of *CM 97/98*'s appeal came from it being the third iteration of the *CM2* engine that he and the team had worked on. By then, they'd perfected it. The next time they would release a third iteration of the same engine was *CM 01/02* – a game almost as beloved as *CM 97/98*, solidifying Cherno Samba as a cult star alongside Taribo West, Sebastien Frey, Roque Santa Cruz, Maxim Tsigalko and Dionysis Chiotis.

THIS WASN'T JUST A COMPUTER GAME. IN A PRE-GOOGLE AGE, *CM* WAS A YEAR-ROUND SCOUTING TOOL FOR FOOTBALL ANORAKS

Ultimately, Samba struggled with the expectations created by his digital persona, and he escaped British football for Spain before returning briefly with Plymouth and Wrexham. Following stints in Finland, Greece and Norway, he played his final game aged 30. As the former Millwall starlet revealed to *FFT* last year, however: "I've read that some wonderkids feel the game contributed to their failed careers, but I disagree. I hate excuses but I struggled to keep my feet on the ground. I'm honoured that people still talk and think about me like they do."

The hype was justified. In reality, Samba had reportedly netted 132 goals in 32 games

as a 13-year-old at Blackheath, and he would later keep Wayne Rooney out of England's under-16 side. Liverpool wanted to sign him.

But not every wonderkid's gold status was deserved. If you ask Miles now why *CM 01/02* was so popular, he gives an honest answer from behind the curtain.

"The truth is, it was pretty easy to play," he admits. "The game had too many players who were overrated. We made too many players world-class, made too many data errors, and that made the game quite easy."

Back then, the now-legendary database was compiled very differently. "You'd get the data back from some team where every player was amazing," chuckles Paul. "For years I was obsessed with that data control and would have arguments with the other coders over it. But that game was a lesson. People compiled that database for the love of the game, so you couldn't just go in and reject all of their data. We were very open to abuse, as people tend to overrate their own teams. After that, we learned that you *need* some kind of control over the database."

Miles explains: "We started going after the fanzine writers, as we felt that they would be ▶

less biased and more balanced. But people love that game. They're still playing it now, 20-plus years later."

Dave Black agrees on the lasting appeal of both games. "There were fairly minor tweaks to the *CM3* game between 1999 and the launch of *01/02*," he says, "so it felt as though they'd been fine-tuning this game and struck gold with how it turned out. It's probably not a coincidence that *97/98* and *01/02* were the end of the cycle and both have stood the test of time.

"Years ago, I was talking about *01/02* with some colleagues from work and the four of us decided to start a network game. It was like being 14 again. It's just so easy to pick up and play, especially now with a modern computer. It's not a criticism of *FM* – I still love the series – but it's hard to find the time to sort out a training schedule and have a chat with six unhappy players while you've got a family to raise!"

CM IS DEAD: LONG LIVE FM

The release of *Championship Manager 4* was a jolt backwards in 2003, with more lag and more bugs than before. For some users, Northwich Victoria would move to a stadium with an 850,000 capacity. For others, the Vics and their division rivals could sign global superstars with ease.

It wasn't a happy time behind the scenes. The development team patched things up with a stellar *2003-04* version, including new playable leagues and the correction of a few farcical mistakes, and it appeared from the outside to be business as usual. Once again, however, there's a universe in which that particular version of the game doesn't exist.

"Our last game with Eidos was supposed to be *CM4*," admits Miles. "We agreed to do one more because it helped us both out. The relationship wasn't good from either side."

It was to be one of the most infamous splits in video game history. In the divorce, Eidos got to keep the name 'Championship Manager'. Meanwhile, Paul, Oliver, Miles and the development team that was now a few dozen strong would go their own way with the code that they had built. Crucially, they had the important database for a new game: *Football Manager*.

"I was worried – I wasn't sure whether to get *FM 2005* or *Championship Manager 5*," says Black. "Whenever anything like that happens, you worry that neither can function as well without the other."

The *FM* team, however, leant into the thing that all good cult products appreciate: their audience. It was in 2005, for example, that *Doctor Who* returned to TV screens on the back of supporters campaigning and keeping the universe alive. The internet of the mid-noughties was teeming with early social networks, fan forums and newsletters sent straight to your email inbox. *CM* had embraced it all.

Seventeen years after its renaissance, it is said that *Doctor Who* is almost unkillable now – even if it's cancelled on TV, there is a cult fandom that will live on. Likewise, as

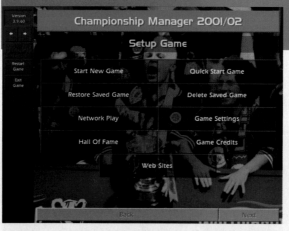

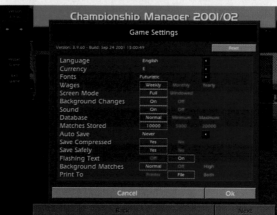

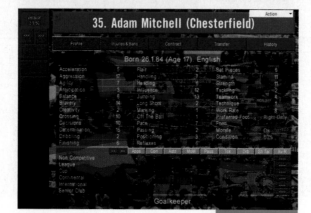

much as Miles, Paul and Oliver believed in the product they had invested in for over a decade, they also believed in the people who would help to keep it alive. Did they *know* a split was right at the time, though?

"No, hell no!" says Miles. "It was a big risk. But we were doing the right thing for us."

Paul explains: "We were pretty confident – as confident as you can be with anything, really – because we would never have done it otherwise." Miles agrees. "We were very confident that the hardcore audience would stay with us," he affirms. "We had built the audience and we were on the internet early as a studio. We'd built up our forums and customer base at a time when other people were still doing postal mailing lists. The community were absolutely essential."

That, and the fact that the first *Football Manager* game was excellent. Eidos bought a match engine and assembled a new team, but they were playing catch-up with people who'd been fine-tuning excellence for years.

"Some would say this is arrogant but I'd call it honest: we'd been No.1 in the market for a long, long time," says Miles. "We knew

how complicated these games are to make. We wanted to be an important part of the publishing setup we went to, and Sega were looking to branch out into that. They hired a bunch of people we knew well and it all came together."

From the start, too, the Collyers had worked with people they trusted. Mark Woodger, one of the first, was a schoolfriend of Paul and Oliver, brought in when the game was being produced in that Cricklewood flat by just six people. He still heads up the data today. The closeness of their team is one of its crucial strengths. Unlike some brothers, there are very few arguments between the creators.

"I've never had a fallout with Oliver over this," Paul insists to *FFT*. "We're quite different, actually: he wants to make something new all the time, whereas I like to improve what we have. He'd get something up and running in its skeletal form, and a long time after he'd be bored with something, I'd be obsessed with that thing and getting it to work. We complement each other pretty well – there was never a professional rivalry. I don't think we've ever disagreed on anything."

"You definitely disagreed on game features from time to time," interjects Miles. "I knew when that was happening because you were both really nice to me..."

GAMING THE REAL WORLD

Bjorn Heidenstrom only appeared four times in the Third Division for Leyton Orient. But he was a hell of a midfielder on *CM* in 1996-97.

"He has since befriended the community online and he's quite happy that he's found 'fame'," Black says of the Norwegian cult hero. "There's even been a heavy metal song recorded about him."

"ANDRE VILLAS-BOAS GETS THE CREDIT FOR BEING THE FIRST PERSON IN FOOTBALL WHO WAS PROPERLY USING THE GAME"

It's funny how a game can touch people in so many different ways. Ben Brereton Diaz – formerly Ben Brereton – was called up to the Chilean national team only on account of *FM* data outlining his ancestry, a detail gleaned from a nondescript Blackburn programme interview by one eagle-eyed researcher.

"You regularly get reachouts from football associations asking for lists of people with second and third nationalities," says Miles. There are hundreds more players, coaches, scouts and analysts with stories of their own. Miles' list of footballers to send the game to each year currently stands at around 3,000.

"Andre Villas-Boas gets the credit for being the first person in football who was properly using it," reveals Miles. "When he was chief [opposition] scout at Chelsea, he was asked about it and he said he was playing a lot of *Championship Manager*. I love that Antoine Griezmann talks about it so much, and that the French national team play the game so

much on trips. It's gratifying whenever anyone tells us that they got involved in football or learned something because of our game. But it's a very natural, normal thing for us now. Most people in football have grown up with it."

It must be weirder for Paul, though, who came up with this idea in a bedroom on a farm with his brother. "Yeah, it is," says Sports Interactive's creative director with a smile. "I mean, I've had enough years to get used to the idea, and you take it for granted in your life, day to day. When I think about it all, though, and when we have these kinds of conversations, it comes back and you get a nice reminder. Actually, yeah... it is ridiculous, isn't it?"

It's very rare: a game with a new release every year, which seems to be getting bigger, better and stronger with every iteration. It's a game about to add women's football, too – and one with no real competitors any more.

"When I see or hear people reminiscing about the games, it's very rarely about the features or the gameplay," says the writer, Black. "Everybody remembers the players who were unbelievable in the game, and that's only magnified if they didn't hit those heights in real life. You can play it your way too, unlike, say, *Tomb Raider* or whatever else people were playing around the time."

It's the ultimate game not for gamers. You can't do it wrong: there's always a team who will take you on after a sacking. But will it last another 30 years?

"I hope we'll be alive to see it," laughs Paul. "But if we could go back 30 years, how could we predict how *FM* would be now? I don't think we would have got anywhere near."

And to think: he could have given it all up for the music. RIP Elevate. ⊙

" I TURNED DOWN THE ENGLAND JOB BECAUSE I THOUGHT IT WAS TOO EARLY. THAT WAS A MISTAK "

Words Andy Mitten **Portraits** Gary Oakley

He didn't get much wrong in his 35-year career, but Bryan Robson still regrets the one that got aw
Captain Marvel earned the respect of a generation of Manchester United players, and even the odd all-tir

Back in May 2019, Diego Maradona was analysing a copy of *FourFourTwo*. The Argentine was managing in Sinaloa, Mexico, and as he flicked through the pages of our humble title, his eyes lit up at the thought of England – but not for the divinely metacarpal matters you'd expect.

"Bryan Robson, he was my favourite English player of that generation," Maradona told us in a sweltering evening heat, reminiscing about days both glorious and not so.

"Robson and Graeme Souness were the best British midfielders. Great players."

Diego talked about a Cup Winners' Cup game he'd played for Barcelona at Old Trafford in 1984, when Manchester United came from 2-0 down in the first leg to win 3-0. "I should have won a penalty!" he protested. "*It was a penalty...*"

Today, Bryan Robson is hearing this story for the very first time. He's talking to *FFT* in a hotel close to his home in Cheshire's ▶

"I LOVE MY LIFE AND MY AMBASSADOR ROLE. I GO TO EVERY GAME AND CAN VISIT THE TRAINING GROUND WHEN I WANT"

footballer belt, reflecting on an immense career in which he was easily United's best player of the 1980s. He represented his country 90 times, 65 as captain.

"I loved Diego but it wasn't a penalty," Robson rebuffs in his soft Durham brogue. "But he was the greatest I played against. He scored great goals, was quick, could go either side of you. Diego had everything."

Robson is 65 now, and works as an ambassador for Manchester United. All the other former players who do work in similar roles, from Andy Cole to Patrice Evra, Denis Irwin to Dwight Yorke, look up to Captain Marvel. United fans still idolise him, and the argument over who was better – Robson or Roy Keane – is perennial. Both heroes were complete box-to-box central midfielders.

But first, it all began with Bovril…

"I GOT LEATHERED ON FOUR PINTS"

"Football is my life," says Robson. "It started when my dad took me to watch Newcastle, and I was so into it. We'd get the bus over to St James' Park from where I lived near Chester-le-Street. It'd take half an hour, then a 20-minute walk from Newcastle station up the hill to the ground. I'd just think to myself, 'I would *love* to be a footballer'.

"I'd get there early and sit at the front of the paddock. Dad would put me there and then give me sixpence for a cup of Bovril and some peanuts, then he'd go to the working men's clubs by the brewery for five or six pints. Dad was a lorry driver and abroad all the time – he could be away for three weeks if he was doing a trip to southern Italy. There wouldn't be any contact with him. He'd do mum's head in a bit when he was back; she was from a farming background, but they were both big Newcastle fans.

"Dad was home one weekend after I'd played a game. I was 13, we were having some lunch and there was a knock on the door, which I answered. It was a scout from Burnley. He came in and invited me down for a week's trial in the school holidays. I loved that idea. I'd been captain of every team I'd played in since I was eight, and always had a good scoring ratio. I wasn't fast, but I loved a tackle and had stamina where I could run for fun – I did cross-country runs for County Durham. We'd race against other counties, and if there were 200 in a race I'd always be in the top six.

"Wyn Davies and Bobby Moncur were my Newcastle heroes. By 14, mum would let me go with my mates. I'd get on the bus with two brothers I knew, and then we'd go in the Leazes End with all the nutters. I'd never take my shirt off in the middle of winter like some, but I'd sing *The Blaydon Races* with pride."

It wasn't long, however, before Robson's own football started to take over.

"I went to Coventry for a week on trial, but it was West Brom who really captured my attention," he explains. "They were the third club I stayed with, and I loved the way they put me up in a hotel and picked me up in a coach. Coventry and Burnley were hostels. At West Brom we trained alongside the first

team, it felt real, then they invited me for six weeks in the summer holidays and treated me like a proper apprentice. It felt like my foot was in the door."

Robson moved into digs in West Bromwich with few distractions – initially, anyway.

"I didn't start drinking until I got into the first team," he chuckles. "We played at York three games before the end of the season [in April 1975] and won on my debut.

"When we got back to the ground, Len Cantello and Asa Hartford said that we were going to celebrate. They took me out and got me absolutely leathered on four pints

of lager. I got back to my room and it was spinning! Len was a Mancunian who looked after me on the pitch. Things were going well, but not well enough to buy myself a place to live, so I sold my car to get a flat.

"Len knew I'd done that, so he picked me up each morning and we'd just chat about games. I'm still in touch with Asa and Len – we have an afternoon out every Christmas."

Robson was just 18 then, but with his talent instantly obvious to all, he grew in stature at The Hawthorns. By the end of that decade, after West Brom had finished third in the First Division and reached the quarter-finals of

> "I SAT AT A TRESTLE TABLE ON THE PITCH, IN A CRAP SUIT, AND SIGNED THE CONTRACT"

Clockwise from left Cup wins were crucial in the '80s; "I've lost my curlers"; a sign of things to come at Old Trafford; "so am I kicking the ball or the camera?"

and get them back. At Manchester United, I went to a charity function in Leeds with Ray Wilkins and Steve Coppell once. We travelled together, but Ray got tired so went for a sleep in the car after a while. We said that we'd join him in half an hour.

"When we did, the car had gone! He'd got a lift back to Manchester and we had to get a taxi from Leeds."

Revenge would come the next morning after training, however.

"I spotted Ray's really nice leather shoes," smiles Robson. "So I asked the groundsman if he had a hammer and six nails, and then banged them through Ray's shoes into the floor. He came back, got dressed, put his feet in his shoes and fell forward!"

DODGY PERMS AND PADDY'S PUB

That was the only direction in which Robson was heading, too. In 1981, having outgrown the West Midlands, he became Manchester United and Britain's most expensive player when he signed for £1.5 million.

"I wanted to win trophies," he says. "We had a great team at West Brom and had beaten United 5-3 at Old Trafford, but the directors weren't true to their word about bringing more players in so that we could challenge for the title.

"So then I signed for Manchester United. [Manager] Ron Atkinson and [chairman] Martin Edwards said they wanted to get the crowd going before one game, so I sat by a little trestle table and signed the contract. I had a crap suit on, which was fashionable in West Bromwich when I'd bought it!

"I was never vain, and if I saw someone wearing football boots which weren't black then I'd be wired up to get straight into them – but who was I to call out anyone when I'd sit with rollers in my hair for an hour when I had a perm?"

Robson's rise to becoming England's best player was slow enough to help him adjust to the new attention, though.

"It wasn't like I was 18 and breaking into Manchester United's first team like Marcus Rashford did," he says. "I got an agent, Harry Swales, who'd looked after Kevin Keegan. Harry would only ever have one client, and stopped working with Kevin when he moved to Germany. He didn't have a contract – he worked on trust. He said if either of us let each other down, then we could walk away. Harry didn't want anything to interrupt my football, and that's why the gaffer [Sir Alex Ferguson] asked me to speak to Harry about representing Ryan Giggs later on."

Swales brought Robson sponsors, and he became the face for New Balance. "Brilliant boots," he smiles. "They made one which I helped design." There was Easy Jeans, too. "Yeah, the modelling bit," he laughs. "The lads took the piss all the time because I was on the side of buses without a top on."

Robson may have been his nation's best footballer, but he didn't play for the nation's best team: Liverpool and Everton won the league, while United managed the FA Cup every few years. Robson knows why. ▶

the 1978-79 UEFA Cup, the Baggies' young star was the subject of a local newspaper petition to get him an England cap.

"I scored a backheel against Liverpool and we won," Robson remembers. "Len had said to me, 'It's a joke that you're not playing for England'. There was some pressure, and Ron Greenwood finally picked me [in 1980]. To be fair, I'd been out for the best part of two years with three injuries – two broken legs and a broken ankle."

Injuries would become all too frequent in Robson's career – a price to pay for his combative, all-action style – but West Brom

proved the perfect platform for his myriad talents. They were good for the soul, too.

"The team spirit was incredible," he says. "Willie Johnston was a nutcase and always doing pranks. One day, we were sat in the pub opposite The Hawthorns, and he was really drunk. Willie decided it'd be funny to take all his clothes off, run across the road and back into the pub.

"I roomed with [Scottish centre-half] Alistair Robertson, who had a thing about fire extinguishers and buckets of water – he liked to spray them about in hotels. If anyone did a trick on me, I'd bide my time

"We didn't win the league because of the lack of depth in our squad," he admits. "We could compete with Liverpool in the cup competitions – we had a really good team when we were all fit. But if we had a few suspensions, we struggled. We won our first 10 games in 1985, then Giddy [John Gidman] broke his leg against Ipswich, before Strach [Gordon Strachan] and Big Paul [McGrath] got injured. I ripped my hamstring playing for England and was out for eight weeks."

Manchester United weren't the only ones with issues in the '80s – football in general was suffering off the pitch, with hooliganism a huge issue.

"We played Liverpool at Everton in the 1985 FA Cup semi-final, and fans put nails in golf balls," Robson recalls. "My missus said she wanted to go to the game but I told her there was no way. That's how bad it got.

"You'd hear about the fights even if you didn't see them. We played in front of cages because of previous pitch invasions. Life was really hard for a lot of people in the '80s and unemployment was high, but that shouldn't have meant people turned to violence. It's more sane now."

None of it stopped Robson from being the team's leader and social convener, mind.

"We'd be regulars in the pubs around Hale, where people would leave us alone because they saw us all the time," he says. "If we went into Manchester it was a bit rougher, but fans were fine and might ask for an autograph. The good thing was that phone cameras weren't around. You weren't being filmed all the time."

The Park, a pub in Altrincham owned by former United midfielder Paddy Crerand, was a favourite haunt. "We'd go in when the pubs were only open 12-2 on a Sunday, and I knew dinner would be ready at half two," he says. "I'd take my daughters swimming and then go in. At first I didn't know Paddy Crerand owned it, and he was there behind the bar. We'd have a couple of pints and it became my regular place. His pub started getting packed on a Sunday, with loads of Wythenshawe lads who supported Man United. Paddy told me that I'd made him a fortune since I started going!

Robson grins wistfully. "We'd have a laugh there. Actually, once I played a cruel trick on Colin Gibson. He was a decent player who always told me that he should be playing for England. Bobby Robson would always ring and congratulate us if we'd made the squad. I phoned Gibbo and told him Bobby had just told me he was going to call him, as he'd made the squad. He wasn't. Gibbo wasn't happy at all – he called me a complete w**ker." Gibson never did play for England.

THE FLEDGLINGS TAKE FLIGHT

Robson, however, was in the first Three Lions team to reach a World Cup finals for 12 years.

"We had a really good team for Spain 82," he remembers. "Maybe not as good as the Brazil of Socrates and Zico who didn't win the tournament either, but if Trevor Brooking and Kevin Keegan had been 100 per cent fit,

we would have been. Kevin would have got goals. We just needed to score in the really tight games. We had players who weren't considered stars, like Phil Thompson and Phil Neal from Liverpool, but they were winning the European Cup with Liverpool and were top players. Trevor Francis, too, with Forest."

Robson scored twice in England's Bilbao opener, a 3-1 win over France where his first goal came after only 27 seconds. Victories over Czechoslovakia and Kuwait sent Ron Greenwood's side through.

"Then there was a second group stage where we played West Germany and Spain in the Bernabeu," says Robson. "We drew both 0-0. Trevor and Kevin both came on against Spain – we needed a goal because Germany had beaten Spain, and only one team went through. We couldn't get one. We went out and were gutted, but that stadium is the best I've ever played in; it's huge and the stands rise steeply. It's easier for a passer like me when the pitch is big, as you have to use your intelligence and pick the right pass rather than get in close and scrap. It's one reason I always liked Villa Park."

England were highly fancied going into the following World Cup in Mexico, but things didn't go to plan there either. "It was always going to be difficult, playing in the heat and at altitude," he reflects. "Me getting injured didn't help, nor did Maradona either, but Gary Lineker and Peter Beardsley were both top forwards around that time.

"In 1990, we had a great chance. The lads proved it by reaching the semi-finals, and it would have been a really close final against Argentina if we'd beaten the Germans on penalties. Gazza was close to being the best player in the world in 1990 – he was that good. If he hadn't gotten reckless with his challenges and got silly injuries, his career would have been different."

Robson left Italia 90 distraught. "My worst injury, easily – Achilles," he winces. "I knew I wasn't going to recover, that it was the end of my World Cup – my third."

He'd been an FA Cup winner with United for the third time that year, but a league title

looked miles away after their 13th-place finish. "I know how it looked, but I could see that Sir Alex was changing the personnel around," Robson says. "Some of the players he'd brought in had quality – a young Paul Ince, Brian McClair, Gary Pallister and Denis Irwin. But it wasn't just players. He brought in Archie Knox, Brian Kidd and Nobby Stiles, and told them he wanted United to go back to the days of the Busby Babes. He wanted all the best kids, especially from the North West, to build the youth system up again.

"The club could see what he was doing in the background and the players could see how good his training sessions were, but we needed that 1990 FA Cup to give the players, especially younger ones, confidence. Those cups were important, but winning the league in 1992-93 was my highlight at United; that first title for 26 years.

"It was a huge step for the club, because it took the shackles off us and showed that we could do it. We won the Double in the next season. That opened up the pathway for Sir Alex to bring his youngsters through."

"WINNING THE LEAGUE IN 1992-93, OUR FIRST FOR 26 YEARS, WAS MY UNITED HIGHLIGHT"

It also meant United were back in Europe's premier competition in 1993-94 – for the first time since 1968-69. "Galatasaray was the most intimidating place that I've ever played," says Robson. "Lunatics! It wasn't just the fans – the police and army joined in.

"We walked up the steps and into the stadium, and the flares were going off. We'd already been met at the airport by a load of screaming fans holding 'Welcome to Hell' banners. But I still enjoyed playing there – I loved the way the Turkish fans would jump up and down, then point to the next stand asking them to do the same."

Robson left United the following season to join Middlesbrough as player-manager in his infamous half-and-half get-up (right).

"I loved it at Boro and had a really good chairman in Steve Gibson," says Robson. "I went to West Brom and kept them up [in 2004-05]. I managed Thailand, which was a fantastic experience being an international coach. At Sheffield United, the fans didn't want to give me time to build a team. I thought I was going the

Clockwise from above Ending 26 years of hurt; following injury against Holland; and at Mexico 86

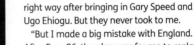

right way after bringing in Gary Speed and Ugo Ehiogu. But they never took to me.

"But I made a big mistake with England. After Euro 96, the plan was for me to replace Terry Venables when he stepped down, after working with him for two years [as assistant]. I had an interview with Jimmy Armfield at my house and he said, 'I'll recommend you to be the next England manager'. But I'd only been at Boro for two years – I was expecting Terry to go into the next World Cup. I said, 'If I'm ever going to manage England, I want to have good experience behind me – I don't want to cock it up'.

"I got that wrong. I should have taken it. At the very least, I should have said, 'Give me a couple of days to think'."

Robson doesn't have many regrets – he's now enjoying life as a grandad and working for his old club. A film about his life, *Robbo*, came out recently. "I love my life now, and my ambassador role at United," he says. "The Glazers take a lot of stick, but they left Sir Alex and David Gill to the playing side while they hit the commercials, which is

what they've done. The fans want to have a go at them, but there are some really good things that they've done.

"I get to all the games to watch the lads, and I can go to the training ground when I want, but I can also go on holiday, too – mainly to Australia, as my daughter lives there. It's been hard not seeing them in the past few years. But in normal times, I can go without football governing me any more."

He's certainly earned it. ◉

MORE ON FOURFOURTWO.COM

• On the hunt for Diego Maradona in Mexico: a thrilling journey to the other side of the world *(by Andy Mitten)*

• Middlesbrough 1996-97: rucks, relegation, cup finals… and training sessions at a prison *(by Rob Stewart)*

• Revealed: Razor Ruddock's 25 hardest players EVER *(by Chris Flanagan)*

AFRAID IN CHELSEA

Roman Abramovich's sanctions plunged Chelsea into disarray, yet 40 years ago fan riots, financial crises and legal wrangling made for a bleaker Stamford Bridge situation. In their time of need came a spiky Ealing businessman who didn't suffer fools – but saved the club

Words Richard Edwards

Usually when a new owner joins a club, there's a bounce, an added energy and some renewed sense of expectation. Enter Oldham Athletic, who arrive for their latest Second Division fixture at a ground that's long since fallen into a state of disrepair, and a short while later will become notorious as the first in the world to try (the operative word – they weren't allowed to) controlling supporters via the subtle-as-a-brick use of electricity.

The date is April 3, 1982. The location is Stamford Bridge. And the natives? Well, let's just say they're as restless as a fan trying to climb over a fence with 12 volts coursing through it. Watching their team is proving a similarly shocking experience.

"Kenneth Bates may well be pondering the wisdom of his recent move southwards," wrote *The Times*. "After moving from Wigan Athletic to become a director of Chelsea and agreeing to erase their debts, he watched his new side squander a two-goal lead against Oldham. The crowd of 8,938 was the lowest of Chelsea's season."

Records, however, are there to be broken, and that figure was depressingly lowered four days later when only 6,196 disillusioned souls reluctantly left the pub to sit through the visit of Cambridge United. If Bates hoped that his £1 purchase would galvanise a club plummeting at an alarming rate, then he was left bitterly disappointed. And if the players thought it would usher in an era of largesse, so were they.

"I earned more bricklaying and playing for Harrow Borough than I did when I signed for Chelsea [in 1980]," admits Chris Hutchings, the future Bradford and Wigan manager who was there when Bates made an atypically low-key introduction.

So desperate was the situation, even the Blues' fundraising lottery was losing money. Forty years ago in west London, no one was feeling very lucky...

FOLLOW THE MONEY

On the morning of the Oldham match, Bates had addressed Chelsea fans to assure them that the club's future was now in safe hands. Before he fed the press, though, the Ealing native had to find his way around a ground that would become his home from home for more than two decades. "I had to ask my way to the secretary's office when I arrived," he told the assembled hacks. "The first thing I can tell Chelsea's fans is that the problems with the club's finances have been resolved."

Sharp-tongued, ruthless and smart, Bates made his fortune by any means necessary: in haulage, in South African land development, in Australian sugar cane, in dairy farming

Above Blues fans were notorious in football's era of hooligan activity **Top** "And up here is where I can turn on the electricity"

and even cement. Oldham had offered his first avenue into football, as chairman in the '60s, before he became co-owner and vice chairman of Wigan. Not all of his business interests had succeeded. In 1976, the Irish Trust Bank he set up infamously collapsed and left thousands of investors out of pocket. After a legal war, Bates escaped unscathed.

Six years on, Chelsea's predicament offered a glimpse into the future – for man and club. The debt which had previously belonged to them, along with Stamford Bridge itself, was switched to a holding company which, in turn, leased the ground back to the struggling Second Division side. Bates then took care to ensure that the seven-year lease could be extended, and that any redevelopment of Stamford Bridge would have to include the club. It meant that if the ground Chelsea had called home since 1905 was redeveloped for any other purpose, then an alternative gaff would have to be found for a team that last won the league in 1955 and didn't look likely to trouble the engravers any time soon. The days of triumphing in Europe – and Chelsea had, lifting the Cup Winners' Cup in 1971 – were as distant as the view to the pitch from a number of stands, which may as well have been on Fulham Broadway itself. Instead, the Blues were losing £12,000 a week and stuck in quicksand.

In short, the club was a mess before Bates showed up – and although their new owner's presence didn't eradicate the difficulties, it did at least make them substantially easier

to solve. Were it not for his intervention at a club that only narrowly escaped relegation to the third tier at the end of 1982-83, then it's more than possible neither Matthew Harding nor Roman Abramovich would have considered investing in an entity that could have been jettisoned from SW6 altogether.

Like most things involving Chelsea down the years, though, the road would be long, winding and littered with potholes. In 1981, the Blues had announced profits of £33,000 on a turnover of £1.3 million, mainly thanks to the sale of several players – most notably Ray Wilkins to Manchester United – that had kept them narrowly out of the red. Interest payments in their various debts, reckoned to be in the region of £4.5m (the equivalent of £14.5m in new money) were, according to club accountant Martin Spencer, "crippling".

The root of Chelsea's financial mess could be traced back to the proposed rebuilding of Stamford Bridge. Buoyed by both FA Cup and European success during the early 1970s, Brian Mears, grandson of the club's original co-founder Joseph, was intent on furnishing one of English football's most swashbuckling sides with an 80,000-capacity home befitting the likes of Peter Osgood and Alan Hudson. The revamped Bridge would boast stands closer to the pitch, an electronic scoreboard and even the potential to pipe warm air under cold seats in the winter. The shining centrepiece would be a new East Stand, the largest of its kind in Britain.

By the time it was completed, however, it threatened to become a monument to folly. "The optimism of 1971 looked like hubris by 1973," noted Rick Glanvill, Chelsea's official historian. By 1974-75, the spiralling costs of rebuilding the stadium meant Chelsea's on-pitch fortunes had nosedived: only four years after their victory in Europe, they were relegated to the second tier.

To compound the Blues' despair, a deep recession bit, making supporters even more reluctant to spend their hard-earned cash watching a desperate band of no-hopers. As Britain lurched into a financial catastrophe and a three-day working week – inflation ballooning from 9.2 per cent to 24.2 per cent in two years – merely servicing the debt on the East Stand was a job in itself.

And it wasn't just the club's cash flow that was rushing out of control.

FIGHT CLUB

Since 1977, Chelsea had been denied ticket sale revenue – ring a bell? – as the result of an away day ban for their fans. It followed violence and off-field chaos in a 4-0 hiding from Charlton at The Valley, leading Denis Howell, Labour's Minister for Sport, to go in two-footed after the latest in an ugly string of incidents that involved not just Chelsea but Manchester United, Nottingham Forest and Luton. For a government desperately scrabbling to solve a problem that wouldn't go away, enough was enough.

"Most Chelsea fans following the club at that point were good blokes, but there was a real hardcore who were just there to cause

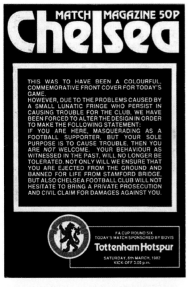

MATCH MAGAZINE 50P
Chelsea

THIS WAS TO HAVE BEEN A COLOURFUL, COMMEMORATIVE FRONT COVER FOR TODAY'S GAME.
HOWEVER, DUE TO THE PROBLEMS CAUSED BY A SMALL LUNATIC FRINGE WHO PERSIST IN CAUSING TROUBLE FOR THE CLUB, WE HAVE BEEN FORCED TO ALTER THE DESIGN IN ORDER TO MAKE THE FOLLOWING STATEMENT:
IF YOU ARE HERE, MASQUERADING AS A FOOTBALL SUPPORTER, BUT YOUR SOLE PURPOSE IS TO CAUSE TROUBLE, THEN YOU ARE *NOT* WELCOME. YOUR BEHAVIOUR AS WITNESSED IN THE PAST, WILL NO LONGER BE TOLERATED. NOT ONLY WILL WE ENSURE THAT YOU ARE EJECTED FROM THE GROUND AND BANNED FOR LIFE FROM STAMFORD BRIDGE, BUT ALSO CHELSEA FOOTBALL CLUB WILL NOT HESITATE TO BRING A PRIVATE PROSECUTION AND CIVIL CLAIM FOR DAMAGES AGAINST YOU.

FA CUP ROUND SIX
TODAY'S MATCH SPONSORED BY BOVIS
Tottenham Hotspur
SATURDAY, 6th MARCH, 1982
KICK-OFF 3.00 p.m.

People

"I NEARLY JUMPED OUT OF A MOVING TRAIN, THAT'S HOW TERRIFIED I WAS"

trouble," says Vic Locke, a member of the Chelsea Pitch Owners and a fan who travelled home and away, despite the ban. "There was all the talk of Chelsea smiles [an infamous knife wound], though that was more a myth, really. But there were fans intent on trouble."

Chelsea's challenges were hardly unique in a decade synonymous with hooliganism. But as time wore on and patience became ever thinner, the ordinary fan was viewed with the same disdain by both police and government.

You could hardly accuse Chelsea of sitting on their hands. In March 1982, an FA Cup tie against rivals Spurs was marked by a solemn programme cover, which laid bare the major obstacle facing English football. On a black background, the Blues used their biggest gate of the campaign (42,557) to issue the threat of private prosecution against anyone whose "sole purpose is to cause trouble".

Such a move didn't come entirely out of the blue. In the previous round, Chelsea had knocked out Liverpool, and their fans had

Clockwise from above "I told you I was peckish..."; the fences that defined the '70s; the programme cover requesting calm from fans

taken it upon themselves to do likewise to the travelling support. "A section of the Britannia terraces occupied by around 500 Chelsea fans, mostly teenagers, went wild like a tribe of savages as they fought with police and opposing fans," sighed John Wasbrough in the *Fulham Chronicle*. It was enough, he said, to "put you off going to football matches". As league crowds plunged, a generation of Chelsea fans knew how he felt.

Bates would assume control of the Blues a month later and, after sorting out the dire finances, he made restoring their appalling image an immediate priority.

"There was something happening every week, not only at Chelsea but up and down the country," says Locke. "I remember once picking up a newspaper and seeing a fan with a dart embedded in their skull. The dart just avoided their eye but it was literally hanging off the side of the person's face. It was grim.

"A bit closer to home, I was on a train from Woking with some pals, heading to Chelsea around the time that Bates took over. All of a sudden, a bloke started chasing us through the train. We ran down every carriage being tailed by this guy with a knife. When we got to the end, I honestly thought about jumping out of the door, out of a moving train. I was that terrified. Then he pulled his lip down, started laughing and showed us the word 'Chelsea' tattooed on the inside of it."

By the end of the decade, Lord Justice Taylor would recommend the introduction of all-seater stadiums in the aftermath of the

Hillsborough disaster of April 1989. In the early '80s, though, Stamford Bridge already had more seats than almost any ground in English domestic football – and was probably the most dangerous place to watch a match in the country. Just ask the Leeds fans who travelled south in October 1982.

"Chelsea's hooligan fans have chillingly exposed the argument that all-seater stadiums will end violence inside grounds," said the *Evening Standard*'s Peter Blackman, as the Second Division meeting concluded in a near-riot. "Their rough-house fans left The Shed for seats along both touchlines against Leeds on Saturday. Clearly, they'll pay more cash to terrorise anyone near them."

Colin Pates was a centre-back mainstay for the Blues from 1979-88. "The ground would be rocking, and just before kick-off I'd turn to the Shed End – all you could smell was the beer coming off the breath of fans behind the fences," he said.

In short, a trip to Stamford Bridge wasn't for the faint-hearted in whatever capacity you found yourself. So, spare a thought for the white-bearded knight charged with overseeing the club on a day-to-day basis.

"Ken was very present," recalls Hutchings. "He was the man who would carry out all the wage negotiations with the players. You'd go into his office with a lump in your throat, and very often he would agree the first figure you mentioned. You'd come out of there kicking yourself – you got the feeling you could have earned another £50 a week." ▶

BATES' HOTEL

Back then, £50 a week was a fair wedge for a club on its uppers. Bates ultimately had bigger fish to fry: his toughest battle wasn't with agents, players or even the hooligans, but a London property company not entirely enamoured by the idea of Chelsea playing at their spiritual home any longer than needed.

On September 23, 1983, chairman Bates awoke to some surprising news. Not that the club had been absolved of blame for another terrace tear-up – this time during a match at Brighton's Goldstone Ground three weeks earlier – but that Stamford Bridge had been sold. The club would likely need an alternative place to play while the most valuable ground in English football, a 12-acre site of prime west London real estate, was redeveloped.

"Chelsea's chairman, Ken Bates, reacted angrily yesterday when he discovered that Stamford Bridge, the ground the club rent from a property company, had been sold to another property company who intend to turf the club out for a couple of years as they develop the site," reported *The Guardian* under the headline 'Chelsea Seek New Digs.'

Given the reputation of their fans, finding a temporary home was unlikely to be an easy task. Of greater immediate concern to Bates was that the freehold had been sold from under his nose. SB Properties were majority-owned by David Mears – the brother of Brian and another grandson of Chelsea's founders – and Viscount Chelsea. When Bates bought the club in the spring of '82, they paid rent to SB Properties, who remained responsible for reducing the debt accumulated as the club rebuilt their East Stand. Flogging the freehold to Marler Estates was their way of clearing it once and for all.

For the new man, it was a bitter pill. "My comment on the way Mr Mears changed his mind would be that his grandfather built the club, but the current generation presided over its decline," said Bates, who was then asked whether Mears would be welcomed back to Stamford Bridge for Chelsea's match against Middlesbrough. "Lepers are more welcome," came his typically barbed response.

It marked the beginning of a long-running battle between Chelsea's chairman and the freehold owners, but Bates found an ally in the form of actor and Oscar-winning director Richard Attenborough. While other ex-board members sold their shares to Marler Estates, Bates and Attenborough made life as difficult as possible for the property company. The 1970s' crash had originally caused many of the issues that threatened the Bridge's future, but another economic collapse – this time in the housing market during the early '90s – eventually secured it, by precipitating the collapse of its freehold owners in November 1992. Chelsea wouldn't have been far behind in the liquidation stakes.

"He's a real bastard to get in a tangle with," David Mellor, the MP for nearby Putney from 1979-97 and a Chelsea fan, said of Bates. "He used the Companies Act at every opportunity.

There are unattractive sides to him, of course there are. But the people who took him on didn't realise how sharp he was."

The man who'd installed an electric fence which was never turned on suddenly had control of Stamford Bridge. "So he set up the Chelsea Pitch Owners (CPO)," explains Locke. "Bates didn't want that situation to ever arise again, so he effectively handed the freehold over to the supporters. That says it all about him and what he did for this club."

With that, Bates could roll out his big Blue vision – adding two hotels, bars, restaurants, apartments, the club megastore and much more. "When I took over I thought to myself, 'We've got 12 acres of land here in the most valuable part of London – and it's only open for business 25 days a year'," he said to *The Guardian* in 2002. "What business can survive on that? Ever since, I've been trying to make it work 365 days a year."

In 2011, Roman Abramovich attempted to wrestle back control of the land on which Stamford Bridge was built, but fell short of the 75 per cent of shares he needed to force through the issue. For those supporters who'd experienced the uncertainty of the 1970s and '80s, the CPO remain a necessary safety net – although 11 years ago, none of those present at that Emergency General Meeting would have imagined what might follow in 2022.

Amid this year's chaos, there are plenty of Chelsea fans of a certain vintage who have seen it all before... albeit with a very different cast of characters. *Crisis?* What crisis? ◉

Below Blue Ken saved Chelsea from extinction through a mix of canny business and a bit of luck

"KEN'S A BASTARD TO TANGLE WITH. PEOPLE DIDN'T REALISE JUST HOW SHARP HE WAS"

TOO BIG TO FAIL?

Chelsea weren't the only powerhouse to slip out of the top tier shortly after post-war success. Despite a true great and a penalty-taking keeper, the same fate befell this trio

MANCHESTER UNITED
RELEGATED 1974

The Red Devils secured the European Cup under Sir Matt Busby in 1968 – yet within six years they'd fallen to the second tier.

An ageing side finished 11th in the First Division in the very next season after lifting Old Big Ears – Busby decided to retire aged 59 only to return briefly 18 months later, taking charge until the end of the campaign after successor Wilf McGuinness was sacked. United came eighth for three consecutive campaigns – the latter under new boss Frank O'Farrell, after failed attempts to recruit Don Revie from Leeds and Jock Stein from Celtic.

That 1971-72 season, the club were forced to play two home fixtures away from Old Trafford after yobs threw knives at visiting fans mid-match – United 'hosted' Arsenal at Anfield, then West Brom at Stoke's Victoria Ground. A fallout with increasingly wayward star George Best and a 5-0 defeat at Crystal Palace led to O'Farrell getting the heave-ho in December 1972, but United still finished 18th under replacement Tommy Docherty. The team found it difficult to score goals – Bobby Charlton top scored with just six and retired that summer, and Denis Law joined Manchester City on a free transfer.

Best remained but featured little as United went down the following season, playing his last game for the club in a 3-0 defeat at QPR on New Year's Day. United again struggled to find the net – goalkeeper Alex Stepney was bizarrely made penalty taker, bagging twice to become the team's joint-top scorer for a period – and went into their penultimate game of the season needing victory at home to City, plus favourable results elsewhere if they were to avoid the drop.

Law's 81st-minute backheel memorably put City 1-0 up – minutes later, United fans stormed the pitch (above) and the match was abandoned. The scoreline was allowed to stand but other results that day meant United were doomed regardless – even a win wouldn't have been enough.

LIVERPOOL
RELEGATED 1954

Seven years after becoming England's first post-war champions in 1946-47, Liverpool finished bottom of the top flight.

The reason for their downfall was obvious. With Bob Paisley in defence, they conceded a league-low 52 goals in 42 games en route to First Division success. But in a miserable 1953-54 campaign, they leaked a league-high 97. Paisley was 35 by then and on the verge of retirement – the club's demise had been coming, after they'd wound up 11th in 1952 and then 17th in 1953.

Don Welsh's side conceded five goals on five separate occasions in relegation and were stuffed 6-0 at Charlton, ending 49 years in the top flight. It would take eight years – and the appointment of Bill Shankly – for the Reds to return to the First Division.

TOTTENHAM
RELEGATED 1977

Glenn Hoddle would become one of Spurs' greatest ever players – but not before his career began with the drop. The teenager was a regular in 1976-77, though couldn't stop their slip towards the Second Division.

Gaffer Terry Neill defected to former club Arsenal prior to that relegation campaign. He'd been an unpopular successor at Spurs for the loved Bill Nicholson, who'd won the UEFA Cup as recently as 1972 and reached the final again in 1974, his last hurrah.

Assistant Keith Burkinshaw took the hotseat from Neill, and while he'd later recruit Ossie Ardiles and Ricky Villa, lead Spurs to two FA Cups and another UEFA Cup, his first season proved a baptism of fire. An 8-2 thrashing at Derby in mid-October was the Rams' first league win – their only other home victory had been 12-0 against Finn Harps in the UEFA Cup.

No one in the division conceded more goals than Spurs that term, as they came bottom and slid into the second tier for the first time in 27 years. Fortunately for them, they immediately returned... and haven't been out of the top flight since.
Chris Flanagan

Below A teenage Hoddle became a regular as Spurs went down in '77

TINO IN TOONLAND

Faustino Asprilla arrived on snowy Tyneside to take Kevin Keegan's Entertainers over the line – then got the blame when it all went wrong. So how is it that the cheeky Colombian is still so adored by besotted Geordies? It turns out guns, girls and hat-tricks aren't even the half of it...

Words Si Hawkins

Now *that's* how to make an entrance. An absolutely Baltic Newcastle Airport in January 1996, and with snow laying roundabout, a vision in furs comes striding across the runway like Elizabeth Taylor on location in Siberia. Faustino Asprilla has touched down on Tyneside, and this land of striker-likers has never seen football like it. Or fashion.

"Those weird T-shirts," sighs his old skipper Rob Lee. "Under that fur coat he was always scruffy, never smart, hunched over. Stick David Ginola in a black plastic bag and he'd still look a million dollars. Tino looked like a bag of rubbish whatever he wore."

Those were the days. Fresh from Italy, this Colombian superstar favoured one famous Newcastle boutique: the Metrocentre Disney Store. Goofy, not Gucci. Still, Tino was far from a Mickey Mouse footballer.

"He was deceptively quick," recalls Lee, switching gears. "He had those bandy legs; one minute you think you've got him and then all of a sudden he'd do something ridiculous. He could do things with a ball you could only dream of."

Off the field, too, there were tales of the unexpected: missing a cup final for kicking a bus. Foiling an assassination. Inventing Jurassic PonyBall. Foisting a prophylactic on a stressed-out Alan Shearer. And yet, despite all these thrills and spills, Faustino Asprilla is often remembered for one half-season as the ultimate misguided winter buy. Which is both unfortunate and not wholly accurate.

It even transcends football, the way Devon Loch's late Grand National collapse became shorthand for, well, what Newcastle did in 1995-96. Cricketer Mark Wood evoked it while pondering whether England should pick eventual match-winner Jofra Archer before the 2019 World Cup. "It was the old Kevin Keegan thing, bringing in Tino Asprilla," suggested the Durham fast bowler. "Does that change the dynamic? Does it mix it up? All of a sudden, you lose the momentum."

But, just like a 93mph yorker, Tino brought the fun in a way most others never could...

MILK IT, TINO

It's easy to forget that Asprilla had won armfuls of medals pre-Tyneside, even if his lifestyle gave managers sleepless nights. It certainly gave Tino sleepless nights, more enjoyably, and his on-field exploits roused the folks back home.

"People would wake up early on Sunday morning, 7am, to watch Parma matches," says Colombian journalist Lucero Rodriguez. "My engineer friend Julian was one, and said to me recently, 'He wasn't the type of player that would disappoint you – he always did *something* to make it worthwhile'."

A gun and horse fanatic, the ranch-dwelling Asprilla properly merits the 'maverick' tag. His hometown of Tulua was a bit Wild West, with gunplay aplenty and a busy trade in "very expensive horses", reveals Rodriguez.

The South American had made his name at Cucuta Deportivo by bagging a brace past Argentina keeper Sergio Goycochea on his debut, then thrived with Medellin-based title winners Atletico Nacional, where he also got death threats as part of the cocaine kingpin Pablo Escobar's club. A move abroad made sense: to Italy in 1992, but not the traditional heavyweights. A new challenger had stormed into Serie A, fuelled by influential dairy giants Parmalat. *Buongiorno, Parma*!

Andrew Gardener, from *bellissimo* Billericay, watched Tino up close back then. Passionate about Parma due to Channel 4's coverage, he started fanzine *One Team in Emilia* – and got enviable backstage access. Gardener remembers arriving unannounced at the club offices once, "and the team manager decided to give me an impromptu tour of the whole stadium".

Parma's less strict vibe suited Asprilla. His free-kick routines occasionally involved aiming at the owner's phone – probably not advisable at certain clubs nowadays.

Still, Italy was tricky initially. "He felt lonely and it was too cold for him," says journalist Rodriguez. "The first impulse was, 'Mom, I'm

Top to bottom
UEFA Cup joy with Parma; "Can I have a wine, Kev?"; Tino's famous celebration

coming back home' and she'd say, 'No, no, no – stay over there until you're successful. If you're successful and still want to come back, come back. But first demonstrate your talents. You can do it'."

And he did. The young Colombian earned worldwide fame with, yes, a mighty free-kick – at San Siro no less, which ended Milan's astonishing 58-game unbeaten streak. He had no clue about the Rossoneri's record beforehand, or their fabled Franco Baresi-led defence, but wouldn't have worried anyway. One constant in Tino's career: an almost superhuman absence of nerves.

The Parma years were incredible. In 1993, Asprilla powered the Emilians to their first European trophy, the Cup Winners' Cup, with two goals in the semi-final first leg against Atletico Madrid. Then life intervened. Back in Tulua, a bus driver crashed into his car. "When I got out, he shut the door on me," Asprilla told *FFT* in 2008. "When I kicked it, my foot went through the glass but got cut as it came back out. If I'd got into the bus, I would have hit him." He missed the final.

Slightly awkwardly, Parma actually trained at the local police barracks. "I got in once and Tino wasn't there," continues Gardener. "He'd had another crash and hit an old lady in a Fiat, which could have been serious. He had a few driving escapades."

The hasty colt was no big-time Charlie, though – certainly with team-mates. In season two he formed a gloriously fluid and frankly unfair attack with Gianfranco Zola. "They were very close off the pitch as well," says Gardener. "I think the club liked that Zola went out with him; [Luigi] Apolloni was another – they were all married, so would look after him."

He still tested patience. Celebrating New Year back home, Asprilla was arrested for unlicensed shooting, while Parma's bus once retrieved him from a roadside ditch. But he still did the business. In 1995, Tino inspired another European success – the UEFA Cup – with three semi-final goals this time, against Bayer Leverkusen. Six months later, the club finally decided to sell their wayward star. Gardener has a theory, though. "We'd signed a pre-agreement with Fabio Capello and he said, 'I don't want Asprilla', so they got rid in advance. Then Capello didn't come."

If he'd only stayed, Newcastle might have won the Premier League title in 1995-96 and still been dominant now. Or not (see Rovers; Blackburn). So how was Asprilla's potential arrival in early 1996 perceived on Tyneside? Well, speaking of Charlie...

"'F**K OFF' WAS HIS FIRST BIT OF ENGLISH. HE'D FALL OVER AND SAY, 'TINO, F**K OFF"

"We'd heard rumours that apparently he was going to fail a medical because he had cocaine in his knee," says Gavin Webster, a Geordie comedian and author, who's now involved with Newcastle non-leaguers Heaton Stannington. Webster would share a pitch with Tino years later, but admits that the Colombian caused plenty of intrigue: "People said naive things then – this wasn't long after the Andres Escobar situation."

Asprilla's exploits with Colombia had been even more erratic than his club form: rows, bans, recalls... but one game that cemented his legendary status for good. In 1993, Diego Maradona belittled Los Cafeteros ahead of a World Cup qualifier in Buenos Aires (the legend was asked, 'Is this a Clasico?' "No," said Maradona. "A Clasico is two powerful rivals"). It backfired magnificently. Argentina were royally battered 5-0, as Asprilla went full gegenpress: winning fouls, forcing gaffes and scoring twice (past old pal Goycochea, no less). It's a wonder he still had puff for the celebratory somersaults.

Colombia were dark horses for USA 94, but they exited early, cowed by death threats which proved tragically prescient. As Asprilla told FFT, the doomed Escobar – no relation to Pablo, but whose own goal effectively ended Los Cafeteros' tournament – warned him on the journey home not to party that night. "So I said, 'All right, I'll stay at home'. And the person who went out was him."

"HE'D BE THE LAST PICK IN TRAINING"

Two years on, Asprilla flew into Newcastle, a whole city in thrall to Kevin Keegan's freewheelers. Had the players heard of him?

"We'd watched some Italian football, as Gazza was there," says Lee. "But we didn't know much. It was out of the blue."

Newcastle were already '95-96's big story. While Manchester United missed the kung fu-banned Eric Cantona, and champions Blackburn wilted, the Magpies soared. With Les Ferdinand nodding home Keith Gillespie's crosses, plus craftier prompting from Ginola and Peter Beardsley, they surged 12 points clear by late January. Why rock that boat?

"I think the idea was to keep Tino on the bench, to eventually take Peter's place," says Lee. Indeed, the new recruit was supposed to just watch Newcastle's next game, against Middlesbrough, and had a glass of wine over lunch. But Keegan couldn't resist naming him as a substitiute. The team was struggling, Kev gambled and Asprilla turned the game.

"His legs at times almost seem to be too long," chuckled commentator Barry Davies, after another loping run and bewildering dragback, with fans already chanting their new man's name. "It was probably the worst thing for Tino," explains right-back Warren Barton. "He was so good against Boro that we thought, 'We've got to fit him in'."

One player with mixed feelings about Tino's arrival was young striker Paul Brayson; Keegan preferred stars over kids.

"We'd won the youth league, cups and the reserve league," he says. "At the time, they had Ferdinand, Beardsley, [Paul] Kitson, then Asprilla, Shearer. You're thinking, 'How am I getting in there?!'"

It didn't do him much long-term harm: at 44, Brayson is still playing – and scoring – for Northern League Newcastle Benfield, led by fellow youth-teamer and non-league stalwart Stuart Elliott. Presumably Asprilla's lifestyle wasn't a huge influence?

"I think we just did the opposite," laughs Elliott. "He'd be the last pick in five-a-sides. Tino's first few words in English were like, 'F**k off' – he'd fall over the ball and just laugh, 'Tino! F**k off!' I don't know if the manager knew what to do with him."

Asprilla wasn't the only big transfer that February. David Batty also arrived on Lee's advice – "Kevin would ask who we wanted to play with" – which caused more tinkering.

Barton enjoyed a fruitful partnership with Gillespie, but "Rob Lee started to drift out to the right-hand side, then Keith got left out..." ▶

Below Tino's Champions League hat-trick against Barça proved to be his final Toon goals

Meanwhile, the freshly returned Cantona was on fire as Manchester United whittled Newcastle's advantage, most significantly a sucker-punch winner at St James' Park in March. Eric – all collar-up haughtiness – was seen as Alex Ferguson's mid-season saviour again. Asprilla – socks down, shirt out – was accused of largely the opposite.

"In some of the lesser matches, he could drive you mad," says Lee. "Against the big teams, you just gave him the ball. When he was off it, you'd try to keep it away."

Were there any motivational techniques for those off days? "We tried, in different languages and different ways," sighs Barton. "Sometimes, away from home when you're under the cosh, it wasn't really for him."

When Asprilla was good, he was very good. An unorthodox finish at Anfield gave the Toon a 3-2 lead, but the Magpies didn't really *do* game management: that eventual 4-3 reverse was disastrous. Newcastle's flair led to unhelpful TV scheduling, too. "United always played on the Saturday," says Barton. "They'd win their game, then we'd be playing on the Sunday or Monday night. The pressure started to mount."

On the manager, especially. Asprilla left Highbury on a motorbike rather than endure another post-mortem (which, he said, were baffling anyway) – then came King Kev's infamous "I would love it if we beat them" rant. They didn't. Manchester United finished four points clear and Newcastle became the Premier League's best-loved losers.

"I'd rather have the medal," says a wistful Barton. "Not a day goes by that I don't think about that."

That said, it was Newcastle's highest finish for 69 years and Asprilla wasn't moping: his doors were always open.

"He'd rented this massive, beautiful gaff," says Stuart Elliott. "There's stuff everywhere. He showed me these two fridges [does gruff Tino impression]: 'One fridge!' – all meat and grub. 'One fridge!' – all beer and champagne. It's an absolute mess, with all these people there. You'd say, 'Who's that, Tino?' and he'd just go, 'Eyyy, no problem!'"

Tino later revealed a canny trick for getting girls round: tell them David Ginola was there. Barton scoffs, "Asprilla didn't struggle in that department – he was ripped. We had a few of them: David, Les... not a lot of room in front of the mirrors."

The Donald Duck T-shirts and sometimes-languorous gait could be deceiving. "Them rubber legs, he was super strong," admits Barton. "A bit like Chrissy Waddle, so difficult to get off the ball."

Would he have enjoyed Barton's previous manor, Wimbledon's Crazy Gang? "He'd have had fun there," chuckles the now LA-based Londoner. "But there was more to Tino. "His English and my Spanish weren't the best, but with a translator we'd talk about the game – he was a student of it. He worked at it."

BULLET HEADERS... AND HOLES

Asprilla enjoyed more mirror time when Ferdinand and Ginola joined Spurs in the

"TINO LIVES SUCH AN INTERESTING LIFE. HE RIDES HORSES DRESSED UP AS A DINOSAUR..."

Above Tino's rubbery style was to the fore in Newcastle's 4-3 defeat at Liverpool in '96

summer of 1997, but the Entertainers were now disbanding. Six months earlier Keegan had left. His replacement, Kenny Dalglish, preferred target men up top – Shearer and Shearer-alike – but Tino's best Toon match was still to come.

Barcelona were Newcastle's first ever Champions League group stage opponents, at St James' in September 1997, and injuries meant the Colombian started. "You could tell he wanted to impress," remembers Lee. "He was unbelievably good – Keith Gillespie, too."

Asprilla's first-half hat-trick – including two bullet headers from pinpoint Gillespie balls – made for one of Newcastle's greatest nights.

But just a few months later, he was gone. Asprilla's January transfer request in the New Year forced his hand. Newcastle were struggling, but Shearer's return to fitness meant Tino's Toon adventure was over, as were his glory days. He allegedly lost his rented house deposit on Tyneside – bullet holes, naturally – and went back to Parma for £6 million. But even they were less fun.

"We were struggling," says fanzine editor Gardener. "I think it was really a signing to appease the fans."

The striker's off-field antics now eclipsed the actual football. He and Paraguay's Jose Luis Chilavert were sent off in a 1997 World Cup qualifier, and Asprilla later claimed that a hitman offered to kill the legendary keeper afterwards. Tino dissuaded him, apparently, but was then sent home from the World Cup for moaning about being substituted in Colombia's opening match with Romania.

The returning icon only played a handful of games back at Parma, then began similarly

Above "You got a dinosaur suit I can borrow?" **Top** His doomed Darlo unveiling

short-lived stints across South and Central America; definitely not his Amazon prime. His second honeymoon at Atletico Nacional lasted mere minutes: a red card on debut, followed by a row with the gaffer.

Weirder altercations were to come. Back in Newcastle for a rapturous on-pitch wave before the Magpies' 2002 friendly against Barcelona, he met George Reynolds: the controversial owner of fourth-tier Darlington. One thing led to another, and Tino incredibly looked set to join the Quakers. Fanzine editor Scott Thornberry wasn't convinced, and his response made headlines.

"If he signed for us, I said I'd bare my arse in Binns' window," he tells *FFT*. "It's a famous shop up here. The old Middlesbrough player, Bernie Slaven, actually did it when Boro won at Old Trafford."

Lord knows what the store's manager was thinking, but Darlo fans were going Tino mad. He was unveiled pre-match against Carlisle, given a squad number, and even Thornberry was buzzing ahead of a potential debut at Hartlepool. "I bought a Colombia flag," he reveals. "But then it all went wrong. So I still took my Colombia flag along, but scribbled 'For Sale' on it."

Reynolds, a former safecracker and jailbird, had made his fortune from selling kitchens.

Signing superstars would also be counter-productive; he'd already been snubbed by Gazza and now Tino did a moonlight flit, contract unsigned. "Faustino has f**ked off," one club employee told *The Guardian*.

Did a night out in Darlington put him off? "It's actually a very well-heeled, quite twee place," rebuffs comedian Webster, who's played a gig there. "I reckon he met George Reynolds and thought, 'There's no way I'm working for this bloke'."

The club had largely liaised with one of the Colombian's Geordie ladyfriends, it transpired, not an agent. "Perhaps a couple of promises weren't kept," reflects Thornberry, who then fell foul of Reynolds: "He used to come round my house quite often, confront me, phone me every night..." Perhaps it's for the best that the ex-safecracker and gun-loving Tino didn't last very long.

Reynolds eventually returned to prison, while Tino continued his South American tour.

"In Argentina, they called him 'Discoteca Asprilla' because he was Mr Party," explains journalist Rodriguez. At Universidad de Chile, he upped the tempo at training by firing guns.

"A joke," Tino later pleaded. "In a shopping centre, I bought a blank pistol like the ones made in Hollywood movies. That day, I took it to training."

It was an alarming technique he seemingly shelved when founding his own team CAFA – Club Atletico Faustino Asprilla, of course – in his hometown Tulua. Funds were raised by auctioning the aforementioned Byblos fur coat – for £2,300 – to a Newcastle theatre producer. Asprilla even made a cameo in her production of *Singin' Alang The Scotswood Road*. Because, obviously.

"EVEN BEZ DASHED PAST HIM"

Decades after his heyday, Asprilla remains newsworthy in his homeland; courtesy of machine-gunning a security checkpoint, posing naked for a men's magazine, shady dealings with a porn star – again – and his own sexy business: Tino condoms. He even offered to donate millions of them during the pandemic, but Colombia's strict lockdowns came down on him hard.

"He recently declared himself bankrupt," says Rodriguez. "Some bad investments."

Former Newcastle youngster Brayson remembers some cash chat at the club gym: "We were talking about Les Ferdinand's Porsche and someone asked, 'Why don't you buy one?' Tino just went, 'Ahhhh! Skint!'"

The bandy-legged icon invariably bounces back: reality shows, punditry... and he still contacts the old crew. "On social media," says Barton. "He's such a likeable guy and he lives such an interesting life. Whether it's riding horses, or riding a horse dressed up as a dinosaur' – while dribbling a giant yellow football, we hasten to add. That seminal footage really should have revolutionised the world of equestrianism.

He still visited Tyneside too, pre-pandemic, and graced some unlikely grounds. Webster was surprised to meet Faustino in the tunnel at Blyth Spartans before a comedians/pros charity game. "He was in town doing some talks for a local impresario," says Webster. "He played the first 20 minutes, pretty awful – I think a few players were trying to do him, nutmeg him. But he wasn't bothered."

That knee was knackered, though Asprilla remained an exceptional night owl. Stuart Elliott recalls a 2016 game for Alan Shearer's foundation, at Newcastle Falcons after a golf day. And night. Great stamina, Tino.

"There's 12,500 there, chock a block, and everyone's going, 'Where the f**k's Tino?!' Keith Gillespie whispers, 'He was still out at half-seven this morning'. Alan's going mad...

"Tino comes walking in the changing room, boots in a Sainsbury's bag, eyes wild – he's had no sleep. Alan's going, 'Get your f**king gear on!' but Tino shouts, 'Shearer! Picture!'"

While posing for a pre-match selfie, Tino whipped out a condom with his face on. "He wanted Alan to look like he was endorsing it," laughs Elliott. "Alan said, 'F**k off!' then Tino started throwing condoms at the lads..."

And how did Asprilla play, after all that?

"He went out, had a little walk about and then went, 'Off! Off!' Bez from the Happy Mondays was playing, just as wired – and even he dashed past him. But everyone was delighted to see him."

That's the thing with Tino Asprilla. Talk to team-mates, compatriots, even disappointed Darlingtonians: there's always a twinkle. Last summer, two years on from his own Asprilla barb, England cricketer Wood was presented with a run out chance against New Zealand. The Geordie ran up to the ball and kicked it at the stumps, gleefully shouting, "ASPRILLA!"

"There's so much pressure on the players nowadays, but nothing bothered him," says Rob Lee. "He enjoyed life. He enjoyed playing football. But he wanted to play his way."

Faustino's way. It'll be back in fashion one day, and football will be more fun for it. ○

MORE ON FOURFOURTWO.COM

• Kevin Keegan on Newcastle's '95-96: "I still have nightmares about how we threw the title away" *(by Sam Pilger)*

• Tino Asprilla, One-on-One: "I don't think we got together as a team enough at Newcastle – we lacked responsibility"

• Argentina 0-5 Colombia, 1993: the game that rocked the world... and embarrassed El Diego *(by Rupert Fryer)*

LIFE WAS BETTER IN BLACK AND WHITE

Alessandro Del Piero made himself an icon of late '90s football in the world's best league, then lifted the 2006 World Cup in an explosive summer for both club and country. The man himself relives his bumpy ride with *FFT*: scandals, Jagger and all

Words Jonathan Holloway

Two months after winning the World Cup, Alessandro Del Piero experienced a humbling reality check. It was September 9, and the mighty Juventus had just drawn 1-1 against 10-man Rimini in front of 10,000 supporters on the Adriatic coast. Kicking off his new campaign in the second tier of Italian football, a 31-year-old Del Piero – a serial winner of seven major trophies by then, including the Champions League – could be forgiven for wondering what kind of alternative universe he'd found himself in.

In the space of a few months, one of the biggest scandals in football history had rocked the game to its core, Italy had become world champions and Del Piero's beloved Juve were condemned to Serie B. Paradoxically, the lowest point in the attacker's storied career followed his greatest achievement by a matter of five days.

"There was certainly bewilderment and disbelief at what was happening, but the World Cup made everything more distant, right from the first days of training with the national team in Coverciano," Del Piero, now 47 and happily enjoying retirement, tells FFT. "I had a goal with my national team-mates – and nothing could distract me."

Such steely resilience becomes a theme throughout an hour in the Italian's company. Scandal, height issues, final heartache and injury agony have given Del Piero enough obstacles to hurdle but, every time, he had the last laugh...

PAINT IT, BLUE

Del Piero wasn't alone in his curious summer of 2006 – fellow Juventus stalwarts Gianluigi Buffon and Mauro Camoranesi were also involved in a national squad full of optimism heading to Germany for the World Cup. In May, the *Calciopoli* scandal of referee rigging had erupted around them, bringing the Old Lady into disrepute alongside Milan, Lazio, Fiorentina and Reggina. But if anything, that ugly episode served only to bring a tight-knit group closer together.

"From the very beginning we believed that we had a chance of winning," says Del Piero. "We flew under the radar without saying anything. But to tell you the truth, game by game, we found even more conviction and more belief. Our confidence grew day after day because we were a united, compact team – everyone was ready to give something for the group. In the end, we felt unbeatable. And we were..."

Such confidence wasn't unfounded: Italy hadn't been beaten since October 2004, and dismantled Germany 4-1 just three months before their first match of the tournament. Two Group E victories and a 1-1 draw took the Azzurri into the last 16, then wins against Australia and Ukraine set up a semi-final showdown with the hosts. Again, Italy got the better of Germany – only this time when it really mattered. After 90 goalless minutes,

"I HAD THE WORLD ON MY SHOULDERS. DID I FEEL SORRY TREZEGUET MISSED HIS SPOT-KICK? NO, I WAS DELIGHTED"

Below On top of the world with the Azzurri against France

Del Piero added to Fabio Grosso's late extra-time opener by ghosting into the box and curling a fine strike beyond Jens Lehmann.

"There's nothing like it," he grins 16 years on. "You can't think of anything else – it's almost impossible to sleep, you just have that goal in mind. Despite the enormous tension, it was a joyful wait [to score in the 119th and 120th minutes]. I'll say it again: we felt unbeatable and wanted to prove it."

Del Piero had plenty to prove. Italy had lost to final opponents France when they last made a major tournament showpiece, Del Piero's Juve team-mate David Trezeguet's golden goal bettering the Azzurri in Euro 2000's historic denouement. Six years later the two juggernauts squared off once more, this time matching each other through 120 minutes. Instead of destroying Del Piero for a second time, Trezeguet struck his shootout spot-kick against the bar. Del Piero scored Italy's fourth, setting up Grosso to convert a dramatic clincher.

"That walk from centre circle to penalty spot was the longest of my life – it wasn't even the first time I'd taken one in a final," he says. "But this was different – here I had my whole story on my shoulders, and the whole world was watching me; especially my country. Did I feel sorry for Trezeguet? Honestly, no, I was delighted. Sure, I'd have preferred it to be someone else's mistake and not David's, but at that moment there's not too much time for feelings."

Three days later, a weird summer got weirder when the music lover appeared on stage in Milan with one of the greatest bands of all time. The Rolling Stones were covering the White Stripes' *Seven Nation Army*, complete with alternative lyrics for a victorious nation. "Mick Jagger and the Stones were playing at San Siro and called

me on stage," chuckles Del Piero. "I don't really know how it happened, but certainly there was a bond – Jagger is a huge fan of Italy and our football."

That 2006 World Cup triumph may be the greatest in his career, but it's impossible to mention Del Piero's name and not instantly think of Juventus. The club's all-time leading goalscorer wore the famous black and white for 19 years, scoring 290 goals in 705 games. But rather than a heroic rise through their youth ranks, his journey to stardom began as a 13-year-old at Serie B outfit Padova.

"When I started playing football, I was the shyest and the smallest, and so it was for years," he recalls. "I used to play everywhere – I played so much with my brother Stefano that my father invented a lighting system to let us play late into the evening! I've always had passion, ever since I was a little kid. The difficult thing was leaving home for the first time at 13 years old, though I wasn't chasing success back in those days – just the desire to play and make my dream come true. First only football, and only passion."

Padova deserve credit for taking on a small, unassuming Del Piero in the hope his physical growth would match his development as a player. The trequartista never made it past 5ft 9in but what he lacked in size, he made up for in skill, determination and smarts. Del Piero only made a handful of appearances for Padova, but that was enough to convince

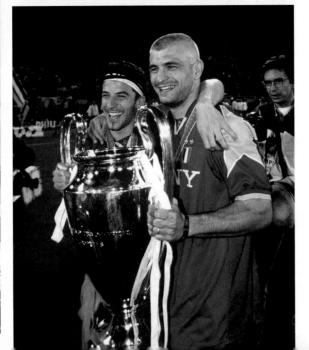

Top to bottom
UEFA Cup defeat to Parma in '95; *Pinturicchio* with his Rafael; "Can I accompany you to Boro, Fabrizio?"

Juve honorary president Giampiero Boniperti to part with a few billion lire. A legendary former diminutive striker himself, Boniperti would later see many of his Juventus records topple at Del Piero's nimble feet. Barely old enough to drive, the latter made a leap from bit-part second tier player to mixing it with world-class talent before his 18th birthday.

"In Turin, I was embarking on not only the best future I could dream of, but I was also joining my favourite team," says Del Piero. "I will always be really grateful to president Boniperti, who unfortunately is no longer with us. He took me to Turin, starting my story in black and white – I don't think I can put into words what I felt then. I wasn't prepared for the fame, but I didn't suffer because of it – mainly because I've always put the game above everything else.

"In those early years, even after the first few goals or even the first Scudetto, I wasn't overwhelmed by the popularity – I was naive and didn't worry about it too much. I thought about playing, scoring and winning. The rest never affected me – I was living my dream."

THE DIVINE APPRENTICE

It didn't take long for that to manifest in reality. The first goal of Del Piero's Juventus career arrived in just his second substitute appearance for the Old Lady; on for Fabrizio Ravanelli in the 80th minute, he rounded off the scoring in Juve's 4-0 September 1993 win over Reggiana within 60 seconds. Six months later, his third start produced a hat-trick against a Parma side packing Zola, Asprilla and Brolin at the other end.

With Roberto Baggio, Gianluca Vialli and Ravanelli for competition, becoming a first-team regular at Stadio delle Alpi was never going to be easy for a 19-year-old Del Piero. The summer of '94 proved a turning point and began the teenager's life as a first-team fixture for years to come.

He watched from home as Italian hearts were broken in the 1994 World Cup Final, seeing club-mate Baggio blast his spot-kick into the stratosphere to hand Brazil victory. Del Piero began 1994-95 in Juve's first team under new boss Marcello Lippi, but quickly assumed bigger responsibilities when Baggio suffered a long-term injury that November. The apprentice didn't disappoint – earning the nickname *Pinturicchio*, as the emerging artist to Baggio's renaissance master Rafael – and played a pivotal role in Juve's league and cup double-winning campaign. It could

have been a treble, had they not fluffed their lines against Parma in the UEFA Cup final.

Twelve months later, Del Piero started up front alongside Vialli and Ravanelli in Rome, as Juve became European champions for the second time. It remains their last.

"It will always be an unforgettable moment of my career, as that cup meant everything to us," he says. "The final at Stadio Olimpico in Rome, only Juventus colours in the stands, and finally European champions once again. It was an extraordinary ride in my first ever Champions League season."

Del Piero had inherited the No.10 shirt from a departed Baggio and scored six goals en route to the final, including a crucial free-kick which levelled their quarter-final tie against Real Madrid. After the Old Lady beat surprise package Nantes in the semis, the final went to penalties after a draw with Ajax. Pencilled in as the fifth taker, Del Piero was eventually spared the responsibility of scoring. "I would have taken it like I always have," he smiles, "but I was delighted to be able to dedicate myself only to celebrating!

"In my time at Juventus, we had several brilliant performances in Europe. If we count the UEFA Cup final in 1994, we reached four consecutive finals, and then another in 2003. Maybe it was destiny that it would go like this. But with the finals, even the lost ones, I can't complain about how things went."

In particular, 1998 was an emotional roller-coaster for Del Piero. In a calendar year that can be split into two distinct and contrasting parts, the 23-year-old ended the 1997-98 campaign with 32 goals in all competitions, the Scudetto and Serie A's Italian Footballer of the Year award. With another Champions League final and his first World Cup to look forward to that summer, he would have been among the favourites for the Ballon d'Or had things gone to plan.

Juve followed 1997's Champions League final woe with a repeat against Real Madrid in Amsterdam, before Italy lost their World Cup quarter-final shootout to hosts France. That November, a season-ending knee injury sustained against Udinese meant a gruelling mental and physical battle in a 10-month recovery. Pace, sharpness, agility – vital to his footballing make-up – hung in the balance.

"I think I would have done the same thing, stretching out to take a shot – I could never have foreseen that ending," he tells *FFT*. "In any case, you don't play thinking about the possible negative consequences of your efforts, otherwise you'd be blocked mentally. ▶

FourFourTwo.com Annual 2023 **89**

"It was another stage on my road which has had many curves and climbs. Perhaps it was even more beautiful that way. Back then, obviously I was distraught, but I got up immediately and thought about how to return – how to react by using all that anger to become even stronger. Today, I can say that I grew up in that moment, almost like a transition from boy to man. I didn't want to stand still. I always tried to evolve, because I never thought the talent I was gifted with would just be enough. I was demanding of myself – it was one of the fundamentals of my entire career."

A new Del Piero emerged. A more tactically minded and mature player, compensating for his absence of speed with breathtaking skill and influence over team-mates. Over the next few years, Juve reaped the benefits of his second coming, enjoying more assists than ever from their talisman. However, one aspect of his game remained a constant throughout. Perfecting the art of cutting in from the left and scoring worldies with his right, the 'Zona Del Piero' – as monikered by Italian media – proved terrifying territory for years. Coupled with a similarly lethal set-piece record, this potent attribute became as synonymous with his game as the No.10 shirt and stripes. With apologies to mirror image Arjen Robben, Alex got there first.

"There's a lot of instinct involved, but also a lot of training," explains Del Piero. "I played a role in Juventus' attack which often led me to be in that position, off-centre at the edge of the penalty area. Goal after goal, I gained more confidence and perfected that move, repeating it even during the week in training. I'm happy that it's become a trademark."

SCANDAL AND DECEIT

Players are ultimately responsible for how a game unfolds on the pitch, but off it, deep in boardrooms where football's great secrets are whispered and protected, egos and self-conceit sometimes rule.

While Del Piero & Co were winning trophies, phone taps investigating accusations of doping at Juve unearthed unexpected and explosive details of an altogether different scandal. In 2006, conversations between club officials at some of Italy's top teams and refereeing officials revealed details of wide-ranging potential match-fixing behind the scenes. Claims of refs being pressured to favour certain sides left Serie A more exposed than a filthy flasher; investigations went on for years, resulting in convictions, acquittals and several long-term bans.

For Juventus, *Calciopoli* stripped them of their 2005 and 2006 crowns, as they were demoted to Serie B and handed a nine-point deduction. Of all the clubs sanctioned, theirs was the most severe. An inevitable exodus ensued that summer, with Fabio Cannavaro, Zlatan Ibrahimovic, Patrick Vieira, Emerson, Gianluca Zambrotta and Lilian Thuram all departing. But the fans knew they could rely on their captain.

"From the first day I made it my duty not to speak, but to do," says Del Piero. "For me,

'doing' meant staying at Juve and bringing her back to the top where she deserved to be. That was what mattered – and only that. I never thought about going anywhere else, I never looked into any offer that came in for me. I had no doubts, not even for a moment. That I can say with certainty."

By this point, Del Piero had already peaked. Becoming a world champion had realised his lifelong dream and put to rest any demons of the past at international level.

"At Euro 96, it was already a lot to be called up for my first major international event with the senior team," he continues. "Everybody wants to play more if possible, but even then the same rule has always stayed with me: for that blue shirt you do everything. Every loss leaves its mark, though – I'm not one of those who could ignore them. I carry them all with me: the disappointments, the lost endings, even the mistakes. I can say I'm privileged to have won a lot of things in my career, but some of that was also because I knew defeat. I always thought there was another match after, another chance to get up again with even more strength.

"The South Korea loss at the 2002 World Cup leaves bad memories, because it was a very strong team – not so different from the one that won the World Cup in Germany four years later. There are many regrets about that tournament, where we never actually played well. That doesn't mean the refereeing against Korea was up to scratch [giving the co-hosts a penalty, disallowing an Italian golden goal and sending off Francesco Totti], but we should have won anyway."

Del Piero used every inch of his experience and leadership to haul Juve out of the 2006

Clockwise from above The 2012 Scudetto; Turin's hero; "You know the Italian for full-kit w**ker?"

doldrums. Celebrating a title-winning Serie B season as the league's top scorer, he followed that feat by bagging Serie A's *Capocannoniere* prize as the Old Lady marked their first year back by finishing third.

"I had nothing to prove, but there was certainly a drive and desire for revenge that drove me for all the years after 2006," says Del Piero. "I focused like never before on the training, on the details, on my role within the team. I knew I still had so much to give, and I proved it. I lived every day after relegation to Serie B with the thought of winning and lifting another cup again."

That wait lasted longer than expected: amid finishes of 2nd, 7th and 7th, Juve blew any hopes of winning the Europa League in 2009-10 after somehow squandering a 4-1 aggregate lead over Fulham in the last 16. For Del Piero, it was the roughest experience in a varied history against British clubs that took him from Ibrox to Anfield.

"The defeat at Craven Cottage, a wonderful stadium, was the biggest disappointment in the Europa League because we had the next round in our grasp," he laments. "My best memories [against British clubs] are linked to Old Trafford, though, for the great rivalry with that wonderful Manchester United team in the '90s – for the goals scored in that ground, and for the standing ovation the crowd gave me at the end of a friendly.

"I had the great fortune of playing in both England and Scotland. For many years, until the opening of the Juventus Stadium I'd say, you had to go there to find that atmosphere – maybe there was only Genoa's Stadio Luigi Ferraris in Italy."

It took until 2011-12 for Juve to end Inter's dominance, thanks to an unbeaten season under Antonio Conte – in Del Piero's final campaign at the club. "Before we'd officially won the Scudetto, I didn't think of anything other than that," he says. "We wanted to lift that trophy so badly – maybe me most of all, because I knew what we'd experienced in previous years and I knew that afterwards I'd be gone. I reflected on my own situation later, but I really had no idea how it would go – I didn't want to think about it. I lived day after day almost in a bubble waiting for

that last game. In the end, everything was perfect. Deep down, I realised that moment wasn't mine alone, because it belonged to the people. It was those fans who gave me an unforgettable day."

Del Piero played on for another two and a half years. First came an adventure Down Under with Sydney FC, before a sojourn in India drew the curtain on a superb career.

"At the end, the question was, 'Where can I live differently from where I've spent almost two decades of my career, almost entirely in the same shirt?'" he says. "Not better or worse, but different. And the choice fell on Australia. Today, I'd do it again, because it was a great life experience which I still remember with great pleasure. Retiring was a decision as natural as it was complicated. There's no doubt that it's a very traumatic moment, to stop doing something you love so much and that was so all-encompassing in your life. I don't think it applies only to us players. But there comes a time when you understand that you must turn the page."

One of the best players to have never plied his trade in the Premier League, Del Piero has fond memories of fixtures in the UK. That's not to say the chance didn't present itself from time to time, with Celtic among several clubs hoping to lure him after he'd revealed his decision to leave Italy.

"I would have liked the opportunity to join a British club, but nothing was stronger than the desire to stay at Juventus," he says of his prime years. "There was a possibility at Celtic after leaving Juve, but I'd already decided to change everything: change football and my life, so I went to Australia."

Before *FFT*'s interview concludes, there's one question left: any regrets? True to form, Del Piero's answer comes with the grace and humility he exuded on the pitch for 23 years.

"If I participated in a television quiz on the theme of 'Alessandro Del Piero goals', I think I would win!" he laughs. "I remember them all, even with all the details. I'm so grateful for everything I experienced that I'd honestly consider it unfair to have regrets. Apart from one – I'd like to play again…"

He may be 47 now, but we bet Alessandro could still do a job. You have been warned. ○

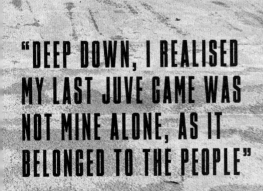

"DEEP DOWN, I REALISED MY LAST JUVE GAME WAS NOT MINE ALONE, AS IT BELONGED TO THE PEOPLE"

THE EVOLUTION WILL BE TELEVISED

Darwin Nunez didn't seem like a natural replacement for Sadio Mané at Anfield, but he's arrived to give Liverpool a very different goal threat. An early red card in front of the Sky cameras delayed the adaptation – fear not though, he's overcome a difficult start before

Words Andrew Murray **Additional reporting** Marcus Alves

arwin Nunez had lost control. It wasn't supposed to be like this.

The Uruguayan's club-record price tag weighed heavily on his square-set shoulders. Playing for a domestic giant, struggling to live up to their pre-season billing as one of the two title favourites, his slow start had burned into his psyche. As an early-evening sunset gave way to a floodlit glow, the frontman's frustration boiled to a crescendo. He knew this was a pivotal moment at his latest club. He had to do *something*.

Drenched with sweat, his red kit clinging to a sinuous frame, the pumped-up Nunez lost his self-control, turned on his heel and embedded his forehead into the torso that stood before him.

Then, he began to cry. Nunez's tears bled into Haris Seferovic's shirt, as his head nestled against his team-mate's chest. The youngster had just put Benfica 5-0 up against Pacos de Ferreira in April 2021, his first goal for two months and just his third in the league that calendar year. He had so struggled with the pressure of being the Eagles' most expensive player that he'd sought help from the club's psychologist and deactivated his Instagram account to avoid the stream of abuse. Self-improvement became a watchword.

Fast forward 18 months, 35 Benfica goals and an £85m move to Liverpool, and Nunez's next momentary loss of control dominated his first steps in England. The 23-year-old's headbutt of Crystal Palace defender Joachim Andersen 57 minutes into his first start may have been a first career red card for violent conduct, but it didn't take long for the fall-out to focus on how Nunez would deal with the Premier League. Surely, thought pundits, fans and almost certainly opposition bosses, this was a sign of a firebrand player unable to keep his emotions in check?

No matter that his footballing education came on Uruguay's notoriously Machiavellian pitches, or that he's faced Pepe on more than one occasion, worries abounded that he'd be subjected to a barrage of dark-arts defending that would make Sergio Ramos blush.

If that's the plan, they're wasting their time. *FFT* has spoken to scouts, fans, ex-coaches and team-mates the world over – the Darwin Nunez they know is dedicated to the singular pursuit of providing for his mother, father and brother back in rural Uruguay. Such a quest is measured by goals and trophies among the elite, a symbiotic relationship that Liverpool hope can help them challenge Manchester City, despite a sluggish Premier League start.

This is what Nunez lives for.

HALF CAVANI, HALF SUAREZ

Artigas is as far away from Montevideo as you can get without leaving Uruguay. Tucked in

a curve in the Cuareim River on the country's northernmost tip, the city depends on the waterway for the rich agriculture it sustains and the transportation it provides of precious amethyst and agate stones, mined nearby to export worldwide. Yet the Cuareim also floods regularly, devastating houses built on banks where cheap land is the only area some locals can afford to live.

It was here, in the El Pirata neighbourhood, that Darwin Nunez spent his childhood. On more than one occasion, floods meant his labourer dad Bibiano had to rebuild the family home using little more than scrap parts and his own nous. To make ends meet Nunez's mother Silvia, a housewife and cleaner, used to walk the Artigas streets collecting glass bottles that she'd sell for change to buy food.

"I don't forget where I come from – a very humble, working family," Nunez later told Uruguayan paper *El Observador*. Money was so tight, Darwin and his older brother Junior occasionally went to bed hungry, but it was their parents who suffered most.

"The one who went to bed with an empty belly most often was my mother," he said, "because a mother does anything for her children, so she went to bed without eating many times, just to give us something."

Nunez's release was football. Each day after school, young Darwin would go to El Pirata's local pitch to train. Shy to the point he was practically silent, his reputation quickly grew beyond Artigas. His older brother Junior was already 600km away in Penarol's academy, and word had reached the Montevideo giants about the younger Nunez tearing it up back home. Jose Perdomo, the club's chief scout

and former Uruguay international who briefly played for Coventry in 1990, drove overnight to see the skinny teenager in 2013.

"Normally, I'd never recommend anyone for the club before watching them a few times, but Darwin was clearly different," Perdomo tells *FFT*. "He was the kind of forward who looked like Europe material – he had a strong presence, but was very good technically too. Even aged 13, you could already see that he was privileged in terms of physical build. At that age, you can't usually tell whether a kid will be a first-team player, but Darwin had all the conditions to get there."

Struck by the speed of the tyro's movement and appreciation of space, Perdomo went to speak to Bibiano at full-time, wanting to take Darwin to Montevideo with him. Silvia said her son was too young to leave, and to return in a year's time.

"Twelve months on I knocked on their door again, but his mother wasn't happy to see me at all," laughs Perdomo. "Silvia was even unhappier after her husband and the kid took my side, and argued that it was important for him to go. She must be very proud of her son. And there's still much more to come – he has 10 years of top-level football ahead."

Yet it wasn't all plain sailing. A 14-year-old Nunez struggled to adapt to the capital and headed home within weeks. A year later, with his parents offering to visit when they could

Above and right
Leading the line for La Celeste; Darwin bagged 34 goals in 41 appearances for Benfica last season

afford it and older sibling Junior more settled in the academy, Nunez went back to Penarol and put on a show.

Studying videos of Edinson Cavani, Darwin terrorised youth-team defences and scored countless individual goals by picking the ball up from deep and running through serried ranks in front of him.

When a family emergency struck in 2015 – it's never been revealed exactly what – and it threatened to cut Nunez's wings just as he was taking flight, older brother Junior stepped in. Despite already training with Penarol's first team, Junior left and returned to Artigas to care for the family, telling his younger sibling as he departed, "You stay here – you've got a future, I don't."

Like his mother's sacrifices, Darwin hasn't forgotten his brother's altruism. He doubled down on his work ethic and was training with the first team when disaster struck. In 2016, while playing for Penarol's second string, he went up for a header. "I jumped up and my knee collapsed underneath me as I landed," he recalled. "Everything went through my head – I was so close to my first-team debut and it was taken away."

He'd ruptured an anterior cruciate ligament and underwent an operation. "Psychologically it was devastating for him – he'd tell me that he wanted to return to Artigas to work 9-5 and was actually close to doing that," reveals scout Perdomo. "He'd say that everyone had

trusted him and he couldn't justify it on the pitch. It took his family, team-mates and friends to talk him out of packing it all in."

Nunez returned to training inside nine months and, highly rated by first-team boss Leonardo Ramos, was soon back in the squad. Still only 18, Nunez knew his own body, that the pain he still felt in his knee wasn't normal. But such was the desire at Penarol for him to succeed, he was persuaded to plough on. In November 2017, Ramos gave his protégé a senior debut as a second-half substitute for former Liverpool winger Maxi Rodriguez. He departed the pitch in tears at the pain. A month later, Nunez underwent a second operation that kept him out until June 2018 – that agonising 27-minute cameo was his sole appearance for 18 months.

"That episode has strengthened his head more than anything," said Ramos. "For a year, he was suffering so much - suffering to run, suffering to train, and crying all the time. He knows about suffering, living with constant pressure that his career was in the balance."

Used primarily as an impact substitute, Nunez scored his first senior goal during an October 2018 defeat of Fenix. Though his only goal of the 2018 campaign, it helped convince his coach to persist with him. "He's half Cavani and half Luis Suarez," enthused Ramos. "Everyone compares him to Cavani because they have a similar style. Darwin is faster, stronger, more intelligent and athletic.

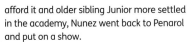

> "EVERYONE COMPARES HIM TO CAVANI AS THEY HAVE SIMILAR STYLES. DARWIN'S FASTER, STRONGER, MORE INTELLIGENT AND ATHLETIC"

He has Suarez's power to go after everyone, to battle and fight with a rival. He's a great union of both.

"He has to play close to the penalty area because he's lethal. He has no respect for an opponent, he knows beforehand where a ball is going to fall and where the goal is."

That may be the player Darwin has evolved into, but his earliest iterations were still hit and miss. After disappointing for Uruguay at the Under-20 Sudamericano championships in January 2019, Nunez took online criticism personally. Only an intervention from the team's psychologist Axel Ocampos turned around what was developing into depression. "I started to take on board the critics and had to speak to Axel – he helped me a lot, but the answer was easy," he explained. "Now I only turn on my phone after games to speak to my family and friends."

Backed by Oscar Tabarez, boss of Uruguay's senior team – "attacking someone online who's struggling is a disgrace, it's like they think it's a sport" – he continued to receive assistance from Ocampos and impressed at that summer's U20 World Cup in Poland. He scored a stunning volley in a 3-1 victory over Erling Haaland's Norway, following it with a cool strike against New Zealand. Uruguay topped the group, while Norway went out, despite Haaland scoring nine times in a 12-0 humping of Honduras.

When Nunez plundered a hat-trick in a 4-0 battering of Boston River upon his Penarol return in July 2019, his purple patch sparked speculation from abroad. Out of his darkest moments, a new European dawn awaited.

ASCENDING IN ANDALUSIA

Upwardly mobile after a recent takeover by Saudi businessman Turki Al-Sheikh, Spanish Segunda Division side Almeria had money to spend. It mattered not that Nunez had scored a modest four league goals for Penarol – the Rojiblancos' new owner had seen Nunez's Norway volley and wanted a piece.

Paying almost exclusively for potential, a three-man Almeria delegation were sent to Montevideo and instructed not to return until they had their man. Following a 12-hour meeting, a €4.5m fee was eventually agreed – the biggest in Penarol's history, after their share of future sell-on fees.

Nunez celebrated by buying a house for his parents in Artigas with his signing-on fee. ▶

A long way from home and in a new city – one where *The Good, the Bad and the Ugly* was filmed – the 20-year-old had played only 45 minutes against Sporting Gijon amid a series of fitness issues by the time he was surprisingly called up for Uruguay's friendly with Peru in September 2019.

La Celeste were losing 1-0 and down to 10 men when Tabarez, in his 200th game in charge, threw on Nunez. Five minutes later, the striker beat his marker and headed in the equaliser, becoming the fastest to score a debut goal for Uruguay since Diego Forlan in 2008. It was a typical Nunez finish too, all bright movement and slick finishing.

"It's unforgettable," he said the following morning. "I started running around without knowing how to celebrate it. I thought about my family who really helped when I endured my most difficult moments with my knee."

That international bow served as a catalyst in Almeria. Soon, Nunez opened his account from the penalty spot against Extremadura, a goal he dedicated to under-pressure Pedro Emanuel, one of four head coaches the young forward would play under in what proved his solitary season in Andalusia. That none of Emanuel, former Real Madrid midfielder Guti, Mario Silva or Jose Gomes has a bad word to say about Nunez is no surprise for someone who was the division's fourth highest scorer on 16 goals, but his willingness to learn was central to each manager's relationship with the nascent forward.

"Fundamentally, any young player from Penarol or other South American clubs will always find it difficult to establish themselves as a striker, as often this role is attributed to more experienced footballers over there," former Reading boss Gomes, the last of his managers in 2019-20, tells *FFT*. "Darwin's speed and potency meant he was initially deployed on the flanks, not close to the goal.

At Almeria you could see his potency. Darwin was the perfect player for their quick counter-attacks. He scored most of his goals taking advantage of the spaces left by opponents.

"He's become a lot stronger, more robust and balanced in terms of muscle – his knee injuries have given him more confidence in duels. I still believe he can improve his first touch a lot. When he's in the central corridor and under pressure from the centre-back, the first touch is key, so he needs to improve his ball control, his positioning and how he adjusts his feet for reception."

In the automatic promotion spots for much of a pandemic-affected campaign, Almeria eventually fell in the play-off semi-finals to Girona. Southampton, Real Betis, Valencia, Roma and Napoli were all interested in the Uruguayan, but president Turki held out for serious money, humble-bragging: "I feel for Darwin in an almost parental way, given he's someone I discovered."

Nunez may have been settled in the city – his partner is an Almeria native, they still holiday there and returned in January this year for the birth of their son, Darwin Jr – but he knew his next step lay among Europe's elite. The €24m Benfica offered in September 2020 was too good for Almeria to turn down.

THE EAGLE HAS LANDED

Benfica's club-record fee was also the most ever received by a club in Spain's second tier. Expectations in Lisbon were high, but Nunez's first few months at the Estadio da Luz were marked by struggles in front of goal, the regularity with which he was caught offside and poor decision-making. In short, he was the erratic, inexperienced youngster he still was – physically brilliant, but lacking finesse.

Crucially, however, he worked constantly on smoothing those rough edges. "It was

> "WE'RE GOING TO HEAR THE WORD 'TRANSITION' A LOT WITH LIVERPOOL. NUNEZ'S SIGNING IS THE FIRST MAJOR STEP OF THAT HAPPENING"

Left Community Shield glory gave Nunez an early taste of success with Liverpool

a whole different culture for him," Evandro Mota, Benfica's then sports psychologist who worked with Brazil at USA 94, tells *FFT*. "I was impressed by him. He said something that I've never forgotten and immediately told head coach Jorge Jesus about.

"Darwin said, 'Look, I know I have a lot to learn and to keep gaining experience'. This from a 21-year-boy. I've been working with some of the best football talents for more than four decades – do you know how many times I've seen a youngster being this mature and humble at this age, even after fulfilling his dream of helping his parents buy a home? Very, very few times."

A bout of COVID and a thigh injury hardly helped matters on the pitch but, following regular sessions with Mota, Nunez's decision to deactivate his Instagram account and avoid a flurry of abuse helped immeasurably.

"When an athlete has the guts to admit he needs some help, it's so much easier to work

with him," recalls Mota. "That's Darwin, a boy way ahead of his age who always kept an open mind and was willing to listen to the right people. When people are dealing with so much criticism, we suggest it's best if they isolate themselves from the environment that's doing them harm. Darwin is a kid who demands a lot for himself and realised the social media stuff would only bring him down.

"He had already overcome a lot in his life, and that episode has helped him become an even better professional. That's what makes him a real gem, not only in terms of technical quality, but also in terms of intelligence."

The tears which followed his goal at Pacos de Ferreira in April 2021, just his fifth league strike for the Eagles, opened the floodgates. Last season, 34 goals followed that difficult maiden campaign.

"Darwin is a forward with a huge physical strength, very explosive and fast," legendary former Benfica marksman Nuno Gomes, now a pundit for Sport TV, tells *FFT*. "These are all physical traits that give an edge in the role he plays. Not to mention that he's one of those players who has his eyes set on the goal the

entire time. Sometimes, he seems to rush his decisions a little bit, but he's still a young man with a big progression margin.

"Benfica supporters are demanding, and naturally wanted to see Darwin scoring a lot of goals. Last season, he delivered that."

Nunez's magnificent brace in Benfica's 3-0 Champions League group stage defeat of Barcelona was just the start of that surge in form. He bullied Eric Garcia all evening, the former Manchester City defender eventually receiving a second yellow card for repeated fouling. The world was taking note of Nunez's rise up the food chain.

"Ever since Darwin was at Almeria, I told Barcelona they had to sign him – I have 15 years' experience in football and know a thing or two about strikers," winked Luis Suarez, the former Blaugrana forward and Nunez's compatriot, who's seldom backwards about coming forwards when a shooing of his erstwhile employers is on offer. "They told me he was very young and only at Almeria. At that moment they'd have paid €15m for him, and now he's going to go for anywhere up to €100m." ▶

BENFICA BOYS

Nunez isn't the first player to have left the Estadio da Luz for the Premier League – some have fared better than others…

DAVID LUIZ
Everyone's favourite Sideshow Bob lookalike spent four years with the Eagles, collecting the Primeira Liga's player of the year award, before heading to Chelsea in 2011. He didn't convince everyone at Stamford Bridge, but Premier League, Champions League and Europa League winners' medals suggest he didn't do too badly. **7/10**

LAZAR MARKOVIC
The Serbian winger landed in Lisbon from Partizan in 2013, dazzled with his dribbling, got sent off for violent conduct, then joined Liverpool for £20m. Thus followed a season when he didn't dazzle with his dribbling, got sent off for violent conduct, then spent the rest of his Reds career on loan at Hull, Fenerbahce, Sporting and Anderlecht. **2/10**

EDERSON
The Brazilian only played 37 league games for Benfica after relocating from Rio Ave – it was enough to hoover up a treble and reach the Champions League quarter-finals prior to Manchester City paying £35m in 2017, then the second highest fee ever for a goalkeeper. Safe to say they haven't regretted it. **9/10**

VICTOR LINDELOF
The Swede sealed his switch to the Premier League just nine days after Ederson, moving to Manchester United for £31m. He had impressed during five years at Benfica but hasn't been able to emulate his old team-mate's success on the red side of the city – kicking off this campaign as the Red Devils' fourth-choice centre-back. **4/10**

RAUL JIMENEZ
The Mexican marksman chose Benfica over West Ham when he left Atletico Madrid in 2015 – he scored 31 goals in three seasons, then was loaned to Wolves and made the deal permanent 12 months later. He netted more prolifically in the Premier League, only for a fractured skull to halt his progress. **7/10**

RUBEN DIAS
The central defender was the Primeira Liga's young player of the year in 2017-18 – his breakthrough campaign after graduating from Benfica's academy. He stood out for two more years before joining Manchester City for £65m, turning around their season and helping them capture the first of two consecutive Premier League titles. **9/10**

By the time Nunez scored in both legs of the same competition's quarter-final against Liverpool, half of Europe were interested. Not least the quadruple-chasing Reds themselves, who would stump up a club-record £85m this summer. "Jurgen Klopp spoke glowingly about him after the Anfield game," Matt Ladson, editor of Liverpool fan site *This Is Anfield*, tells *FFT*. "He was a handful - one of those physical, quick forwards that play on the last man, who Liverpool tend to struggle against. He definitely made an impact."

Sadio Mané had already told Klopp about his desire to move on in 2022. With Luis Diaz adapting quicker than expected following his January transfer from Porto, the German boss decided to return to Portugal, a country where he sees value. No.2 Pep Lijnders and elite development coach Vitor Matos once worked for Porto, while new sporting director Julian Ward also has good links there – Klopp calls them his 'Portugal department'.

"He was already on the list – we knew he was very interesting, but didn't really think about signing him then; we weren't in talks," Klopp said recently. "We had two, three or four years where it was always clear before pre-season that we start up front with Sadio, Bobby [Firmino] and Mo [Salah]. Now the door is open for pretty much everyone. That's really cool and that is what we have to use. With Darwin, it was kind of clear he's a pretty good striker. We don't go for the fancy stuff, we

> **"I THINK THERE WAS AN OVER-EAGERNESS TO LIVE UP TO THE PRICE TAG. THE WORRY NOW IS HE'S PUT A TARGET ON HIS BACK"**

want to go for the right stuff. That'll make us completely difficult to study before a game."

NO IFS OR BUTTS

Nunez's unpredictability was paramount to Klopp's plan. Carlo Ancelotti summed it up best after Real Madrid beat Liverpool 1-0 in May's Champions League final, saying the Reds were "easy to decipher".

"Ancelotti was pretty accurate," concedes Ladson. "You want to be unpredictable in the attacking half, which is something Liverpool need to vary, especially against teams with a low block. Look back at why we didn't win the league last season and it always comes back to draws with Brighton and Brentford.

"Last season it was only really Divock Origi coming off the bench that gave us something entirely different – a player who got beyond the centre-half and actually put himself in the box to unsettle sides. If you're comparing Nunez to a forward in last season's squad, he's basically a more refined version of Origi, who'd create chaos by occupying defenders and offering a physical threat."

The early signs were good. Nunez came off the bench to score against Manchester City in the Community Shield, then bagged a first Premier League goal in a 2-2 draw at Fulham on the opening day. Yet the switch to playing with a more defined No.9 may not be as easy as Erling Haaland has made it look at City.

"We're going to hear the word 'transition' quite a lot this season with Liverpool, and Nunez's signing is the first major step of that happening," adds Ladson. "The age profile of the attackers needed to change – Nunez and Diaz have eight or nine years on the players they're replacing. There's barely an attacker that's gone into a Jurgen Klopp team he's not improved, though it does mean a change in style in the interim that might take longer than some fans would hope."

Nunez's former Almeria coach Gomes can only see positives. "Darwin fits like a glove –

Right and top
The Uruguayan newbie nets at Fulham; before getting sent off against Palace

INSTANT HEROES

Before Darwin Nunez, these were the last 10 players to net on their Liverpool debut

VIRGIL VAN DIJK	2018
MO SALAH	2017
SADIO MANÉ	2016
JORDAN ROSSITER	2014
VICTOR MOSES	2013
DANIEL STURRIDGE	2013
ANDRE WISDOM	2012
LUIS SUAREZ	2011
GABRIEL PALETTA	2006
CRAIG BELLAMY	2006

he and Liverpool are a perfect marriage," he tells *FFT*. "I have no doubt he's prepared for the challenge ahead. He also has the kind of players by his side who will remind him every day that he must work hard, otherwise he won't make it at that level.

"Darwin's move to Liverpool was no surprise because he's a super athlete with incredible speed and enough quality to score inside the box. He's not one of those quick players who can't score. That's what makes him valuable."

What has surprised Gomes – and every journalist, coach, player and scout *FFT* has spoken to in the past month – was Nunez's third Liverpool appearance. That's right, we need to talk about the headbutt.

Crystal Palace defender Joachim Andersen may have been needling the Uruguayan, but Nunez's upbringing in his native country had surely prepared him for antagonistic tactics? "I couldn't believe what I was seeing," Jorge Senorans, who interviewed the striker for *El Observador* in 2019, tells *FFT*. "That's not the Darwin I know. He's always been very correct in everything he's done. This is how we play in South America, especially us Uruguayans!

"When we spoke, he was still very young, but what struck me more than anything was how much time he had for other people, how

he wanted to share his story of self-growth from Artigas, to prove himself and be worthy of the faith people put in him. I'm certain it was in his mind that night – he lost control by trying too hard."

Ladson agrees. "I think there was an over-eagerness to live up to the price tag, and it boiled over," he says. "The worry now is he's put a target on his own back by saying, 'You can get to me'. He'll have to rise above that and stay clean."

Klopp quickly reminded his player of his responsibilities in the immediate aftermath, while ex-Red Suarez spoke to his compatriot, telling him what to expect now. "They'll come after you three times over – I'm telling you as an idiot who made a mistake and paid for it," said the former Anfield star.

Nunez missed three games at a time when Liverpool desperately needed to recover from a slow start – the Reds' record-equalling 9-0 humiliation of Bournemouth sandwiched either side of a limp defeat at Manchester United and fortunate win against Newcastle. Nunez apologised in the dressing room and extended that contrition to Twitter. "I know I had a bad attitude," he wrote. "I'm here to learn from my errors. It won't happen again."

"That proves just how humble he is," sports psychologist Mota tells *FFT*. "When you don't admit your mistake, you make up excuses. But you'll never be able to correct your error if you never admit it. He doesn't give a damn about what other people will think, his main priority is to grow up as a footballer and keep gaining experience. He's already featured in all sorts of competitions – competitions like the ones in South America, which are way tougher than the Premier League in terms of provocation and violence – and only once before had he been sent off, in the Spanish Segunda Division. So don't believe he's that player based on one single episode.

"We can expect defenders trying to get in his head more now, but I've absolutely no doubt he'll be a big hit in the Premier League and this won't happen again. Having gone through so much in his life, he appreciates each step he takes forward and will seize his opportunities. He's a special lad."

It's that vital life experience, from Artigas floodplains, career-threatening injuries and borderline depression at Benfica, which most inform Darwin Nunez and ensure his role in Liverpool's evolution.

"I spoke to his father recently and he was extremely anxious about this move to the Premier League, because this is much more than they'd ever dreamed," says Perdomo, the Penarol scout who started the journey in 2013. "Darwin has changed his family's life. He bought his parents a big house in Artigas, so they don't have to worry about money in their lives. They suffered a lot, it wasn't easy, and Darwin doesn't forget it. Everything he does is with his family in his mind."

Providing love, food and shelter for those closest to him. You might say it's Darwinism in its purest form. ○

THE BARÇA GENT

Twenty-five years ago, Bobby Robson and his plucky translator pitched up at Barcelona to replace the great Johan Cruyff. But in a season which brought the popular Englishman together with Jose Mourinho, Ronaldo and Pep Guardiola, not even success was enough to avoid a bitter ending in Catalonia

Words Mark White **Additional reporting** Andrew Murray

"Everybody should see the sea, or a mountain, or walk in the woods each day of their lives," Elsie Robson had told her husband, Bobby. And so each morning, the former England boss would drive along the promenade, looking over his right shoulder at the endless azure of the Mediterranean before hitting the motorway to training.

Twice before, Robson had declined this delightful way of life. He'd rebuffed Barcelona's advances out of loyalty to Ipswich during their early-80s pomp, and later honoured his national service with the Three Lions, suggesting Terry Venables to Blaugrana chiefs instead. Aged 63, he didn't say no a third time in the summer of 1996, although life in Catalonia wasn't exactly his way of taking his foot off the accelerator and accepting a more relaxing job.

Johan Cruyff had just left the Camp Nou. Robson couldn't speak a lick of Spanish, instead relying on his trusted translator at Sporting and Porto: the younger, dashing Jose Mourinho. The new Barça boss once described himself as a gunslinger arriving into the Wild West, and having to convince a saloon full of towering figures to follow his lead. Robson was acutely aware of how intensely integrated the club was to Catalan culture, likening Barça games to battles; away grounds to foreign fortresses to storm. It was also a fractured city, with the recently dethroned Dutch sheriff's silhouette still looming large. This town wasn't big enough for the both of them.

Someone had to succeed Cruyff, though, who had been dismissed after a series of spats with president Josep Lluis Nunez. "Robson came in at a difficult time," says defender Abelardo, who had joined the club from Sporting Gijon two years earlier. "Cruyff had been such a massive part of Barcelona for getting on a decade – it was never going to be easy taking a job where the previous coach had established such a huge reputation."

Nor was it straightforward to split Cruyff from the club he had come to define. The face of Total Football had become a mercurial architect in middle age, reshaping Barcelona in his image from foundations to skylights. He had delivered Los Cules' first European Cup in 1992 and written the blueprint for how youngsters at La Masia would learn to play the game. He wasn't sacked so much as overthrown.

"Cruyff was the ghost in the machine – he haunted my early days," Robson later confessed. Cruyff frequently watched ▶

matches from the stands, while his son Jordi was on the books when Robson arrived, only to join Manchester United for £1.4 million in the Englishman's first summer.

Robson and Mourinho had marched into a club mired in political turmoil; one with egos and outrageous talent, but no major trophy to show for two seasons' toil and backbiting. It was a team fully in transition: captain Jose Mari Bakero was featuring less and less, with a 25-year-old Pep Guardiola starting to wear the armband regularly. It was also a side that would perhaps never really feel like Bobby Robson's, whatever he might achieve during his two-year contract.

The pressure was immense. At least those morning drives along the sea could help take the edge off.

"RONALDO'S NOT A MAN, HE'S A HERD"

"Bobby," notoriously frugal president Nunez snapped, "You know your job depends on this?" Robson's seat in the dugout was still cold, yet Barcelona had just broken the world transfer record on a 19-year-old, simply on his recommendation.

"When Ronaldo came to Barça from PSV, there wasn't the internet or social media, but there was a *runrun* – the buzz about him was gigantic," recalls writer and LaLigaTV pundit, Graham Hunter. "There was a feeling of lots of elements all coming together in a cocktail,

"HONESTLY, THAT GOAL WAS A DISGRACE. ROBSON PUT HIS HANDS ON HIS HEAD, BUT WE ALL DID. THE BEST I'VE SEEN"

and there was a festival atmosphere about the Bobby Robson era."

Laurent Blanc, Luis Enrique, Fernando Couto and a returning Hristo Stoichkov had signed that same summer, but there was no doubt who claimed top billing. It took the Brazilian just five minutes to announce himself as the new matador in town. With little more than a swivel and burst of pace, he danced past two defenders before unleashing a 25-yard opener in the first leg of the Spanish Super Cup against Atletico Madrid. By full-time he'd destroyed Los Colchoneros with another goal, following a glorious elastico assist for Ivan de la Pena in his side's 5-2 win.

The carnival had arrived. A supercharged Ronaldo plundered 13 goals in just 11 league appearances as Barça reached the summit, two points ahead of Real Madrid.

Below Robson staked his own reputation on signing teenage talent Ronaldo

"I once saw Ronaldo score a goal for Barça where he beat five or six players," Robson later reminisced of one such early match to *FourFourTwo*. "Diego Maradona at his best was the best I ever saw. Ronaldo would be a close second, though."

That goal remains a vivid postcard moment two and a half decades on. The north-west city of Santiago de Compostela is the final destination of a 500-mile Catholic pilgrimage from southern France, and one night there in October 1996, Ronaldo gained possession by the halfway line and mimicked the route. Zigzagging past a handful of defenders, he picked up speed, then spun out of their orbit. By the time the ball hit the net, Robson's look was one of astonishment. The reaction is as iconic as the goal itself.

"Honestly, that goal was a disgrace," says Abelardo. "You can see Robson putting his hands on his head in disbelief after Ronaldo scored, but we all did. I remember looking around and everyone was in the same pose. The best I've seen, totally unrepeatable by nearly any footballer alive. Maradona against England, Messi against Getafe and Ronaldo against Compostela. That's it."

Barcelona were beginning to click under Robson, with the festival feeling still flickering into autumn. Ronaldo followed his mesmeric Compostela strike with a sublime hat-trick at home to Valencia, battering through players like a wrecking ball through condemned buildings. Los Che boss Luis Aragones could only snarl on the touchline, perhaps aware that he would be replaced within weeks by Jorge Valdano, who famously declared of his predecessor's tormentor, "Ronaldo's not a man, he's a herd."

An 8-0 October annihilation of struggling Logrones was to define Robson's tenure in many ways. The Camp Nou's Cules *olé'd* their appreciation, but critics were less impressed with Bobby's bulldozing Barça.

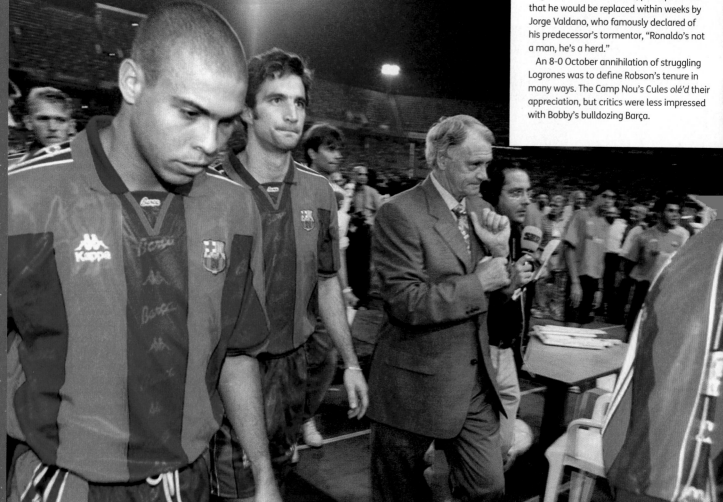

"The headline the next day in *Diario Sport* was '*Muchos goles, pero muy poco futbol*'," reveals Hunter. "'Lots of goals, but very little football'. There was a bit of snobbery from some sections, although it wasn't a rebellion against him. There were plenty who adored Sir Bobby because they thought he was *un caballero* – a gentleman."

Robson took the stick personally, however, calling it "cracking comedy". He saw the split in the press as a reflection of a split fanbase, many of whom still mourned Cruyff's more measured methods. Despite some factions not warming to their new coach, the team were still flying in La Liga by mid-November and into the Cup Winners' Cup quarter-finals after despatching both Larnaca and Red Star Belgrade. Increasingly leading video sessions and compiling opposition scouting dossiers, Mourinho had become a media master.

"He didn't manipulate the journalists, but he was very clever in making sure his profile was high," explains Hunter. "He served Bobby well in that he had a knack of steering press conferences into safer waters."

Barcelona managed to stay unbeaten long after Robson's seaside excursions had turned chillier, until they surrendered their run at the hands of Athletic Bilbao in late November. Mourinho wasn't quite so diplomatic on that occasion, contesting decisions and squaring up to Athletic's lollipop-wielding coach Luis Fernandez. Mourinho's swagger was simply

Top to bottom
Ronaldo sets off before scoring his wonder goal at Compostela; Robson's team went on to win two cups, and look happier...; "It's nice, but it's no Whitley Bay"

staggering, and Fernandez – a Doberman of a boss – couldn't believe the bottle. Guardiola had to drag the Portuguese away.

A 2-0 loss in December's Clasico followed, before Barça squandered a two-goal lead at home to relegation fodder Hercules, losing 3-2. By now they were playing catch-up in the title race and jeers had replaced cheers at the Camp Nou. Meanwhile, Ronaldo – now the youngest ever recipient of the FIFA World Player of the Year prize – was embroiled in rows with club chiefs about when he could depart for international duty.

"It was a paradise of great football and great people," says Hunter. "Yet for Bobby, plenty of s**tty things were also going on."

CALL IT A COMEBACK

Carrer d'Elisabeth Eidenbenz is a narrow road just behind the Camp Nou, with portly palm trees and overgrown grass. There's a car park behind a mesh fence on one side, but it used to be the site of a training pitch.

This fence was a window into the world of Robson's Barcelona, and the pavement used to be where fans, journalists or smitten girls, there to catch Ronaldo, would congregate.

"My only manager was Cruyff until Bobby arrived," right-back Albert Ferrer tells *FFT*, "but Bobby didn't want to be the protagonist – he just wanted to be the coach of a team and create a good atmosphere."

Robson and Mourinho's dynamic was that of a headmaster and teacher overseeing the class. They worked perfectly together. Bobby's first instructions to Jose at Sporting were, jokingly, that he was too handsome to stand near him. Even five years later in Catalonia, Robson maintained a professional distance from his players, while Mourinho was more matey with the group.

As a fellow native Portuguese speaker, Jose proved an ally for Ronaldo, and would often talk tactics and philosophies with Guardiola and Enrique. The former became Mourinho's closest cohort; they hailed from markedly different backgrounds, yet their footballing philosophies were rooted in the practical ideals of building play from a solid foundation at the back.

"We saw and heard lots of things," recalls Hunter about those days on the pavement. "Mourinho had come over from Portugal with Bobby and learned from him; Guardiola had a fantasy about what life at traditional old English football games would be like. I can't tell you if they considered each other outright

friends, but they were two very bright minds with a degree of international curiosity and experience. There was a click."

Anglophile Guardiola was a favourite pupil of Robson's, who appreciated his midfielder's courage in speaking up at half-time. Pep in turn adored his manager, even writing to him years later asking to join Newcastle.

"The squad had many strong personalities," continues Ferrer, now a LaLigaTV pundit. "Pep Guardiola, Hristo Stoichkov, Luis Figo, Ronaldo, Giovanni, Laurent Blanc, Luis Enrique, Juan Pizzi... but players with this personality helped us through any challenge."

Robson's biggest challenge at the Camp Nou came in March 1997 against Atletico in the Copa del Rey quarter-final second leg. Disapproval boomed in the giant bowl after a dreadful first half where Atleti had strolled into a 3-0 lead; Barça fans waved their white handkerchiefs en masse.

"I thought it was snowing in the stadium," remembered Robson of that night. Atletico and Barcelona were frosty enemies as it was, but unbeknownst to the manager, Blaugrana directors had decided to sack him should the scoreline remain. Those inside the dressing room insist that Robson was unusually calm. What happened next took the Camp Nou's collective breath away.

"Well, I guess Ronaldo happened," laughs Abelardo, who played that night. "He scored twice and within little more than five minutes we were back to 3-2. [Milinko] Pantic quickly scored a fourth for Atletico, then Figo and Ronaldo brought us back level before Pizzi's late winner. With players of that class you're never out of a game. Beating a team as good as that Atletico 5-1 in just one half shows the level we were at that season."

Barça's comeback was as exhilarating as anything the venue had ever witnessed: pre, during or post Cruyff. Still, though, the press suggested that Robson's players had staged a half-time rebellion in the dressing room. It took Guardiola, captain in the extraordinary *remontada*, to rubbish that theory the next day. "I thought, 'I want to be a manager' because of how he handled that situation," he glowed years later.

Atleti and Barcelona faced each other six times that season, scoring 37 goals. On that March night, there was plenty of football too.

BACKSTABBED IN THE BOARDROOM

Spectacular or sober: those were the two states of Robson's Barcelona. In mid-April, ▶

Doomed Hercules needed little fight to beat a Ronaldo-less Barcelona 2-1 on June 1. The Brazilian's last goal for the club came a week prior against Deportivo La Coruna, his 10th scoring league game in succession mere days before he was called up for Le Tournoi. As the title slipped from Barça's grasp in his absence, *O Fenomeno* agreed to join Inter for another world-record fee. It was Figo, not Ronaldo, who inspired that Copa del Rey triumph, R9 having left a week earlier.

"That was a huge surprise for everyone," says Abelardo. "We all thought Ronaldo could define an era at Barcelona, similar to what Leo Messi would do a decade later. We were shocked that the directors would let a player like that leave, one who would guarantee 30 goals a season."

Robson wasn't amused either, but worse was to follow. Amid whispers about his own future, he asked Mourinho to eavesdrop into conversations that the directors were having. His worst suspicions were confirmed before the Copa del Rey final. Louis van Gaal was to replace him; an overlooked clause in Robson's contract gave Barça the right to move him upstairs to an ambassadorial role.

This *caballero* was seldom as distressed. He was the calmest man on that fretful night against Atletico, took the slugfest Betis final in his stride and didn't get overly involved in Ronaldo's intra-club conflicts. A few months previously, he'd turned down an offer from his beloved Newcastle to stay in Catalonia ("no one sacks Barça," Nunez had retorted). Now, Robson was white-hot with fury. "I'll tell you what you can do," he told a sheepish Joan Gaspart, Barça's vice-president tasked with breaking the Van Gaal news. "Get rid of him. I want the job."

Robson hadn't exactly failed. Barcelona missed out on the title to Real by two points, though the Copa del Rey celebrations at the Bernabeu – which doubled up as Robson's

another Ronaldo hat-trick obliterated Atleti's barricades in a 5-2 win; a month later, Barça ground out a disciplined, mature 1-0 Clasico victory to close a yawning gap behind Real Madrid to five points.

Las Palmas were slain 7-0 on aggregate in the Copa last four, while Barça beat Gabriel Batistuta's Fiorentina in the Cup Winners' Cup semis. They may have been fighting a losing battle in the league, but were competing on three fronts with a stacked squad. "Bobby kept things simple," says Ferrer. "He wanted to keep the momentum."

Barcelona had two final dates circled in the calendar: the Cup Winners' Cup against Paris Saint-Germain in May, and the Copa del Rey against Real Betis in June. Each night, Cules got to see the two faces of their team.

"Beating PSG was amazing," says Abelardo of the first finale in Rotterdam. "They were

the defending champions and had a great team, but I do think we were better on the night, even if it was only a Ronaldo penalty that sealed the trophy for us."

Guardiola and Mourinho embraced at the final whistle, bouncing up and down on the spot. Ronaldo held one arm of the trophy, Robson the other, a big smile spread across the manager's face. The celebrations were controlled, unlike the raucous Copa del Rey final at the Bernabeu in Madrid.

"I sat behind the goal with Barcelona fans and it was absolutely mental," remembers Hunter. "It was 3-2 and went to extra time; it was a slugfest, it was fantastic, all the fans were going crazy. When Barça finally won, they played the club anthem in the Bernabeu over and over again."

The two showpieces were six weeks apart. In between, worlds came crashing down.

leaving bash – perhaps softened the blow. The Cup Winners' Cup victory had restored their European reputation and, after putting his neck on the line for Ronaldo, the striker had delivered 47 goals in 49 games. What more could Bobby do? Despite everything, he still felt like he'd embarrassed his bosses.

IT AIN'T WHAT YOU DO...

In 1989, Johan Cruyff and Louis van Gaal fell out over a misunderstanding at a Christmas dinner. The Ajax legends never reconciled. Cruyff viewed himself as an expressionist; he saw nothing of himself in Van Gaal's football, despite their shared roots and similar values.

It must have grated to see Van Gaal in his dugout far more than it ever had watching Robson. However, perhaps the latter's tenure reaffirmed something to all three of them: it's not just what you win at Barcelona – it's how you do it.

More than a decade later, in 2008, Robson's protégé would learn this. The outstanding candidate for the Camp Nou throne following stellar spells at Porto and Chelsea, European heavyweight Mourinho was overlooked in favour of Barça B boss, and old pal, Guardiola. Mourinho, like Robson before, was furious – he felt belittled.

Barcelona knew Mourinho was more than capable of delivering trophies, while both he and Guardiola shared a raging intensity for rigour and detail. But it still wasn't enough, and nor would it ever be: Guardiola was given the nod because he was a certified *Cruyffista*. Where once the pair were comrades on that training pitch tucked behind the Camp Nou, they would soon be very public adversaries.

Robson had no such time for bad blood after his own betrayal, wishing Van Gaal the best and accepting Nunez's offer to become director of signings. He encouraged Jose to stay and learn from his successor.

"HE WAS WOUNDED – I DON'T THINK HE WAS URGENTLY KEEN TO GET BACK IN THE DUGOUT"

Clockwise from top "Hey, what's the Spanish for 'football?'"; Cup Winners' Cup joy with Ronnie and Mou; Pep loved his English boss

"The decision to move Robson on felt very strange," Abelardo tells *FFT*. "We still noticed him around the club, but there wasn't the same day-to-day contact with him any more. I don't know whether he enjoyed it or not, but he still seemed his usual happy self."

Robson travelled the world in his new role. By day, he'd sit near the pool of whichever five-star hotel Barcelona had sent him to; by night, he'd scout. He had time to read, time for golf. It was a much-needed sabbatical.

"He was so wounded that I don't think he was urgently keen to get back into coaching," admits Hunter. "He definitely pushed the idea with anybody he talked to that his gentle revenge on the club was to keep taking their money for a wonderful job that allowed him to sit by the beach. There was a point where he said to me, 'You know what? This is the greatest job in the world'."

For a while, Robson took Elsie's advice, saw more of the sea and took more walks in the woods. He would soon get back in a dugout, though; shortly before, Hunter had bumped into him at a Fulham restaurant.

"I'd written a column about why it was the right time for Bobby to go into management again," says Hunter. "He soon responded by ringing me at home. I said, 'You've lived the good life for long enough – you're a people person. It's about what gives you satisfaction and what you like doing.'"

Robson took the advice, first for a second spell at PSV, before making it to Newcastle after all in 1999. Management wasn't just what he liked doing: he was exquisitely good at it. So good, in fact, that he said yes to one of the most difficult jobs in Europe – following the idolised Cruyff – and did so well that he forced his bosses to uneasily promote him.

That season's Camp Nou cocktail remains one of Barça's most memorable campaigns. Bobby had delivered two major trophies, won the fans' respect and signed a phenomenon to remember for years to come.

Robson never did work alongside Ronaldo, Guardiola nor Mourinho again. *O Fenomeno* would fulfil his immense promise as a World Cup winner, always speaking fondly of his former boss. Guardiola received a letter back from Robson wishing him good luck ahead of the 2009 Champions League Final against Manchester United, meanwhile. Two months later, the old master passed away aged 76 after a long battle with lung cancer.

"If he's half as good a manager as he was a player for me, he'll do OK," Robson once remarked of his midfield general.

Mourinho also ensured he kept in contact with his mentor, after the 1996-97 season prepared him for the future turmoil in which he would revel. It was those experiences at Barça which taught 'the Special One' how to survive on a touchline in the heat of Clasicos and cup clashes; how to handle the preying media; and what a dressing room crammed with world-class players looked like up close.

Perhaps Mourinho learned some deeper truths from that year in Catalonia too. Make time for yourself, enjoy nature, always be the calmest man in the room and try to remain a gentleman when you can. And remember: success doesn't necessarily deliver what you deserve. Even if, like Sir Bobby Robson, you take on the impossible job and win. ◎

LaLigaTV is the only place to watch all of the action from the 2022-23 La Liga campaign

MORE ON FOURFOURTWO.COM

• The making of Jose Mourinho – how did he go from 'the translator' to 'the Special One'? *(by Andy Mitten)*

• Year Zero: Ronaldo's stunning 1996-97 for Barcelona *(by Nick Miller)*

• Nine managers who made the critics look stupid *(by Chris Flanagan)*

THE

AGENTS OF

CHANGE

Mino Raiola's death was global news in April, given his extraordinary reputation for doing deals for football's top stars. From pizza restaurant to mega-broker, Raiola became the face of super-agents – an eye-watering phenomenon 65 years in the making. *FFT* finds out more...

Words Huw Davies

Mino Raiola's family understood the brief. When the world's best-known football agent died earlier this year, aged just 54, their statement made no attempt to separate personal tragedy from professional swagger. "In infinite sorrow, we share the passing of the most caring and amazing football agent that ever was," it read. "Mino fought until the end with the same strength he put on negotiation tables to defend our players."

It's what he would have wanted. Super-agents are super-aware of their importance, which is natural: you don't justify collecting a reported £41 million from a transfer deal with bashful false modesty. Less natural, at least to football fans, are the figures involved. FIFA say agents received nearly £375m in fees from cross-border deals alone in 2021 – more than in 2020, despite total transfer fees falling. English clubs were responsible, or otherwise, for more than £100m of that.

For Manchester City, Erling Haaland is such a steal at £51m that even hefty bonuses for his father (Alfie) and agency (Raiola's, now run by Rafaela Pimenta) make it a still-cheap £85m. Borussia Dortmund, who paid £17m for him in January 2020, will make roughly the same profit as Pimenta and Haaland Sr.

Such bumper payouts have their logic – the aforementioned £41m bonus was Raiola's reward for talking Manchester United up to £89m in their ultimately 'successful' 2016 bid for Paul Pogba. They have their defenders too.

"I can justify it any day of the week," Jon Smith, football's first super-agent, tells *FFT*. "I understand that the commissions and wages are offensive to supporters, but they shouldn't be. These guys bring in billions, so they should be paid millions. The football fan isn't an unintelligent human being any more. They understand the game. But the nuances need to be explained better."

We'll do our best, Jon. We'll also look at the power struggle that has led to FIFA's efforts to curb intermediaries' income and influence, a situation which resulted in agent Jonathan Barnett saying, of global football's governing body, "We're not little boys. We are equal to them in every shape and form."

How the hell did we get here?

BOSMAN BREAKS THE MARKET

It was a scandal. For purists in both proud footballing nations, an Italian club buying a player from an English club was an affront to all natural laws – even if that player was Welsh. Signing John Charles was tricky, sure, but Leeds would find that persuading Gigi Peronace to take a hint was, too.

Snubbed, the Italian agent took to propping up the bar at the Railway Tavern in the Leeds suburb of Beeston, talking to landlord Harold

Williams, who happened to be Charles' former team-mate. Then Peronace started appearing at Charles' semi-detached house in Morley to woo John and his wife, Peggy. It took two years, a British record transfer fee and a signing-on bonus 1,000 times what English clubs might pay (with Charles telling journalists he looked forward to "a new car and a flat with coal and lighting laid on"), but in 1957 he joined Juventus, courtesy of Peronace's persistence.

As the striker scored twice in his farewell to Leeds, the *Yorkshire Post* wrote: "The black eyes of Gigi Peronace, there to take delivery of John Charles when the match was over, glistened with excitement and satisfaction whenever the great man got the ball. 'That's my boy,' they seemed to say."

England imposed a maximum wage for its footballers. Italy didn't. Peronace did the maths. He tempted Denis Law to Torino and Jimmy Greaves to Milan – decades later he'd add an Irishman to his Welshman, Scotsman and Englishman by organising Liam Brady's switch to Juventus. He spoke fluent English, having arranged kickabouts between Allied soldiers and Italian locals in the Second World War. Indeed, so Anglo-Italian was Peronace, he literally invented the Anglo-Italian Cup.

He also looked exactly how you'd picture him: Ritz-eating, suit-fitting, shoes-gleaming. Greaves, with typical understatement, said, "He always had a cigar the size of a chair leg protruding from his mouth. The only time he removed it was when he laughed, and when he laughed, he sounded like a hyena that had heard a bloody belter from another hyena." The cult of the agent was born.

Still, they were mainly representing clubs, not players, who'd been able to switch sides since the Victorian age – but thanks to 1893's Retain and Transfer System, only with the club's say-so. In 1963, however, the 'retain' element was finally scrapped. No longer trapped following an expired contract, players moved clubs and agents moved the players,

"WHEN HE LAUGHED, HE SOUNDED LIKE A HYENA THAT HAD HEARD A BELTER FROM ANOTHER HYENA"

Above Italian agent Peronace (middle) meets Spurs stars (from left) Alan Gilzean, Alan Mullery and Jimmy Greaves

though still with their options limited by their employers. Then came Jean-Marc Bosman.

The Bosman Ruling, made in December 1995 after a five-year legal battle, allowed players to negotiate with new clubs during the final six months of their deal, then take their pick and leave for free. They could have their cake and eat it, and the cherry on top was that their current club would want to favourably renegotiate terms earlier in their contract. Win-win. In his book, *The Deal*, Jon Smith writes: "I said to Paul Stretford, 'This is pension-fund stuff, now. For the players and for us.'"

"The Bosman ruling completely changed things," says Erkut Sogut, prominent agent to Mesut Ozil and more. "Agents became a big factor. Players had more power, so agents had more power." Not just power, as Daniel Geey, sports lawyer and author of *Done Deal*, explains to *FFT*. "Free transfers allow money that would otherwise be in a transfer fee to be redistributed into the player's hands," he says. "Elite players can benefit from being out of contract, with much higher wages and agent commission as a result."

Agents were getting rich as well as famous – and they *were* famous. Stretford is best-known now for bagging 20 per cent of Wayne Rooney's off-field earnings and a record commission, but he was making headlines back in the early-90s. Eric Hall, who declared, "I'm not a one-man band; I'm a one-man orchestra," even had his own catchphrase: "Monster monster." It was a simpler time. Before them came Dennis Roach, who was Johan Cruyff's agent/groupie (depending on ▶

Above "Keep that fella Veiga off my nice tie"

who you ask) after meeting him on holiday, later negotiated football's first ever £1m transfer fee, and in 2001 responded to an FA investigation into bungs by seeking a High Court ruling ordering that only FIFA had the right to charge him.

And, leaving the music industry behind him to represent Diego Maradona and the England football team – in 1986, no less – there was Jon Smith.

MENDES, MOU AND MINO

"I was breaking the British transfer record every year," Smith tells *FFT*. "We'd do deals in motorway service stations. Tony Cottee's record move was a big story – was he going to Arsenal or Everton? – and when we were finishing it off, there were people coming into South Mimms services saying, 'Oh, all right, Tone?' We were writing these figures on a napkin; they'd look and go, 'F**k me, is that what you're getting? Well done, mate'. After a while, we started using private jets and hotel suites."

Smith is a hive of stories. He tells *FFT* how he brought product placement to football ("Nothing like I did was ever done"); how his telling England's players to celebrate in front of Coca-Cola hoardings led Gazza to invent diving; how he helped to launch the Premier League; how he watched Barry Hearn offer to settle a million-pound dispute at Leyton Orient by tossing a coin. A "big deal" taking a German player to England collapsed after nine months' work, Smith says, because just as he was about to arrive, the player learned that his dog would be quarantined for six

months. "We told him he could see the dog every day," he says, "but the deal fell down."

If anyone were to suggest that such stories are embellished for the after-dinner circuit, they'd be missing the point: that an agent could be on the after-dinner circuit. Erstwhile administrators became VIPs, as the Bosman ruling melded with millions in broadcasting revenue to make transfers as big a part of football as the football itself. Smith may be the original super-agent, so says his LinkedIn page, but he wasn't the last.

Jorge Mendes is synonymous with the term 'super-agent'. He claimed responsibility for 68 per cent of player transfers involving Portugal's Big Three (Benfica, Porto, Sporting) throughout the 2000s, before taking up near-permanent residence inside Jose Mourinho's office when his client managed Real Madrid – and five Mendes players – while other agents waited three days to receive a visitor's pass. He took players, managers and even

owners to pastures new, and most of those clubs were very grateful: Braga president Antonio Salvador insisted their success was "thanks to Jorge".

A key moment came in 2002. Mendes and agent Jose Veiga, Luis Figo's representative, exchanged pleasantries during a flight and, Portuguese newspaper *Record* recalled, "had a fight, grappling with each other on the floor, Mendes on top and Veiga grabbing his tie". Mendes picked up Veiga's phone amid the melee – allegedly. Either way, within months, the mother of 17-year-old Cristiano Ronaldo had replaced Veiga with Mendes, who sold the Sporting sensation to Manchester United just a year later.

Veiga would have been unable to grab hold of Mino Raiola's tie. The no-nonsense Dutch-Italian, who spoke eight different languages and learned his interpersonal skills as a child while waiting tables in his family's pizzeria, wore T-shirts instead of suits to ensure people

"WE WERE WRITING ALL THESE FIGURES ON A NAPKIN; PEOPLE WOULD LOOK AND GO, 'F**K, IS THAT WHAT YOU'RE GETTING?'"

underestimated him. It worked. Raiola's successful transfer of Zlatan Ibrahimovic to Juventus began with Juve general manager Luciano Moggi asking the agent, "What the hell are you wearing?"

Ibrahimovic remained his best client. He respected directness, and after their initial meeting Raiola had told him, "Sell your cars, your watches and start training three times as hard, because your stats are rubbish." The Swede was one of four Raiola players signed by Manchester United in 12 months under Mourinho, including Pogba's £41m bonus.

Such sums have turned super-agents from famous to infamous. A 2021 survey by CIES Football Observatory found that 89 per cent of fans thought agents were overpaid; only 66 per cent said the same about top players. That year, Premier League outfits forked out £272.6m to intermediaries – over a tenth of their television revenue and 19 per cent of the period's transfer fees, though agents also receive bonuses for deals being renegotiated and, in the case of Brazilian attacker Willian at Arsenal, even terminated.

Are we simply jealous? Does football lack perspective, or do we? "I don't think anyone would have an issue with multimillion-pound players paying their agents significant sums," continues Daniel Geey. "In US sports, players pay their agents directly. It's the narrative around football clubs having to pay players' agents that makes it a problem. There's also disproportionate attention given to outliers, which perpetuates this idea that every agent makes tons of money."

Below Super-agent Stretford chews the fat with his walking pension fund Wazza

Some agents don't really help their cause. Dimitri Seluk's complaints about Manchester City's mistreatment of Yaya Toure, included reference to "an African curse" preventing Pep Guardiola from winning the Champions League. Unscrupulous agents may pretend they've got their client a big boot deal, only to buy a few pairs off the shelf, leaving the player to promote the brand on social media while tagging a bewildered manufacturer. Others in the UK may neglect to mention that although it's the club that pays their agent's fee, the player owes 45 per cent tax on it. Cue a sudden six-figure bill.

But dodginess is self-defeating. "It should never be about money – it's about career progression," says Phil Korklin of Momentum Sports Management, which he co-owns with ex-player Brian Howard. "If everything goes well, the money will come, but that can't be the only driver. You might succeed once but you won't keep succeeding."

Anyway, super-agents would insist such practices give agents a bad name (and they have plenty). You could never accuse Raiola of not being upfront – his first response to Ibrahimovic's interest? "Tell this Zlatan to go f**k himself."

"CLUBS SEE US AS A NECESSITY"

Agents don't just handle transfers. Well, some of them do. "We call them brokers," explains Erkut Sogut. "They broker the deal, take the commission and go. We're a family-based agency. Yesterday I was on a Zoom call with one of my agents, a player and his parents, trying to guide them to the best option not just financially, but for education. Football can't guarantee them a career where they'll never have to work again."

Sogut also repeats Geey's warning about confirmation bias. "A lot of new agents think they'll be millionaires within a year," he tells *FFT*. "They read articles in the media saying agents make millions – that's 0.05 per cent of agents, and it took them 20 to 30 years. The reality is much different." ▶

What *is* the reality, then? Korklin's agency represents 50 Football League players and every day is deadline day for them. "You're giving footballers the right tools to learn how to manage their own finances and look after themselves," he says. "Mortgages, insurance, investments, a car, other personal stuff – you need to know the right people, so they're not ripped off by someone who thinks players earn shedloads of money and therefore have shedloads to spend."

There's a duty of care involved. "During the pandemic, when the structure and routine that football provides was taken away from them, we held Zoom sessions with all of our players and a mind coach. Jacob Brown said it changed his life. He was at Barnsley, went to Stoke and was called up by Scotland, and he flagged our session about reading books, listening to podcasts and not spending too much time on your phone. He messaged us a week after it to say, 'A notification just said

I spent 50 per cent less time on my phone, and I've finished reading three books'."

Agents live on the road. "You're travelling to games, and the most enjoyable thing is watching our players play," reveals Korklin. "You're meeting people, speaking to clubs, networking with other agents."

Many interpret 'networking' as 'not working', but for agents it's crucial. "On deadline day, a club might sell your player only if they find a replacement, but they won't say who it is," says Korklin. "You have to find out who and ask the agent, 'Is your lad the replacement?' When he says, 'Well, yeah, but he's not going there', you know your player isn't getting out. Clubs see us as a necessity, not a hindrance. They need information."

That extends to data. Yes, even agents use xG. They know what their client offers and which teams need it. Swindon's Scott Twine signed for League One MK Dons last summer when many expected a Championship move,

but as Korklin explains, "We looked at heat maps, where they created chances, and if you placed him on top then scientifically it was perfect. MK Dons told Scott that being in a creative team would give him a platform." Twine, 22, was named League One Player of the Season with 20 goals and 13 assists.

"Ten years ago," says Korklin, "I'd mention our players' goals per minute, not per game, and people would insist I was just trying to make the player look good. Now, clubs buy into it. Data makes clubs accountable, and players accountable to clubs."

Accountability goes for agents, too. Clubs and managers don't forget good work that's gone before, especially from those without extensive scouting networks.

WAR OF THE SUITS

In 2015, FIFA made a mistake. We'll narrow it down: they deregulated a football agent

RAIOLA WORE T-SHIRTS OVER SUITS SO THAT HE WOULD BE UNDERESTIMATED. IT WORKED

to the latter two would have lowered Raiola's commission for Pogba's transfer, as he could not have negotiated with Juventus.

The response has been both explosive and predictable. Gareth Bale's agent Jonathan Barnett raged that FIFA should "stay away from what they don't know" and Raiola said he "will not accept it", before his April death. Agents are already suing FIFA, though their first attempt wasn't the best, with attempts to obtain an injunction from German courts dismissed on the basis that there is nothing to serve an injunction on just yet. Barnett and Sogut claim that FIFA invited only two small agencies for talks, in Uruguay right at the end of the transfer window, before putting out an unapproved press release that implied much greater consultation. FIFA's response: "It is difficult to say we don't talk to agents when they won't talk with us."

And so it goes. While FIFA's reforms rumble through the courts, bonuses will keep making their way to the pockets of agents and super-agents, including the myriad intermediaries who represent footballing family members. Hiring relatives as representatives is regular among young players starting out, but Geey believes it's "a major risk... not only do you probably not have the negotiation skills, but you don't have the network, either". Yet the roster of players represented at least in part by dads, mums, brothers and wives includes Messrs Messi, Mbappe, Kane, Icardi, Rashford, Rabiot, Pulisic and Alexander-Arnold. Some are brilliant. Some... less so.

These are the big dogs. Lower down, there's fear that smaller commissions might make deals less viable for agents brokering smaller transfers, potentially leaving lower-league players without a competent representative. Will they be collateral damage in the battle between FIFA and the super-agents?

We'll see. But as Smith tells us, "My crystal ball shows no downturn in football finance in the coming years. The world is in a s**t place financially, but football has a humongously large audience. That's not a criticism because I helped to create it. During a recession, the take from individuals may be smaller, but the numbers are getting bigger. And the more the world goes to s**t, people go to church less and their TV sets more."

What a cheery thought. ◦

industry that had been in place since 1994, optimistically hoping national associations would take the baton. Agents were classed as 'intermediaries' who no longer required qualifications, when they'd previously had to pass background checks and an obscenely tough entrance exam, including questions evaluating capability, adaptability and legal knowledge, which 70-75 per cent failed.

In the space of 18 months, England went from having 350 licensed agents to at least 1,600 – and, stresses Geey, "If nobody needs to have the requisite knowledge, things go wrong pretty quickly."

Now FIFA are keen to restore regulation. Proposed reforms will cap commissions at 10 per cent – one bonus last year was 118 per cent of the transfer fee – and put a stop to payments to family members who aren't licensed intermediaries, while preventing agents from representing all three sides in a deal: seller, buyer and player. Being limited

Above Mino's first response to Ibra's interest? "Tell him to go f**k himself" **Above right** Erkut Sogut, Ozil's agent and now an author, has big ambitions

"YOU TRICKED ME INTO LEARNING"

How to spread insights into football's dark secrets: jot them down in a novel

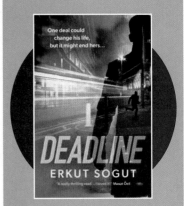

A 'holiday read' is an action-packed thriller or an insightful dive into real-world problems. *Deadline* **is both... and it's written by Mesut Ozil's agent.**

Featuring deadly rival representatives, a secret cabal of criminal super-agents and a kidnapped daughter, Erkut Sogut's account reads like *Taken* crossed with transfer deadline day, only more factual than the former and less boring than the latter. Nor is Sogut from the Steve Bruce school of 'writing', as he tells *FFT*: "I read so many books about how to write a novel – creating characters, writing locations – and visited courses online."

But... how do we put this... why? "I've always wanted to share my knowledge," explains Sogut. "My passions in life are teaching and writing, not being an agent. I've experienced so much in this business and I wanted to write about what's really going on. If I do it in fiction, I teach people while they read an enthralling thriller. People die in the story! But you also learn how deadline-day transfers work."

Nepotism is *Deadline*'s murky subject. This is the first of three books Sogut has planned; the next are human trafficking in football – he's already gone to Africa for research – and racism in Germany. On *Deadline*, he says, "I name people. I name things that happened. They're not hidden: with the Fergusons, I got everything from the *Panorama* BBC documentary. I'm not a whistleblower. I'm bringing some facts together in a fictional story."

Football fiction has had mixed success. Bruce's Partridge-esque mysteries, called "a laughing stock" by the man himself, read as if put through Google Translate a dozen times. Philip Kerr's Scott Manson trilogy stars a sleuthing fixer-turned-coach-turned-manager-turned-detective who tries to protect his London City FC side from distractions by solving the odd murder. Can Sogut transcend the genre?

ART IS

The *Picture of Dorian Gray* attracted such controversy in the early 1890s that Oscar Wilde wrote a preface to defend his only novel's reputation. That prologue has come to be as famous as the work it precedes as a manifesto for art for art's sake, praising something utterly useless as long as its beauty can be admired intently.

Take a look at Zinedine Zidane's list of club honours and your first reaction is probably disappointment. In the modern era of Lionel Messi and Cristiano Ronaldo, three league titles, one Champions League, one Ballon d'Or and a goal every five-and-a-bit games is meagre. Sure, France's 1998 World Cup and Euro 2000 victories are impossible without Zidane, but at club level, the bare figures are far from earth-shattering. Yet Zidane exists in the bracket of all-time greats with Johan Cruyff, George Best and Alfredo Di Stefano.

Why? Art. Such was Zizou's ludicrous talent and leonine grace that, in his late '90s and early noughties prime, the man with the monk's haircut produced as close to art for art's sake as any footballer in history. You can't count the balletic roulettes which extricated him from tight situations, the ▶

Twenty years ago, Zinedine Zidane's impossible swoosh of a left boot led to the greatest goal in Champions League history; the signature act of a footballing icon in motion. And yet, for all his magic, this gritty son of Marseille often diverted attention from the conflicted soul within…

LIFE

Words Andrew Murray

unnecessary flicks on the halfway line or a crowd's moments of hushed awe as stats because they're not direct contributors to the brutalist function of winning matches. But you could *feel* them.

Twenty years ago, however, Zidane came as close as anyone before or since to showing how doing something just because you can may also provoke something spectacularly useful. On May 15, 2002, Zizou watched a ball plummet from the Scottish night's sky, swivelled on his right foot and thrust his weaker left to shoulder-height. The volleyed goal of such startling, impossible beauty that followed deserved its own museum. It also won Real Madrid the Champions League and beatified a modern football god.

"Without your art, you are nothing"

Goals like Zidane's against Leverkusen just shouldn't happen. These showpiece events are usually littered with an unremitting drudge of mediocrity between two teams desperate not to make a costly mistake. Individuality and creative thinking are actively discouraged at the expense of team shape, limiting space and eventually finding a way to win. Playmakers in Champions League finals exist as an afterthought, like a work experience kid tossed a throwaway crumb to keep them busy: get the ball, see if you can do something with it, but mainly remember your responsibilities to your co-workers.

Forty-two years before the howitzer that ensured Zidane's deification, on the same Hampden Park pitch in Glasgow, his Madrid forebears proved there was another way in a European Cup final if you were touched by a higher power. When Alfredo Di Stefano and Ferenc Puskas scored every Real Madrid goal – the latter four, to the former's three – in a 7-3 destruction of Eintracht Frankfurt in the 1960 final, ingenuity triumphed over pragmatism for Los Blancos.

Madrid were under intense pressure in Glasgow in 2002. That March, a faltering side had lost the Copa del Rey final to Deportivo La Coruna – staged at their Bernabeu home to mark the club's centenary – in one of the greatest upsets in Spanish football history. Later, Madrid won just one of their final five league games as they gifted the league to Rafa Benitez's Valencia. Zidane's arrival for a world-record €78 million at the beginning of the season – 12 months after Luis Figo's controversial defection from Barcelona for a then-record fee – was supposed to herald a deluge of trophies for president Florentino Perez's Galacticos project, not a series of embarrassing near-misses. The Frenchman, too, was feeling the pressure. After four goals in his first six games of the campaign, Zidane – an intensely private man – struggled to display his sublime skills to an unconvinced public which mistook his inherent shyness for aloofness.

"The first three months were difficult," he later admitted to *FFT*. "The media chased me everywhere, photographers were everywhere, and I thought, 'What is all this?' I remember at one point saying, '*a lo mejor me voy*' –

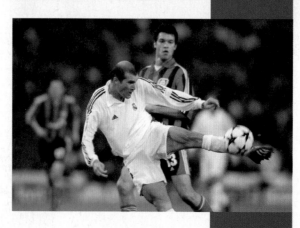

maybe it's better if I go. In the end, though, it passed. Everything always passes."

The Champions League semi-final against bitter rivals Barcelona – the first time there had been a European Cup Clasico since 1960 – proved a turning point. The first leg was at the Camp Nou on April 23, the festival of Catalonia's patron saint Sant Jordi, when it's tradition to exchange roses and books. As the Madrid coach approached the ground, however, most Barça fans swapped flowers and Shakespeare for rocks and actual spears. Zidane and his team-mates threw themselves on the floor as missiles rained down on the bus and through its windows. This was war.

Above Zidane waits for the ball to drop at Hampden Park; and whelps it in the top bins

"I lived that for [former club] Juventus against Fiorentina, too," remembered Zizou. "*Bang, bang, bang, bang.* 'Maybe this is normal,' I said to myself. 'They just want to attack you; they don't love you'. But it maybe gives you more tension, more motivation. You get into the zone."

Channelling his inner Hulk, Zidane scored a delicious second-half dink over Roberto Bonano to put Los Blancos on their way to a superb 2-0 victory. "What I will always remember was the return to Madrid," he later told *FFT*. "There were 5,000 people at the airport, saying '*gracias* for the goal!' The people wanted to eat me."

The Madrid fans finally onside, Zidane went one better in the final. On the stroke of half-time, and the score at 1-1 after Lucio had equalised Raul's early opener, Zidane faced his destiny. In 1960, Di Stefano, Puskas & Co had an entire 90 minutes to create their masterpiece – Zidane had the three seconds it took Roberto Carlos' looping cross to drop out of the Hampden sky.

"What I'm thinking is, 'I'm going to shoot'," he told *FFT* in 2013. "I shift sideways and look to see where the goal is for a second, because I have time to think. First time. I'm going to hit it."

What followed was Nijinsky, Nureyev and Baryshnikov all rolled into one. Zidane's wife Veronique gave up a career as a professional

ballet dancer for the man she first met as a 17-year-old in Cannes in 1989 – her future husband had clearly been taking notes. On the edge of the box, Zizou pirouetted *en pointe*, raised his left foot and met the ball with a volley of such technical precision that even this Bolshoi principal couldn't believe it. "*Toma, toma, toma!*" he shouted ("have it, have it, have it"), before sprinting 60 metres around Hampden in total delirium.

"Zizou knew instantly it was a work of art, and he celebrated the goal in a way I hadn't seen him celebrate ever before," Madrid's left midfielder that day, Santi Solari, later recalled. "For people to remember goals and make the jump from sports to the wider

Above "Will you be showing *Zidane: a 21st Century Portrait*"
Top Ol' Big Ears gets ready for a Glasgow kiss

public, there has to be something extra. In this case, the finish is so artistic, it's in the 45th minute, on the 100th anniversary of the club, in the Champions League final... and it's the winner."

Mortals would have controlled the ball and passed. On the biggest club stage of all, only the true artist would even consider shooting.

"I tried to score the same way again later, even during shooting an advertisement," Zidane later revealed. "It never happened again. Never. I tried in training, but it never happened. It was perfect that day."

That it secured *La Novena*, Real Madrid's ninth European Cup, only added to its allure. "That goal was really important because of everything that built into it," Zidane told *FFT*. "The thing I didn't have was the Champions League. I'd lost it twice with Juventus – that was the only thing that I hadn't won. When a club pays €78m for you, it's because you have to do something very big! People say, 'Well, he cost a lot of money but he won the Champions League.'"

It also cemented the sort of crossover appeal that had been building but was yet to take off. The year before, Zidane had found himself in a hotel room next to Andre Agassi, but was too shy to knock on the eight-time Grand Slam tennis champion's door. He didn't possess Ronaldo's impish brilliance, Luis Figo's suave mannerisms, nor David

Beckham's rock star appeal. Frequently monosyllabic, Zidane's art was based on football as a meritocracy, centred solely on the pitch. The move to Madrid, however, brought him to global attention.

"One of the most inspiring nights of my life," said basketball royalty Magic Johnson after watching Madrid beat Depor 3-1 in January 2002, six months before the volley that changed Zizou's life forever. "Zidane is a phenomenon, as good as me and Michael Jordan put together."

Four years earlier, before France's home World Cup of 1998, there was little to suggest that Zidane's name would ever be spoken of among his contemporaries, let alone the biggest names in sport, with such reverence. Infamously, Blackburn chairman Jack Walker is reported to have asked "why do we need Zidane when we've got Tim Sherwood?" after manager Kenny Dalglish requested the Frenchman's signing back in 1995, while Newcastle turned down Zizou a year later.

Though he scored twice on his debut for Les Bleus to rescue a 2-2 draw against the Czech Republic in August 1994 – the first a staggering dribble and left-footed smash from 30 yards – Zidane played second fiddle as playmaker until Eric Cantona kung-fu kicked his way out of Aimé Jacquet's plans. Despite winning the Ligue 1 Player of the Year award for Bordeaux which earned his ▶

Clockwise from
above "See ya
later, Scholesy";
Zizou's headed
World Cup final
brace endeared
him to a nation;
"Allez les fleurs!"

move to Juve, Zizou was unable to replicate his domestic form at Euro 96 as France exited in the semi-finals, after successive goalless draws in both knockout rounds.

When World Cup warm-up Le Tournoi came around in 1997, the knives were being sharpened after Paul Lambert's man-marking job had nullified Zizou in Champions League final defeat to Borussia Dortmund.

"He failed in the European Championship and failed in the European Cup final in Munich. Is Zidane, like Eric Cantona – the man he superseded – not up to the big occasion?" wrote the *Independent* about France's No.10. "However, his Champions League performances for Juventus suggest otherwise, as Manchester United found out for themselves. It is hard to believe he's still only 24 and thus still learning. This will be another step in his footballing education, and in our knowledge of him."

A year later, everyone's knowledge of this nascent talent would be plenty better. His two headers in the 1998 final against Brazil were brutal in their simplicity, but at Euro 2000 he was at his game-controlling peak for France, winning the Golden Ball as the tournament's best player. "Zidane has an internal vision," Jacquet enthused of his playmaker's zenith. "His control is precise and discreet. He can make the ball do what he wants. But it's his drive which takes him forward. He is 100 per cent football."

Left-back Bixente Lizarazu, World Cup and Euros-winning team-mate, said the players' plan was altogether simpler: "When we don't know what to do, we just give it to Zizou and he works something out."

Mostly stepovers, feints and roulettes but like the best artists, Zidane also helped unite a country. A second-generation Algerian immigrant, he was part of a French team comprised of "*black, blanc et beur*" (black, white and Arab, a wordplay on the red, white and blue colours of the French flag) players which promoted racial diversity. Patrick Vieira, Marcel Desailly, Lilian Thuram and Youri Djorkaeff were also from immigrant backgrounds, but Zidane was the star,

once topping a poll of 'the most popular Frenchman of all-time' in *Journal du Dimanche*, the French equivalent of the *Daily Mail*. On the Champs-Elysees, an Algerian flag flew alongside the French tricolour.

That this came at a time when Jean-Marie Le Pen's far-right Front National party had support in the country – a situation with eerie recent parallels as his daughter Marine did equally well in the recent French general election – was testament to Zidane's appeal.

Yet, even at France 98, Zidane's latent dark side – a hangover from his upbringing – was seldom far from the surface.

"Art conceals the artist far more completely than it ever reveals him"

For more than 30 years, Dorian Gray's hedonism in pursuing his heart's desires over a life of late-Victorian morality courted high-society scandal, rumour and intrigue, all while he maintained his impossibly youthful beauty. What the world didn't know was that Gray's Faustian pact had ensured his own portrait, rather than he, would grow old, fade and bear the hideously deformed scars of his libertine lifestyle. After all, nothing that beautiful could possibly be responsible for his rumoured crimes, could it?

To watch peak Zidane was to see multiple personalities competing for dominance over the other. His was an unsolvable paradox of serene skill and uncontrollable temper that brought 14 career red cards. It was as if every moment of genius was designed to obscure the true man within. "Magic," he once said, "is sometimes very close to nothing at all."

Born in La Castellane, a council estate on the northern suburbs of Marseille formed of dusty streets and high-rise tower blocks, Zidane never forgot his roots. The district is what is known in French as a *quartier difficile* – a sensitive zone with high crime and unemployment rates, but one that also fosters a strong sense of community spirit.

"I have an affinity with the Arabic world – I have it in my blood, via my parents," Zizou once said. "I'm very proud of being French,

but also very proud of having these roots and this diversity. I'm first of all from La Castellane and Marseille. Wherever I go, La Castellane is where I want to go back to. It's still my home.

"It's true that it's still a difficult area. But there's also a special culture there. Marseille is probably a place like Liverpool, very vibrant and very tough. My passion for the game comes from the city of Marseille itself."

Zidane's father, Smail, would work in a warehouse by day and as a department store's nightwatchman in the evenings to give his family a comparatively easy life in their rough neighbourhood. Little Zinedine – still known by his middle name Yazid among his close family and friends – used to suffer from terrible nightmares when his father was on night shifts.

Watched by his mother Malika from the balcony of their flat, a five-year-old Zidane began playing football on Place Tartane, an 80-by-12-yard slab of concrete that served as the estate's main square. Soon, he was showing the sort of technique his hero Enzo Francescoli displayed every week for Marseille,

and joined local clubs US Saint-Henri, then SO Septemes-les-Vallons whose youth team coach persuaded the club director to sign an 11-year-old Castellane kid. Smail drove his youngest of five children to training in the family's battered Renault 12.

"Every time he played, I had to produce a piece of identification that proved his age," Zidane Snr later recalled. "His opponents thought he played under a false licence."

Sent by Septemes to a three-day training camp in Aix-en-Provence run by the French FA, a 14-year-old Zidane was spotted by Cannes scout Jean Varraud in the summer of 1986. "He spoke with the ball," said Varraud. "Believe me, I've never seen anything quite like it. Yazid had the warrior quality of his impoverished community. He was hungry."

A six-week trial led to a place at the club's Mimont academy. Zidane spent much of it cleaning – a punishment for punching an opponent who'd mocked his ghetto origins, the first act of uncontrolled rage which sought dominance over the artist.

Varraud worked hard with Zidane to curb his mentee's raw temper, after further attacks on spectators who insulted the youngster's race. Eventually, a spell living with Cannes director Jean-Claude Elineau's family helped calm Zidane down.

"My greatest memory is Cannes, my apprenticeship, the six or seven years I spent there," he recalled. "I watched the pros play, I trained every day and I said, 'Kid, if you work, if you're serious, you can do something here'. I didn't go to the cinema, or the beach to show off to girls. I knew what I wanted."

It was at Cannes where Zidane made a friend for life. He hit it off with David Bettoni immediately; they raced each other home to Lyon and Marseille respectively in their battered Ford Fiesta (Bettoni) and

Renault Clio (Zidane) the day they first met. Zizou may be painfully shy, but he's also fiercely loyal to his intimate circle. When he joined Juve a few years later in 1996, Zidane and the Old Lady arranged for Bettoni to join third-tier sides Avezzano and Alessandria so their star man had a familiar face around along with his young family ("I can't tell you about all the to-ing and fro-ing!" he later said). Bettoni was also Zidane's assistant manager when he took over at Real Madrid. They still speak most days.

Zidane was merely 16 when he made his Cannes debut in May 1989, in a Ligue 1 fixture against Nantes. The 1990-91 season proved his breakthrough year, as he made 31 appearances and scored his first goal – also against Nantes – in February 1991. At a party after the game, president Alain Pedretti came good on a promise to give Zidane a car after netting for the first time. The outrageous talent Varraud had first seen – "he'd go past one, two, three, five, six players; it was sublime" – was now wowing Ligue 1, not least when Cannes finished fourth to qualify for the UEFA Cup. It remains their best performance since finishing second in Ligue 1's inaugural 1932-33 season.

A 20-year-old Zidane joined Bordeaux in the summer of 1992. There, manager Rolland Courbis recognised the brooding intensity of the introvert in his fellow ▶

"I WOULD RATHER DIE THAN SAY SORRY TO MATERAZZI. IT WOULD DISHONOUR ME"

marseillais, and the necessity to shape a raw talent into something special. Courbis is also credited with channelling Zidane's emotions and coining the Zizou nickname. The latter helped Zidane establish an alter-ego – Yazid from the Castellane ghetto was dead, Zizou the flawed genius was his reincarnation.

"You could see he was an extraordinary player straight away," Courbis later said, "but it was a moment in his career when you couldn't afford to do just anything with him. For example, you couldn't just give him his head and burn him out in a season."

Zidane's 10 goals in 35 Ligue 1 games in his first season were testament to Courbis' influence, but it was after his mentor's exit that the prodigy came to world attention. In 1995-96, Bordeaux became the only team to reach the UEFA Cup final after qualifying for it by winning the much-maligned Intertoto Cup, but lost 5-1 to Bayern Munich on aggregate after knocking out Real Betis and Milan en route (Zidane provided two assists in a 3-0 tonking of the Rossoneri, one with the amusing aid of a ref's backside). Bordeaux finished Ligue 1 in a disappointing 16th, but such was Zidane's supernatural talent that Europe's elite were chasing his signature.

Juve won the fight – and in Turin, he scaled world football's summit. In his maiden season, 1996-97, Zidane won Serie A and was voted the league's inaugural Foreign Footballer of the Year. The following year, the Old Lady retained their title as Zizou scored or assisted on 14 occasions. Yet, because of Champions League final losses

to Dortmund, then a similarly anonymous display against Real Madrid in 1998 – "we were s**tting ourselves at facing him," Raul later revealed – he was never truly loved in the Italian Alps. It didn't help that Zidane preferred to spend time with Veronique and nearby Cannes pal Bettoni, unlike compatriot Michel Platini's outward gregariousness in carousing the city during his 1980s peak.

Zidane's irritability also returned. He'd react to the sort of niggly fouls that grizzled Serie A defenders in the '90s specialised in, and even carried it into France 98: Zidane's World Cup was nearly ruined by a pointlessly petulant stamp on Fuad Anwar when Les Bleus were already 2-0 up against Saudi Arabia. They barely made it through the last 16 against Paraguay without him. No World Cup would have meant no Ballon d'Or.

In what proved his final Juve season in 2000-01, Zidane headbutted Hamburg's Jochen Kientz in a 3-1 October defeat to earn his second red card of the Champions League group stage. UEFA threw the book at him, banning Zidane for five games. Typical of the coexisting violence and beauty at the heart of his story, Zidane ended up serving four games of that suspension at the start of the following season for Real Madrid. By the end of 2001-02, the 29-year-old had scored the greatest goal in tournament history.

"Each of us has heaven and hell in him"

That Zidane only won one La Liga title and one Champions League at Real Madrid, and

Aboce Zidane's football was never beige, unlike his dress sense...
Top Los Galacticos won fewer titles than you'd expect

nothing of any consequence post-2003, seems almost impossible. The Galacticos defined an era, as first Figo, then Zidane, Ronaldo and Beckham followed in successive summers to create the Harlem Globetrotters of football. There was no better way to watch the best players in the world.

"He dominates the ball, he is a walking spectacle and he plays as if he had silk gloves on each foot – he makes it worthwhile going to the stadium," said the notoriously brusque Di Stefano.

"I enjoyed playing in that team so much," Zidane told *FFT*. "The opposition scored two? *No pasa nada*. We'll score three. It was fun."

Yet the fun couldn't last. The financial necessity brought of the '*Zidanes y Pavones*' – star names supplemented by youth teamers like Francisco Pavon, who lacked

ein Andenken von Z

"I was a bit disappointed with the film," he told *FFT*. "They sold me the idea of the cameras, the sound, the montage. It wasn't their fault because I wasn't able to give everything to the project. That game was a bit sh**ty and obviously finished with the sending off. I can see from their point of view that they wanted to end on that dramatic point, but I'd have preferred a more football-related intensity or emotion."

Did he enjoy giving himself over to art? "If I'm playing in a way that is elegant, great – I like that. It's nice that they say that. But I'm first of all a footballer and I hope people enjoy me as a footballer on the pitch: a competitor, not a dancer. I'm not there to show things, I am there to win."

By the end of the following season in 2005-06, Zidane blamed himself for Madrid's third successive trophyless season and decided to announce his retirement.

"You say to yourself, 'I'm an important player in this team and it's three years,'" he told *FFT*. "I'm responsible for that. I might have stayed longer if we'd won more. In the end, you tire of it. In a hotel, in your room, before every game. I couldn't take it any more. I left: that tells you. I had lots of offers to carry on. But I left it."

For the first time in his career, Zidane cried before his final game at the Bernabeu in May 2006, a 3-3 draw again against Villarreal.

"I had a bad day," he told *FFT*. Despite scoring, the fact there was nothing riding on it mattered more. "Right from the start to the end, I just wasn't there. I was thinking, 'It's over, that's it'. And the game wasn't a good one. It was a game that didn't matter and I was thinking so much about the end, what there was afterwards, what would happen next. That can happen to people, but not to me. I just burst into tears."

That summer's World Cup would be his last act, beginning it still aged just 33. Zidane had already retired once from international football after a surprise quarter-final defeat to Greece at Euro 2004 solidified a feeling of despair that began two years earlier – then, the defending champions hadn't made it beyond the group stage of the 2002 World Cup. Not only that, Les Bleus had failed to even score, with a half-fit Zidane injuring a thigh in the build-up to the tournament. When France were struggling to qualify for 2006, Zidane (as captain), Thuram and Claude Makelele all reversed their decisions as they eventually made it to the finals.

In Germany, France opened with two draws. Zidane, booked in the second against South Korea and knowing he'd be suspended for the must-win third against Togo, kicked down the dressing room door in Leipzig. Instead of replacing it, local officials have drawn a golden frame around the mangled door, stud marks front and centre.

France defeated Togo without Zidane, but he returned for the last 16 against Spain and delivered a goal and an assist. In the quarter-final against Brazil, he set up Thierry Henry's winner in a man-of-the-match display. He then scored a nerveless semi-final penalty to beat Portugal 1-0.

Then came the final against Italy. In the seventh minute, Zidane opened the scoring with a dinked Panenka penalty of glorious artistry. He was in thrall to Yazid again, playing with the raw instinct he'd hidden since the streets of La Castellane, and would win another Golden Ball as player of the tournament. But, with 10 minutes of extra time remaining, it happened.

"If you want my jersey, I'll give it to you at the end," spat France's No.10 at Marco Materazzi, scorer of Italy's 15th-minute equaliser and doing what Azzurri defenders learn in the cradle. Depending on who you believe, Materazzi either insulted Zidane's sister or mother – the latter was seriously ill in hospital at the time. Either way, the departing playmaker turned on his heel and headbutted the former Everton centre-back's chest with a visceral potency felt across the world. The image of Zidane walking down the tunnel, past the World Cup trophy, remains one of the great photographs in football history. France lost the ensuing penalty shootout.

"If you look at the 14 red cards I had during my career, 12 of them were a result of provocation," he later reasoned. "This isn't justification, this isn't an excuse, but my passion, temper and blood made me react." The wrongs he still felt from that childhood racism burned hard and were seared into his soul. No amount of elegant creativity could hide it. Yazid made Zizou do it.

By the end of *The Picture of Dorian Gray*, the titular character can no longer see a way out. Unable to carry the secret of his Faustian pact any longer after one affair (and murder) too many, Gray eventually drives a knife through his portrait, not only killing himself and transforming his body into a withered, loathsome pile of skin and bones, but also restoring his picture to its beautiful original form.

When Zidane embedded his head into Materazzi's chest, he did so knowing he was taking a knife to his own career, yet he did it anyway. Why? Because he followed his heart.

"If I ask Materazzi forgiveness, I lack respect to myself and to all those I hold dear," he later explained. "If I say 'sorry', I would also be admitting that what he himself did was normal. But to him I cannot. Never, never. It would be to dishonour me. I'd rather die."

Like Dorian Gray and his picture, Zidane knew no amount of headbutts could diminish the art he had helped to create, nor the immortality he'd ensured. Perhaps, as one left-foot swish 20 years ago proved, not all art is useless after all. ◎

elite talent – meant Los Blancos fell away. The names became more important than a team that was allowed to age, but Zidane's art continued to be indulged.

On April 23, 2005, 17 cameras followed Zizou around the Bernabeu for a league game against Villarreal – the resulting documentary film *Zidane: a 21st Century Portrait* was a real-time deep-dive into what it was to be an ageing superstar. If all art is quite useless, this is the epitome – it's impossible to follow the game itself, just the balding, shuffling, monosyllabic genius who sweats profusely and flits in and out. Late on, Zidane hares halfway across the pitch to defend Raul, who is surrounded by Yellow Submarine defenders, one of whom he headbutts. It's an eerie harbinger of what would happen some 15 months later.

Top to bottom Zizou's mark is forever left on a Leipzig door; "Have it, Marco"; the World Cup that got away

MORE ON FOURFOURTWO.COM

• Year Zero: The making of Zinedine Zidane at Juventus, 1996-97 *(by Nicky Bandini)*

• 14 pieces of Zidane's most majestic skills *(by Louis Massarella)*

• Quiz: Name the 50 Real Madrid players with the most Champions League appearances

WHEN THE MUSIC STOPS

Footballers experience a life of adulation in their playing days, but it's a whole different ball game after retirement. Adjusting to a new existence can be really tough, as Dean Windass & Co reveal to *FFT*...

Words Ed McCambridge

Dean Windass can still remember the first time he didn't have to get up for training. While his team-mates, fresh back from their summer holidays, trudged in for day one of a gruelling pre-season schedule, the then 41-year-old stayed tucked up in bed.

A few months earlier, the striker had played his final professional match, calling time on a two-decade career that took in 10 clubs, including spells in the Premier League and Scotland's top flight. Windass scored more than 200 goals and had lived the dream at hometown team Hull City, where he's still idolised to this day. Understandably, he had never wanted it to end.

"I prolonged my playing days for as long as I could," Windass, now aged 53, tells *FFT*. "I never took being a footballer for granted. At 20, I swapped working on building sites for an apprenticeship at Hull and always had that other path – the one I didn't take – at the back of my mind. I enjoyed every single moment because I knew it easily may not have happened. But 20 years goes by very quickly. I really didn't want to retire, but we all have to at some stage."

It's a sentiment that will be so familiar to many. Coming to terms with life after football is hard, as Mark Crossley, a veteran of more than 500 games for clubs such as Fulham, Middlesbrough and Nottingham Forest can attest. "I had no plan at all," he explains to *FFT*. "Football tells you where to be, what to do, when to be there, what to eat, when to eat it, what time the coach is leaving, what time we're reporting for pre-season, where we're going for pre-season. Then it all goes overnight. I got up one morning to drive to work, and I wasn't even working there any more. It was weird."

Not many people get to experience the adrenaline, adulation and, in some cases, eye-watering salaries that come with being a professional footballer. On the other hand, not many of us have our careers taken away at such an early age. Footballers have their incomes, friendships, support networks and even their purpose pulled from under their feet when their bodies are no longer up to it. It's no wonder so many struggle.

Windass' transition was made tougher by a divorce from his wife and the sudden death of his father, a man who had watched him ▶

play "every week between the ages of four and 41". Following the loss, Windass started to suffer from depression and began drinking heavily. On more than one occasion, he tried to take his own life.

"I was going through a very bad time with my dad's passing," admits Windass. "I was absolutely devastated and that was the key cause of my depression. Looking back, I see how losing the daily structures in my life, the support football offered me – my dressing room relationships and my reason for getting up and keeping healthy – all added up on top of that."

Like so many professionals coming to the end of their careers, Windass tried his hand at coaching, serving as player-assistant manager under Colin Todd at Darlington in 2009 before the pair left after nine league games in charge.

"I just didn't get any opportunities after that," he continues. "Coaching had been my dream but it was over all too soon – people didn't trust what I had to say. I later joined *Soccer Saturday*, working as a pundit on TV. I did that for two years, but after my dad died I was unable to carry on. I started drinking a lot, ended up in rehab, and that was that with Sky. I was tarred with a brush and never got a chance again."

In his own mind, Dean Windass the player, the manager, the pundit, became... plain old Dean. That loss of status is one of the most challenging things for any retired professional footballer to come to terms with, whether they've been in the Champions League or the National League.

"All they've known throughout their entire lives is football," explains Dr Michael Bennett, director of player well-being at the PFA. "They focus on football 24/7, year in year out. From a young age, that's all they've ever dreamed of. They've strived, given up their childhoods, given up friends and sacrificed everything to focus on football. So when they leave the game, and they're no longer a footballer, they struggle massively because that's their identity. It's who they are."

Not every player is as fortunate to have had a career as accomplished as Windass'. The Englishman totalled more than 100 outings for Bradford, Middlesbrough and Hull in the Premier League, one of the most lucrative divisions in world football. The same can be said for Crossley, who played more than 200 times in the English top flight for Nottingham Forest and won eight caps for Wales. Further down the pyramid, a loss of status can be the least of retired players' concerns.

"It's something a lot of people don't think about when players retire," adds Bennett, who played for a number of clubs including Charlton, Wimbledon and Brentford before retiring and joining the PFA.

"Beneath the Premier League, you've got loads of players who spend their careers on one-year contracts, going from club to club. One day that can suddenly stop. They've got wives, mortgages and kids to look after. They spend plenty of time fretting about all those things while simultaneously being asked to perform at their peak. When they don't get

a new contract, their world comes to an end. They've been under so much pressure to stay in the game, that they haven't thought about what comes next."

Even those with some savings in the bank can soon find themselves in financial distress while they adjust to their new lives outside of football. It's no surprise then, that money management is one of the major areas that Bennett and his colleagues at the PFA, plus several other organisations, concentrate on with ex-professionals.

"Numerous former pros have never had to worry about financial decisions throughout their careers," says Bennett. "They've always had everything done for them, from buying

houses to booking work trips and holidays. We've had some retired players who've lost everything – either squandering their cash, failing to plan for the future or racking up big debts through poor investments, gambling or drinking."

Organisations such as the PFA try to pick up the pieces when retired footballers lose their way financially. "We run courses that teach players how to budget, how to save money and how to make their finances go further," says Bennett.

The simple fact is, unless you're a Premier League stalwart earning tens of thousands of pounds a week, it's likely you'll need to find new sources of income once your career

Right Bullard found a new career in TV, but not everyone has the opportunity nor the charisma to be a big success **Below** Hometown hero Windass lets Hull's 2008 play-off final victory sink in

"I LOST ALL THE DAILY STRUCTURES IN MY LIFE, MY DRESSING ROOM RELATIONSHIPS AND THE REASON FOR GETTING UP AND KEEPING HEALTHY"

draws to a close. Many players assume they will either transition into coaching or become full-time bosses when that time eventually arrives, but there aren't enough positions to go around. Others imagine life as a TV pundit, but not everybody gets the opportunity or has the charisma to do so. Those that do can count themselves lucky.

"I was itching for something to keep me busy when I stopped playing," former Wigan, Fulham and Hull midfielder Jimmy Bullard, now a presenter of *Soccer AM*, reveals to *FFT*. "I didn't know what to do with myself at first. But I was fortunate that I was seen as a bit of a joker during my playing days.

"I got invited on to *I'm A Celebrity... Get Me Out of Here!*, then more TV offers followed. It's something I love doing and I don't take it for granted. Many of my mates have suffered from depression after they've hung up their boots. It's been tough to watch, but I can see why they've struggled. It's not easy leaving football behind."

What to do, then, for those that don't stay in the game, in one way or another? The vast majority of ex-pros don't possess the savings to live out the rest of their days on holiday, enjoying the high life.

Some find their own solutions. After retiring in 2009, former Derby, Middlesbrough and Leeds striker Malcolm Christie became a car salesman for Jaguar, although he gradually realised he'd ventured down a path he wasn't completely satisfied with. "I ended up in the motor industry, but it took me eight to 10 years to see it wasn't what I wanted for the rest of my life," he later confessed.

Christie's is not a unique case – replacing football with a 'normal' job can be a shock to the system. The feeling of scoring a last-gasp winner in front of thousands is, by definition, impossible to replicate in another job. Finding the right line of work, a new calling that can stimulate in other ways is crucial. Sadly, few players are fully prepared when the moment comes to start the next chapter.

"So many of these guys have always been Steve or Dave the footballer," says former West Bromwich Albion defender Paul Raven, education executive at the PFA. "It's all many of them care about while they're still playing – they don't want to focus on anything else. I often go around clubs and speak to players, and I'll tell them, 'Listen, you're a footballer only 10 per cent of the time – you're playing football for a lot less time than not playing, ▶

"WE DON'T WANT PEOPLE COMING TO US IN FINANCIAL DIFFICULTIES – WE WANT TO HELP THEM AVOID THAT"

so make the most of that freedom to plan for the future'. But not nearly enough use their downtime wisely.

"Even just three hours a week would make a big difference in the long run and help them adjust more easily to life after football. So many people end up in a tough situation that could have been avoided with more forward planning. They'd be ready to start something fresh and wouldn't feel the blow of missing football so emphatically."

Today, young players at professional clubs have to complete a BTech or NVQ alongside their football education, plus basic coaching courses that will give them the platform to explore that path when they retire. However, Raven and his colleagues encourage players to go the extra mile – anything from learning a different trade to studying for a degree at a local university or college.

The PFA also provides a pension scheme for members. For every year of a male member's playing career, £6,400 goes into a personal non-contributory fund – while female players currently receive less, moving towards parity is a target for the near future. If a member's career lasts 10 years, they will have amassed more than £60,000 by the time they finally call it a day, easing the immediate financial shock of retirement.

Retired players are able to take advantage of advice and funding from the PFA as they search for a new occupation.

"Nothing's off limits," says Raven. "We have some marvellous data around what players undertake in terms of academic or vocational qualifications following retirement. There are something like 40,000 roles out there, and I'd be surprised if there isn't an ex-footballer in virtually every one of them. Players have trained to become paramedics, pilots, train drivers, doctors and even dog groomers – all sorts of weird and wonderful vocations. We do our best to help them achieve their career goals, with funding assistance available for any number of courses."

Above Ex-Leeds star Brian Deane launched Phoenix Sports in 2016 to help players pick up vital life skills

Despite their efforts, there are people who feel the PFA still isn't doing enough to help footballers transition into life after football. Former Sheffield United, Leeds and England striker Brian Deane, who scored the Premier League's first ever goal back in August 1992, thinks they should be doing far more to stop the biggest problems at their root.

"They're reactive, not proactive," explains Deane. "They will wait for players to come to them with problems that could have been avoided a lot earlier. They're usually nowhere to be seen for players until they're already experiencing major problems."

In 2016, Deane co-founded Phoenix Sports and Media Group, an organisation that allows

WHAT THEY DID NEXT
Not everyone goes into coaching – some take up more surprising vocations...

ARJAN DE ZEEUW
After retiring in 2009, the ex-Barnsley, Wigan and Portsmouth centre-back returned to his native Netherlands and began training as an investigative detective, specialising in forensics.

KEVIN KYLE
As well as entering the BDO Scottish Open darts tournament, the former Sunderland striker became a ferry storeman, working on a ship housing oil workers in the Shetland Islands.

KEN MONKOU
A popular defender for both Chelsea and Southampton, the Dutchman reinvented himself post-retirement as a pancake chef, owning the Old Town Pancake House near Rotterdam.

TIM WIESE
The six-cap Germany goalkeeper's career came to an end in 2014, his physique described as better suited to bodybuilding than football. So he turned to WWE wrestling, of course.

former players to gain vital skills they might otherwise have picked up, had they not been pro footballers. Phoenix works directly with clubs, including Liverpool, Derby and Crystal Palace, giving players an opportunity to learn other trades on the side.

"We provide a range of specific courses," outlines Deane. "We're offering cyber security courses, which give players the tools to move into a growing job market when their careers end. We know this generation of footballers are into computer gaming and technology, so it's something they're often interested in.

"We also go into the clubs and host money management workshops, so they know how to handle their money during and after their careers. We're not waiting around for them to come to us in financial difficulties, we want to help them avoid that scenario. We don't have anything close to the same budget as the PFA, but we do what we can and we feel like we're making a real difference."

Deane believes football needs a shake-up, with the FA and clubs putting more money aside to educate players while they're active, and the PFA taking on greater responsibility for its members.

The PFA is no stranger to such criticism and concedes it can always do more. Yet Raven is quick to reiterate the role the organisation plays at professional clubs, and the variety of services, advice and funding on offer to those who need it. He also stresses the importance of players coming to the PFA and making the most of the expertise available, should they feel they ever need it.

That final point is something Windass says he could have done sooner, to ease his own struggles. "I was a member of the PFA, but I didn't open up for a long time," he reveals. "I was always the big man in the dressing room when I played – a prankster and joker. I never thought I was someone that actually needed any help."

"The PFA does its best to reach out and talk to players," says Bennett. "But we can't see everything. Sometimes players need to get in touch and let us know the difficulties they're going through. Admitting there's a problem is an important step." Thankfully, Windass eventually got the support he needed. After speaking up, the PFA arranged for the former striker to attend rehab and, ultimately, he kicked the booze. It was a huge achievement – one that went a significant way to restoring some clarity in his life. His fans were thrilled to see him doing better.

"After I sorted myself out, I started posting videos on social media to let everyone know I was OK and on the mend," recalls Windass with a smile. "I told all my followers, 'I've just made my bed and I've put my pillows on top'. It was just a bit silly – I wanted people to see I was up and about and living my life again. The catchphrase sort of stuck and now I have to finish every video by saying, 'I've made my bed and put my pillows on top'."

However, his real post-playing purpose was yet to come. Those who watched Windass in his pomp – a forward that could bully central defenders with strength – would be forgiven for thinking he's found his zen doing boxing

Above Windass, Crossley and more former pros have embraced walking to keep fit and maintain purpose

or weightlifting. They'd be wrong... Windass is a walker. He's got a friend to thank for that.

"The walking was all Mark Crossley's idea, really," Windass tells *FFT*. "He'd gone through a bad time himself and discovered walking. He knew I'd been through the mill myself, so he reached out. That was a massive thing for me – I'm very grateful."

Crossley realised the joys of walking shortly after his own post-playing career – a role as a goalkeeping coach at Chesterfield – ended in January 2020. "I was struggling mentally – the week I came out of football, my dad got diagnosed with cancer," he says.

"My mate said, 'You don't seem yourself – you need to come walking with me'. I began doing that and soon became addicted to it – I got a dog, started walking and targeted 40 to 50 miles a week. It was helping to keep my fitness up, keep my weight down and, mentally, it was benefitting me loads because it releases endorphins. I found my niche and it's carried on."

Aided by Windass and a few other old pros, Crossley has set up a fundraising organisation called WATCH (Walking And Talking Charity Hikes), which collects cash through sponsored walks using the hashtag #walkingsbrilliant. After a gruelling coast-to-coast trek last year, a group featuring Chris Kirkland, Jon Parkin,

Steve Howey and Nigel Jemson did the Three Peaks Challenge this summer, climbing Ben Nevis, Scafell Pike and Snowdon, joined by ex-boxer Tony Bellew. They've set their sights even higher in 2023: scaling Kilimanjaro.

"We try to support others who haven't been as lucky as us," says Crossley. "I knew a lot of people were struggling, especially during lockdown. Everybody jumped at it and it's just grown and grown in the space of two years. We've raised more than £100,000 and made half a dozen donations to mental health charities. That's where we get our satisfaction from now. It takes up a lot of free time, but it's so rewarding."

Windass, Crossley & Co have found a new purpose in life, something everyone – former players, the PFA and Phoenix – agree is key to dealing with the shock of losing a career in professional football.

"I'd advise any active player to think about what their next step may be when they hang up their boots," concludes Windass. "It's all about finding a new challenge. Retiring from football can be the start of something new, of something very different. Losing your playing career doesn't have to be the end." ○

For more details about Crossley's fundraising and to donate, head to walkingsbrilliant.com

"WHAT'S LANCASTRIAN FOR 'GALACTICO'?"

First Youri Djorkaeff saved Bolton Wanderers from trouble, then came a motley crew of stars searching for something special. In a humble corner of the North West, the Trotters' unconventional rise delivered plenty of pleasant surprises...

Words Chris Flanagan

One humdrum weekday afternoon in February 2002, a lone footballer stood in the middle of the Reebok Stadium pitch.

Just under four years previously, he'd helped his country to win the biggest game in world football, in front of a crowd of 75,000 and an estimated television audience of a billion. Today, a totally deserted stadium surrounding him, Youri Djorkaeff had something he wanted to do.

A couple of hours earlier, the Frenchman had completed one of his opening training sessions with Bolton Wanderers. Then he headed over to the Reebok, accompanied by a member of the backroom staff, before wandering onto the pitch with a football.

When asked to play a few gentle passes for Djorkaeff to jog after, in various areas of the playing surface, the staff member was puzzled. "What are you doing, Youri?" he asked. "I'm looking at all the advertising boards," said Djorkaeff. "Then at any time, I'll know where I am on the pitch."

In that moment, it became clear that things were about to change for Bolton. A World Cup winner had arrived, and not only was his attention to detail beyond anything the club had ever seen, he was also absolutely determined to succeed. Signed on a deal until the end of the season, Djorkaeff helped promoted Bolton stay in the Premier League by four points.

"Then came the most important thing of all," Sam Allardyce tells *FourFourTwo*. "He went to the 2002 World Cup that summer, rang us up and said, 'Can I come back?'"

Djorkaeff would be followed to Bolton by Jay-Jay Okocha, Ivan Campo, El-Hadji Diouf, Stelios Giannakopoulos, Fernando Hierro and Nicolas Anelka, in the most remarkable era that the Lancastrian town had seen since the trophy-winning days of the 1950s. Led by Allardyce, Bolton's Galacticos propelled an unfashionable club into the upper reaches of the Premier League, then the knockout stages of European competition. In a few short years, an eclectic mix of entertainers ensured cult hero status for life.

SHEEP'S TESTICLES AND TOILET RACING

Things were different when Allardyce took over as manager in October 1999, with the club mid-table in the second tier. "It was fate, as my first game was on my birthday," recalls the 67-year-old, who'd previously represented Bolton as a player.

In his first full campaign, Allardyce guided them to the top flight with victory over David Moyes' Preston in the play-off final. Three games into their Premier League adventure they were top, having beaten Middlesbrough and Liverpool following a 5-0 opening day triumph at Leicester.

The latter was so emphatic that the club's backroom staff had to eat sheep's testicles – an agreed wager if the team ever won by three goals or more. Other bonding exercises included a day trip to the Lake District, where

Below "Could you stop taking the piss out of us sometime soon please, Youri?"

players raced downhill while sat on toilets. As the 2001-02 season went on, though, Bolton slid closer to the relegation zone. Allardyce knew he had to add extra talent to complement team spirit.

"We wanted more quality but had a limited budget, because the club was £45-50 million in the red when I first took over – when I left, I was in profit," he explains. "The best way was to find players who could come on loan or were coming out of contract – either they wanted to leave the club they were at, or the club wanted to get rid of them."

In Djorkaeff, the Trotters found their man. Frozen out at Kaiserslautern, the 33-year-old wanted regular football to secure his place in France's squad at a World Cup only months away. The midfielder held talks with both Manchester United and Liverpool, but it was Allardyce who swayed Djorkaeff by flying to Germany and offering him a pivotal role in Bolton's survival bid.

"I thought it was going to be difficult to get him, but I had to have a go," the former Bolton boss says now. "I visited him to sell it,

Top to bottom
Jay-Jay brought the fantasy to Bolton; "When can I meet my indie band?"; Stelios was a Big Sam stalwart

"WE PUT TOGETHER A VIDEO FOR PLAYERS. THE ONLY THING IT DIDN'T SHOW WAS THE TRAINING GROUND – IT WAS A S**THOLE"

rather than making him come to me – Youri wouldn't have known where Bolton was. Our IT lads put together a great video for players, about who we were and what we were. The only thing it didn't show was the training ground – at that time it was a s**thole...

"We showed them the stadium and where they could live, either locally in the town, or a bit more of the high life in Manchester. We were also in the Premier League, the most popular league in the world."

Within weeks of his arrival, Djorkaeff was masterminding Bolton's move away from the drop zone. "Signing him was such a big moment," says Gudni Bergsson, who'd been in the squad since 1995. "That showed the ambition of the club."

By the time the Frenchman returned on a new two-year deal that summer, Allardyce had begun to look for more overseas stars.

"We spent all our time flying into Europe watching players," he recalls. "I remember going to three games in a day in Spain one Sunday – an agent felt it was so important that he put on a private jet for me.

"We signed Ivan Campo, who'd won the league and the Champions League with Real Madrid, but had been bombed out there. All the idiots here called him a clown at first, but he soon turned that around.

"We also got one of the best entertainers in world football."

Jay-Jay Okocha was 28 when he arrived on a free from Paris Saint-Germain, but his debut didn't go well – subbed at half-time at Loftus Road against Fulham, with Bolton 3-1 down.

"In the dressing room it was like he'd seen a cat run over – he was still in shock," says Russell Byrne-Fraser, the club's kit man. "The game passed him by. He was like a rabbit in the headlights and I remember him saying, 'I've got a lot of work to do'. That might have broken a lesser character who could have thought, 'God, what have I done by coming here?'. But he rolled up his sleeves, he was patient and he learned."

Wanderers were rock bottom of the table in November, but by the closing stages of the 2002-03 campaign, Okocha had become one of the Premier League's best players in spearheading the club's rise to safety – the Nigerian netted a brilliant solo goal to beat West Ham, the team that went down instead. If Bolton ever needed to wind the clock down, he'd dazzle with an array of tricks, including a rainbow flick that totally befuddled Arsenal midfielder Ray Parlour.

"It was just joyful," reflects Bergsson, who hung up his boots after Okocha's free-kick helped to seal survival against Middlesbrough on the last day of the season.

The club sold 'Jay-Jay: so good they named him twice' T-shirts, while Campo wigs were

also available. After initially struggling in the centre of defence, the Spaniard's popularity blossomed after he converted to a holding midfield role. A north-west indie band were even named in his honour.

"EL-HADJI DIOUF? ANNOYING..."

In the summer of 2003, more cult heroes joined the fun in the form of Diouf (out of favour at Liverpool), Kevin Davies (released by Southampton) and 5ft 8in winger Stelios.

"I was in my seventh year at Olympiakos and about to win a seventh title," the latter tells *FFT*. "I knew clubs were keen on me – Bolton were less prestigious than the others, not the big club that everyone was dreaming to play for, but they were the most serious. I sensed I was wanted, and also saw they had these big-name players. If they'd gone to play for Bolton, they must have spotted something attractive."

Soon, Stelios saw exactly what they'd seen – a club on the rise, and a collection of stars that were forming a formidable team. That campaign, Bolton reached the League Cup final against Middlesbrough – aided by an overhead cracker from the Greek, plus two stunning free-kicks from Okocha in the semis against Aston Villa – and also finished eighth in the Premier League.

"We had several international players, big characters, players who'd lifted trophies," says Stelios. "They were serious winners and all the big names gelled together."

Allardyce was essential to such unity. "We had players from a lot of different nations, but he created a family environment," former Jamaica international Ricardo Gardner tells *FFT*. "No matter where you were from, once you entered that dressing room we were all in it together."

An unusually large backroom staff paid dividends. "Sam really looked after us," says keeper Jussi Jaaskelainen. "He demanded a lot but had a lot of staff who looked after everything, from daily life to the football pitch. He gave us the best chance to play to a high level week in, week out."

That wider expertise had been part of Allardyce's philosophy from day one. "Having 28 backroom staff, or 32 in the end, was openly criticised at the time," he remembers. "People said, 'Who needs all those staff?' But the analysis group, the psychologist... it was covering every department in football that they talk about now. We had Prozone, which not everyone had then. We even had the first cryotherapy unit in the country.

"We had World Cup winners, Champions League winners, and it was so fascinating listening to them talking about where they'd been and what they'd done – it taught me ▶

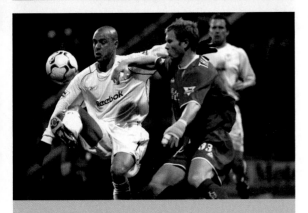

a lot. But they actually said, 'You do a lot of things we've never seen before'."

Bolton's success was also the result of an ingredient that has been crucial for decades – man management. No matter the star, Allardyce could handle them.

"A manager needs to be extremely good in one-to-one management," says Stelios. "This is the difference big managers have – they cope with big personalities on big contracts, they motivate them and inspire them to play well, which isn't easy. Big Sam had that at a very high level."

He was assisted by performance director Mike Forde, later headhunted by Chelsea. "It was about looking at each individual," says Allardyce. "Mike introduced a profile form – there was only one company in America who'd give you feedback on the profile that the players filled in, and that gave us two people. As an individual, we have the way we act in company, but when we're on our own at home, we act differently. Someone might be outspoken and funny, but more reserved when they're at home.

"Instead of having to work out a player's personality yourself, you got an idea of who he was before you even started with him. I'd already done a long interview with them, too – I'd never sign a player without interviewing him on his own, just me and him. Then their profile form helped me to deliver a technique of man management."

Even Diouf, a notoriously difficult player during his controversial career, thrived under Allardyce. "Dioufy was the type of character who'd fill in the profile form and maybe just tick a few boxes – well, that would still be his profile," continues Allardyce. "It would maybe come back as, 'Doesn't quite concentrate enough', 'flamboyant', and that was him on a day-to-day basis – annoying!

"But I had a lot of staff managing all the players, which gave me the time to do what I needed to do. As a manager, your time is only to be spent on the most pressing things for you that day, and when those things are finished, you go home – then you've not got people knocking on the door wanting a piece of your time.

"You can think about ideas you want to put in place – now, next month or even next year. Without that, you're less creative than if you give yourself thinking time and you debate. We'd sit in a hotel for a day with the staff. That was Mike Forde's idea – we'd turn our phones off and talk about the previous three months, what the next three months might look like, and by December or January we'd be looking at what next season looked like."

'RIVALDO? NO THANKS...'

In 2004, the next season briefly looked like it might bring the arrival of Brazil star Rivaldo. The attacker was among several other names – Luis Figo and Dennis Bergkamp included – that Allardyce investigated signing.

"The main one we just missed out on was probably Samuel Eto'o," he says now, of the then Mallorca marksman who was in his early 20s. "Rivaldo was a no from me based

"WHEREVER YOU GO INSIDE MY HOUSE, YOU SEE MEMORABILIA AND PHOTOGRAPHS FROM THAT BOLTON ERA. I WON'T FORGET!"

on our meeting in Manchester. I met him at the Lowry Hotel – that was the first time that the player came to meet us, rather than the other way around. Talking to him, I felt we were being used so it would attract a bigger club, because it got leaked into the press. It didn't seem right, so we moved on."

Rivaldo eventually joined Olympiakos, but Bolton did sign Gary Speed from Newcastle and ex-Real Madrid skipper Fernando Hierro,

BOLTON
WANDERERS

out of contract after leaving Qatari outfit Al Rayyan. Speed, who won the league with Leeds in 1992, was a model of consistency; 36-year-old Hierro, just like Campo, turned from struggling centre-back to a Rolls-Royce of a midfielder.

Both moved the team up to another level, combining with Okocha and Kevin Nolan to help Bolton remarkably challenge Everton and Liverpool for a place among the top four. They ended up in sixth, level on points with Rafa Benitez's Reds in the year they won the 2004-05 Champions League.

Hierro retired after a home win over Everton on the last day of the season, and received a standing ovation by both Bolton fans and a number of visiting Real Madrid supporters when he was substituted – only to be shoved off the pitch by an irritated Duncan Ferguson who was keen to get on with the game.

Sixth meant a place in the UEFA Cup – the first time Bolton had ever qualified for Europe. It was also enough to attract interest in the club's stars, including Stelios, who'd won Euro 2004 as a Bolton player and was wanted by Liverpool and Manchester City.

"City weren't the team they are now – they were at the same level as us, so I didn't even think to leave Bolton for them," he says. "The only situation was Liverpool, but eventually it didn't happen because it wasn't in my hands, and Bolton gave me an amazing offer to renew my contract. I was more than happy to do that, and stayed for another three years."

Clockwise from above Liverpool get bit by old boy Dioufy; Anelka shone at Bolton; "I can't wait to play with Nicky Hunt"; Hierro's farewell in 2005

He would help Bolton reach the last 32 of the 2005-06 UEFA Cup, as they emerged unbeaten from a group containing Sevilla, Zenit and Besiktas.

Not all of Bolton's signings worked – Mario Jardel joined out of shape and never scored a Premier League goal, while Japanese icon Hidetoshi Nakata started 14 league games before retiring at the end of his season-long loan from Fiorentina, aged 29.

But Allardyce's success rate was impressive. In 2006, Bolton paid a club-record £8m to sign a 27-year-old Nicolas Anelka, who was viewed as being on the way down following a spell at Fenerbahce. "Nicolas was the icing on the cake because he guaranteed goals, the one thing we were missing at the time," explains Allardyce.

Nicknamed 'Le Sulk', Anelka was a world removed from his reputation. "We never had a problem with him," says Byrne-Fraser. "I'd met him before, when he filmed a Reebok commercial at our ground. Two weeks later, I was walking through Manchester and saw him in a jewellers – he came rushing out to see me, rather than the other way around, which I was blown away by. I thought, 'What a nice guy'. I never found him any other way – I'm still in touch with him now."

With the Frenchman on fire, the Trotters sat third in January, behind only Manchester United and Chelsea. Allardyce was hoping for funds to push for the Champions League spots – instead, he could only sign free agent midfielder David Thompson. Bolton fell away.

They were sixth with three matches to go – out of Champions League contention but on the verge of another season in the UEFA Cup – when news emerged that Allardyce was about to quit, frustrated the club's ambition no longer matched his own.

Fittingly, Wanderers drew 2-2 at Jose Mourinho's Chelsea hours later, in Big Sam's last match in charge. His team had developed a habit of surprising the big boys – during Allardyce's reign, Bolton also won at Stamford Bridge, triumphed at Old Trafford two seasons in succession, and earned four victories each over Arsenal and Liverpool.

"There was a cost to upsetting the big boys,

though, which was rather sad," remembers Allardyce. "People called us a long-ball side, despite all the great players we had. I should have slaughtered them for even suggesting it. They were making excuses to cover their deficiencies. Rarely would a manager give us credit if we beat them."

Without Allardyce, Bolton reached the last 16 of the 2007-08 UEFA Cup, drawing 2-2 at Bayern Munich and beating Atletico Madrid under Gary Megson, but the club slipped into a Premier League relegation battle. Anelka was sold to Chelsea. The great era was over.

The memories live on, though, and were rekindled recently when a number of stars returned for a charity match. Allardyce and Okocha jigged on the touchline, just as they had done after Bolton avoided relegation in 2003. "He's a top bloke, and we had a little dance together again," smiles Allardyce. "My time as Bolton manager was my greatest achievement, without a doubt. It was a great journey – simply fantastic."

The feeling is mutual for the overseas stars who helped to make it all happen. "If you come to my house in Greece, you'll see how special my time at Bolton was to my whole life," says Stelios. "Wherever you go, you see memorabilia and photographs from that era – even if you want to forget, you can't!

"Bolton felt like my second home, and I still feel that now because I live back in the area with my family – this is our second year since we returned, and every time I drive past the stadium, I remember all the great moments we had. No matter how many years pass, I'll always feel the same."

Djorkaeff's arrival to Allardyce's departure was just five years. For everyone involved, it's an era that will be cherished for a lifetime. ⊙

A number of former stars returned to Bolton recently for a charity match to raise money for the mother of current player Gethin Jones, who has motor neurone disease. Funds were also raised for the Darby Rimmer Foundation, set up by ex-Bolton and Liverpool defender Stephen Darby, who's battling the same illness. For details and donations, visit *justgiving.com/crowdfunding/karen-jonesmnd* and *darbyrimmermnd.co.uk*

NAKATA
16

FourFourTwo.com Annual 2023 **131**

HEROES & VILLANS

In February 1982, Aston Villa's greatest manager Ron Saunders resigned. Within four months, the Villans stunned Bayern Munich to become European champions – and now, 40 years on, their heroes tell *FFT* how. Just don't read over dinner...

Words Mat Kendrick

"We were a very close squad, and we had to be — we only had three toilet seats..."

Aston Villa were in the quarter-finals of the European Cup when their finest ever team found themselves passing round in-demand bits of their hotel bogs.

Tony Morley bursts into laughter as he recalls a European adventure a long way from the glitz and glamour of today's Champions League extravaganzas. Transported back to that last-eight clash at Dynamo Kyiv in March 1982, Villa's top scorer in their historic march to glory describes a hotel so grotty that the lavatory seats were in short supply.

Villa's squad moved a handful of circular sit-upons from room to room, sharing them with the care and attention they'd usually reserve for passing a football. And don't get Morley started on the "f**king chicken soup", or the bread roll his close friend Gordon 'Sid' Cowans dared to break open.

"It was a disgrace," Morley grins in mock rage. "It was hot water poured over a raw chicken. I thought it was going to fly off my plate. I'd been all around the world eating meals with Sid, but not that one. I remember him saying, 'I'm not eating that, I'll just have a roll'. True story: he then opened his roll and a cockroach was in the middle of it. I yelled, 'Eat it quickly before it runs away!'"

Ultimately, Villa's 1981-82 tour of Europe would conclude with captain Dennis Mortimer getting his hands on the only souvenir Aston Villa coveted from their continental trips. That was just as well – these were certainly no sight-seeing city breaks.

"If anyone went behind the Iron Curtain in those days, they'd quickly want to come out," says Mortimer. "When we went to Berlin and Kyiv, there was one colour – monochrome. It was bland and that's all we saw. It was so abysmal to the eye that we wanted to get out of there as soon as possible."

Villa supporters were sadly used to seeing things in black and white, though: until Ron Saunders' revolution of the 1970s and early '80s, all the Midlanders' former glories were more sepia-tinted than beautiful multicolour. Even now, Villa's most recent FA Cup triumph dates back to 1957; until Saunders, they'd failed to rule the land since six pre-war league titles – and we're talking the First World War ▶

here. But everything changed when an out-of-work bloke from Birkenhead arrived on June 5, 1974. Toilet seats and cockroaches were all the rage...

BARTON'S ARMY

That Villa Park is still without a statue of Ron Saunders can only be down to a four-decade shortage of granite as hard as the iconic late Villa boss. There can be no other reasonable explanation for why the club's greatest ever manager, who passed away aged 87 back in December 2019, hasn't been immortalised properly before now.

In his first season in 1974-75, Saunders set the tone by leading Villa – a third-tier side as recently as three years earlier – to promotion from the Second Division, plus League Cup glory at Wembley. It was his third consecutive appearance in that showpiece with as many clubs... but the first time he'd tasted success. By season three in 1976-77, Saunders had added another League Cup and set about establishing Villa in the top half – a position they would occupy throughout his tenure.

His place in club folklore was complete when the squad he painstakingly created won the 1980-81 First Division championship. "Do you want to bet against us?" are the seven words forever etched on his footballing epitaph, summing up his unwavering belief in the underdogs who edged out title rivals Ipswich against the odds.

So far, so great. Until February 9, 1982, that is, when Saunders stormed out of Villa after a bust-up with the board over transfers and his own contract. Birmingham's biggest twist since the Spaghetti Junction continued as he rocked up 3.4 miles down the road at Villa's fierce second city foes just over a week later.

"I almost fell off my chair," central defender Allan Evans tells *FFT*. "He'd had problems with the board, but Ron was very strong and you expected him to carry on going. It must have taken something dramatic to walk away at that stage of the season. It was a big shock to everybody. I was in the dark and thought, 'What's going to happen now?'"

By then, Villa's league form had stumbled. After triumphing in '81 with just 14 players, including seven ever-presents, injuries finally caught up with them during the following season's title defence – when Saunders left, they were 15th in the table. Still, there was the small matter of the European Cup to have a go at. Saunders was a man of principles, but must have considered the extra eminence he was potentially sacrificing.

His stubbornness was both a blessing and a curse for the Villans – a curse because the uncompromising son of a Liverpool docker was no longer around to finish what he had started; a blessing because his authoritarian intransigence had left behind a supremely talented group with an unshakeable belief in themselves and each other.

Despite reeling from the manager's exit, chairman Ron Bendall recognised Saunders' continued legacy within the dressing room – a realisation resulting in the masterstroke appointment of Tony Barton as his successor.

Shifting from unassuming assistant to team boss was straightforward enough for Barton, whose total lack of ego allowed his simple approach to flourish.

"Tony didn't come straight in and give us any ultimatums," explains Mortimer. "We all knew him anyway. He just needed to guide us. We didn't need a new manager coming in and taking over – we were in charge of us. Our destiny was in our hands. The greatest tribute we can pay Tony is that he kept things simple, trusted us and we repaid it."

Barton, who'd been at Villa since reuniting with his old Portsmouth team-mate Saunders in late 1975, was more than a fly-by-night Roberto Di Matteo at Chelsea type of interim, mind. Sticking around as gaffer for two years and four months, on top of the European Cup victory, the softly-spoken manager's stint also included a famous European Super Cup win over Barcelona.

Rather than imposing himself on a well-drilled dressing room of champions, Barton was selfless and savvy enough to ensure that most Saunders hallmarks remained – including defensive parsimony. Villa's title success had been built on conceding just 40 goals in 42 games, and their European Cup exploits followed similar meanness. In their nine-game march to glory in '82, Villa kept seven clean sheets. No team has conceded fewer than Villa's two in lifting Ol' Big Ears.

A series of two-legged aggregate wins began with a 7-0 rout of Icelandic side Valur, before Villa progressed on away goals after an anxious 2-2 draw against Dynamo Berlin. After Saunders left, they beat Dynamo Kyiv 2-0 in the quarter-finals and then Anderlecht by a single goal in the semis. The second leg in Brussels was marred by crowd trouble with a glut of arrests, prompting genuine fears that sanctions might include Villa's expulsion from the European Cup final.

Clockwise from top "Who thinks Withey shinned it?"; Spink steps up to replace an injured Rimmer; Saunders laid the foundations for Euro success

"The newspapers are all full of Villa possibly being bounced out of the tournament," wrote Colin Abbott in *Barton's Army: Conquering Europe with Aston Villa*, a gripping fan account of the 1981-82 adventure. "In time, we find out the punishment meted out: a fine and a behind-closed-doors fixture the next time we are in Europe. The relief is immense. I'd set my mind on going if we reached the final from the get-go. And I will."

MAKING PLANS FOR NIGEL

Abbott travelled to Rotterdam with another 12,000 or so Villa fanatics, who witnessed history being made as their side beat Bayern Munich 1-0 at De Kuip on May 26, 1982. "The final wasn't much of a spectacle – there were two events," continues Mortimer, referring to the surprise introduction of rookie goalkeeper Nigel Spink on just nine minutes, and Peter Withe's 67th-minute winner.

Spink, summoned from the sidelines when Jimmy Rimmer succumbed to a neck injury, went on to produce a match-saving display against the German behemoths, stepping out from the oblivion of one past senior outing two and a half years earlier to achieve lifelong notoriety. "If you're watching mum, this is the best day of my life," he grinned ecstatically into a television camera after making a string of vital stops, his favourite being a second-half dive to deny Bernd Durnberger.

"Spinksy had an absolute blinder," chuckles midfield playmaker Cowans. "He played very well and kept us in the game," agrees Morley, insisting squad players such as Spinks were so well-rehearsed in training that deputising was (ahem) "like putting on a glove".

The most memorable moment was Withe's second-half clincher. A banner quoting Brian Moore's commentary from the ITV coverage still takes pride of place on the North Stand

at Villa Park: "Shaw... Williams prepared to venture down the left... There's a good ball played in for Tony Morley... Oh, it must be. And it is! Peter Withe!"

"People always say it bounced up and hit Withey's shin," grins Mortimer. "God, I wish I'd have scored it."

Withe reiterates for the umpteenth time it definitely, absolutely, without a shadow of a doubt did not come off his shin. "It hit a divot and shot off at a right-angle!" he protests to *FFT*. "But the more you watch it, the more you see that it wasn't off my shin. I made good contact. Jimmy Greaves asked how I managed to hit the post from there – I told him I was trying to play a one-two but the net stopped it coming back!"

Morley, however, remains unconvinced, insisting, "It's the luckiest goal he ever scored and the most important in Villa's history. If he meant that with his right foot, it would've gone over the bar! He just stuck his leg out and it went in," he smiles, before adding with a wink, "It was a very good cross, though..."

Taking the piss clearly comes more easily for Morley than it did for both Withe and Ken McNaught, whose participation in the post-

Above Spink becomes the unlikely hero with a string of super saves **Below** Withe scores what proves to be Villa's winner

game festivities was delayed by a protracted drugs test. Fortunately, the duo started their own party to speed up their urine samples. Marched off to a little caravan under a stand, Withe and McNaught were plonked opposite Bayern opponents Klaus Augenthaler and Wolfgang Dremmler when officials produced a receptacle big enough to display flowers in, let alone store their pee.

Withe spotted a stadium worker clutching a crate of beer destined for the Villa dressing room. Pointing to the lion on his club crest, the match-winner convinced him to hand it over. The Bayern players declined his offer of a drink with him.

"I sunk mine and then headed back to an empty changing room," recalls Withe.

"There was no one left except Jim Paul the kitman, who gave me a bottle of champagne. The bath still had water in it, so I climbed in. I remember thinking, 'We've won one of the world's biggest competitions and I'm sitting here drinking on my own'.

"Before we know it, Jim comes back to tell us that if we're not ready in 10 minutes, the coach will go without us!"

Villa's sixty and seventysomethings are in their element as they remember how they celebrated, sniggering like schoolboys as they describe the pranks, calamities and slapstick moments that soon followed. Distinguished gentlemen of their vintage probably should know better, but their everyman appeal is rooted in the fact that they absolutely don't.

Many of the stories – rehearsed, possibly slightly misremembered or even embellished over the decades – involve the trophy itself. Momentarily losing it on the team bus and discovering Withe had stowed it in the toilet for safekeeping, for example; Mortimer trying to fill it with eight bottles of bubbly at their Amsterdam afterparty before realising it was too heavy to drink from; Cowans calling the police to retrieve it after the prize was stolen from a Midlands pub while he was boozing with fans at the bar. Morley can't contain his delight when he pictures Cowans scrabbling around on his hands and knees after their plane home touched down on the tarmac at East Midlands Airport.

"He's horrible isn't he?" eye-rolls Cowans. "I was on the plane trying to find my medal. I thought I'd lost it and there's him [Morley] sat there with a big grin on his face."

"Careful, careful," says Morley, still laughing his head off all these years on. "He lost it – it fell out of his pocket!"

"Hold on a minute, *it fell out of my pocket?!*" says Cowans. "He put his hand in my pocket. So he'd nicked it and I was in bits." ▶

"IT'S THE LUCKIEST GOAL WITHEY SCORED AND THE MOST IMPORTANT IN VILLA HISTORY – HE STUCK HIS LEG OUT AND IT WENT IN"

"ONE MAN F**KED IT"

It's no wonder that Villa's players still cherish their club mementoes so much. The 12 who played in the Rotterdam showpiece were only awarded 34 caps between them: Withe (11), Cowans (10), Morley (six), Rimmer and Spink (both one-cap wonder keepers who earned 45-minute cameos) account for the majority of them with England, while Evans (four) and Des Bremner (one) got theirs for Scotland. But captain Mortimer, golden boy Gary Shaw and Kenny Swain were completely overlooked for senior Three Lions honours, as were Gary Williams and McNaught north of the border.

But that didn't stop them doing their bit for England. Extending the country's European Cup stranglehold into a sixth campaign was a major motivator for Villa after Liverpool's trio of victories in 1977, 1978 and 1981, and Nottingham Forest's back-to-back double in between. Not that fans on Merseyside were particularly impressed when Morley showed off the trophy at his local pub in Ormskirk. "Typical Liverpool supporters – 'We've already seen that three times', they went," he recalls. "Shut up will you, lads?"

Back then, Villa's squad was more Scouse than the cast of *Brookside*. Saunders' troops included a quintet who started the 1982 final: Morley, Mortimer, Withe, Rimmer and Swain. Morley's allegiances lie in the blue half of Liverpool, but the proud Toffee reckons Villa should have challenged his boyhood team for mid-80s dominance. Instead, Everton won

the First Division championship in 1986-87 while Villa finished bottom. By then, Howard Kendall's charges had already captured the league title and European Cup Winners' Cup in 1985, plus the 1984 FA Cup.

"Everton went and won everything," reflects Morley. "But man for man I think we were far better. Villa could have had a similar thing to Manchester United when Gary Neville, Ryan Giggs and David Beckham went in with great

Top to bottom
"Hi there, this is Captain Mortimer speaking"; boss Barton steadied the Villans' ship; "Hey, will eight bottles of bubbly fit in this thing?"

players like Steve Bruce and Bryan Robson – we had the chance to become a superclub and it was lost.

"I'm gutted because I'm a selfish footballer. I wanted another couple of trophies in my cabinet – an FA Cup or another league title. We'll never know now. We had a platform, and a foundation... but one man f**ked it."

Which man could he possibly mean? "Doug Ellis destroyed it," confirms Cowans.

'Deadly Doug' had been on a three-year hiatus from chairing Villa during the finest glory years the club has ever known. "That really stuck in his craw," ex-club secretary Steve Stride would later tell the *Birmingham Mail*. "He didn't give that period in the club's history the attention it deserved and tried to move on from it."

By the time Villa humiliatingly tumbled out of the top flight, just five years on from their finest hour, only a handful of European Cup winners remained. Instead, Ellis put his own name on a stand at Villa Park in 1994.

Forty years on from the club's halcyon days, a paltry two League Cups in the mid-90s have been added to an increasingly musty trophy cabinet. As the anniversary arrives, by neat coincidence Villa are now entrusting their immediate future to a European Cup-winning Scouser born in the early '80s.

"When Steven Gerrard took over, people were saying he's using it as a stepping stone to go to Liverpool," says Withe. "I don't look at it that way. He's been given an opportunity to manage in the Premier League and it's not just any team. Aston Villa are a big club.

"Knowing Steven, he'll want to win things. He knows what's happened here in the past and he'll be reminded of it more than ever this year with all the celebrations. He's used to winning in his playing career at Liverpool and as Rangers manager. It's in his nature. If you don't dream about winning trophies, then you shouldn't be managing Aston Villa."

House of Fun was at No.1 when Villa lifted the European Cup in May 1982. No matter how well Gerrard does, it's Madness to think there will ever be a cover version anywhere near as good as the original. ✪

"VILLA COULD HAVE HAD A SIMILAR THING TO MAN UNITED AND GONE ON TO BECOME A SUPERCLUB, BUT THAT CHANCE WAS LOST"

DISCOVER THE BEST OF WOMEN'S FOOTBALL WITH OUR ESSENTIAL GUIDE

Packed with in-depth features on the USWNT, LGBTQ+ inclusivity, the rise of Ada Hegerberg, the 50 greatest female players ever, and more, plus exclusive interviews from the *FFT* archives with the likes of Marta and Megan Rapinoe, this is a must-have for fans of the beautiful game

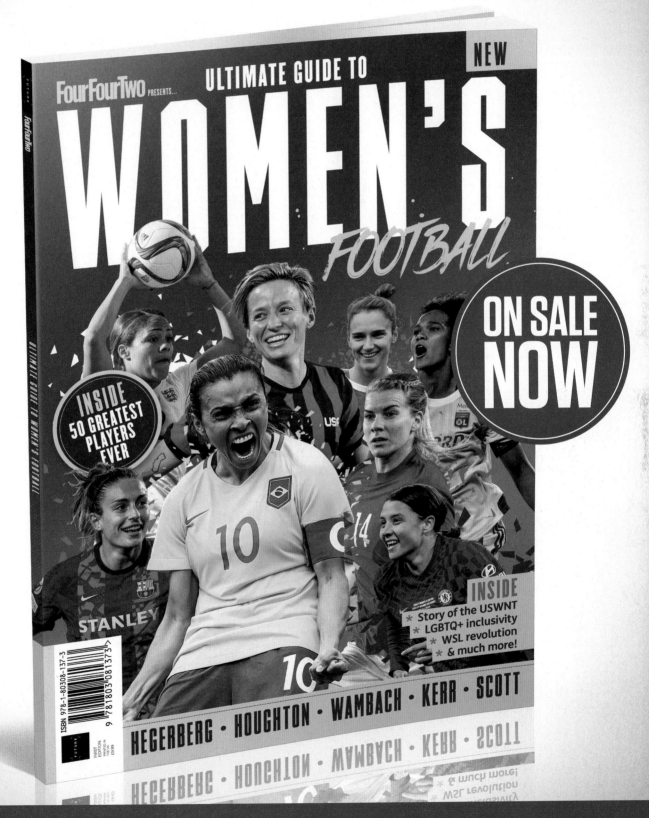

"GETTING RECOGNISED BY ENGLAND, SCORING GOALS AT CLUB LEVEL, WINNING TROPHIES... WOW. IT WAS THE TIME OF MY LIFE"

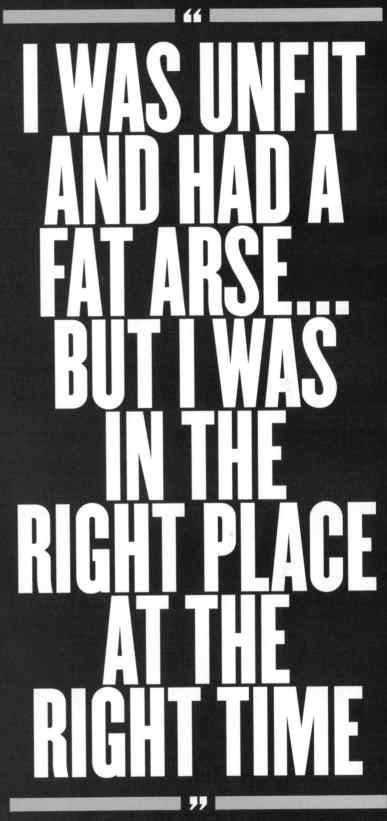

" I WAS UNFIT AND HAD A FAT ARSE... BUT I WAS IN THE RIGHT PLACE AT THE RIGHT TIME "

Sir Geoff Hurst provided English football with its greatest day, scoring a hat-trick in the 1966 World Cup Final – but how did he get there in the first place? And why did he anger a bloke while doing insurance sales later? *FFT* chats to the Three Lions legend himself...

Words Leo Moynihan

Less than an hour before we're due to speak to Sir Geoff Hurst, an email arrives informing us that he's having problems with his Zoom, and instead could we simply have our chat over the phone? We've all been there. Who over the last two years hasn't screamed in frustration at some online video conferencing malfunction? So, maybe he's just like all of us. Maybe, Sir Geoff *is* an everyman after all.

Let's face it, though: he's not, is he? Sir Geoff Hurst is unique. In almost one hundred years of World Cup football, Hurst's two feet and forehead remain the only part of any man's anatomy to have conjured up a hat-trick in a final. The England icon turned 80 in December, but he remains sharp, warm and friendly – normal, even.

But there's no escaping it: Hurst's seismic feats on that July afternoon at Wembley in 1966 continue to give him exclusivity when it comes to world football's greatest event. It's a day that defined life as he knew it forever, and continues to define English football to this day. How's that for a legacy?

HOWZAT, RON?

It's hard to imagine plain old Geoff Hurst before July 1966 – the hardworking and talented, but much less lauded striker in Alf Ramsey's squad.

But that's exactly what he was. With only five international caps in his collection going into the tournament, and up against scoring stalwarts in Jimmy Greaves and Roger Hunt, there was no reason for a 24-year-old Hurst to feel any strain of expectation.

"That's true," he tells *FFT*. "There wasn't any pressure because frankly, I didn't even expect to play in the first place..."

Hurst was born into the game of football, but a world away from global gongs and the royal honours list. His father Charlie was a pro before him; a centre-half who plied his trade in the lower leagues at Bristol Rovers, Oldham and Rochdale, before moving the family to Essex when Geoff was six for a stint at non-league Chelmsford City.

Like many post-war boys, a young Hurst alleviated the effects of rationing and the leftover rubble of conflict with an obsession for sport. His father's profession ensured that a football was never far from his toes, but there was also a love for cricket which might well have curtailed his – and his country's – footballing destiny. Having joined West Ham at 15, playing as a centre-half or midfielder, Hurst's fondness for the whites and willow almost knocked his other ambitions for six.

"I enjoyed playing for the Essex second XI," the former striker remembers. "It was football in the winter and cricket in the summer, but looking back, during my early days at West Ham it was detrimental to me being a success in football. I'd miss most of pre-season and my fitness wasn't right.

"In the 1962-63 season, I was struggling in the reserves. Ron Greenwood [West Ham's manager] came over to me one day – I was expecting a bollocking because I was clearly not fit. Instead, he told me, 'We're playing Liverpool tonight, we've just sold our forward and I want to try you upfront'. I gave it a go, we won 1-0, I played OK, my shorts looked like they'd been dipped in water because of my unfit fat arse, but I played the rest of the season as a striker and scored 15 goals. Once that happened, football took over and the cricket was out the window."

Hurst puts much of his achievements down to chance, but it seems as though his road was destined to reach Wembley in July 1966. "Right place, right time," he says with a shrug – but despite a feeling of inevitability, those who were watching over him, teaching him from a young age, were in fact shaping that famous summer afternoon's events.

First of all, there was his dad. "He always encouraged me to use my left foot, and we'd practise again and again on it," Hurst recalls. "And I guess you could say that came in useful with [England's] fourth goal in '66."

And then there was Greenwood at West Ham, a forward-thinking coach who was pulling his players towards modernity. After he replaced Ted Fenton in 1961, Greenwood didn't just inspire unprecedented success at Upton Park – he also laid the foundations for England's greatest day.

"Ron coming to West Ham was a blessing," Hurst says. "He came in and one of the first things he did was to take the running spikes away from us, as we used to do all of our sprints in them. That shocked us as we'd grown up with them, but his emphasis was more on the ball."

Old-fashioned work was out, then – but silverware was soon in. First came the FA Cup in 1964, followed a year later by the Cup Winners' Cup with victory over West German side 1860 Munich. Both games were won at Wembley, each with a champagne style of football that would in time earn its very own moniker: 'The West Ham Way'.

Integral to its end product was Hurst. After 25 goals in 1963-64, another 20 arrived the following campaign... but still no England cap. If Ramsey was looking for more from his frontmen – quite reasonably, given that Greaves and Hunt had struck a combined 141 goals across those two campaigns – then he certainly got it as his Three Lions geared up for World Cup duty. In 1965-66, Hurst managed 40 goals for West Ham in all competitions; by February, it had been enough for Ramsey to hand him his first cap – against West Germany, naturally – in the same month Greaves made his long-awaited comeback for Tottenham following a nasty bout of hepatitis.

"That was a great time to be playing the game, the swinging sixties," Hurst recalls. "We'd recovered from the war, the crowds at games were huge, there were very attacking matches and the world was changing. It was an unbelievably brilliant time.

"For me, scoring goals at club level, getting recognised by England, playing at a club with great players and winning trophies... Wow. It was the time of my life."

Left At West Ham, Hurst's – and England's – destiny was being shaped

The likes of Hurst, fellow Hammers Bobby Moore and Martin Peters might have been enjoying themselves on and off the field, but day by day, training session by training session, they were also being schooled by Greenwood – a man who knew where the game of football was heading.

"He was an exceptional coach," Hurst says. "Ron knew so much and he always wanted to innovate. In terms of my own game, when I asked him why he'd moved me upfront, he simply said that in me, he saw a player who liked getting forward but didn't like getting back quite so much…"

It was a trait that might have been tagged to West Ham's team as a whole, however. Hurst believes that with the emphasis so heavily on attacking football, league titles were never really on the cards.

"It's true that we became more of a cup team," he explains. "Ron was all about attack and that maybe cost us in terms of the consistency needed to win the title, but there was no doubt he was changing the game – things like taking quick free-kicks and the near-post cross. Ron invented the near-post cross… and of course, both would benefit England."

Below Plain old Geoff Hurst gets a taste of winning at Wembley in the 1964 FA Cup Final

JIMMY'S IN STITCHES

There were six days between England's final warm-up game and the opening match of the 1966 World Cup at Wembley. For Three Lions players, they were six days to wonder about Ramsey's preferred starting line-up.

But while many may have been on edge, Hurst was armed with a calming sense of serenity. England had played four warm-up matches in 10 days approaching their home tournament, on a tour of Scandinavia and Eastern Europe, but Hurst hadn't scored in either of his two starts. The fact that Ramsey had handed him and Greaves the squad numbers (10 and 8 respectively) they played with at club level may have raised his hopes, but such was No.21 Roger Hunt's form that it came as no surprise when Ramsey selected the Liverpool man to partner Greaves in England's opening fixture – and indeed all three of their group tussles.

"I sat on the sidelines for that first game against Uruguay," Hurst remembers, "and was just so happy to be there. Roger and Jimmy were exceptional and had played better than me in the warm-up games, so that was that. The opposition had no intent to attack at all [in the first match], so it was a frustrating 0-0, but I hadn't realised until I watched that game again recently just how loud the booing was from the England fans."

Such reactions were never going to shift Ramsey's focus. He'd predicted English glory that summer, and an early hiccup wasn't going to damage the team ethic he'd worked so hard to instil within his squad.

"Alf honed us into a fighting machine," Hurst says. "He got rid of players who didn't want to be part of the group mentality, and the best thing he did was pick those who could fit into and complement his system. Before Alf, selectors simply picked the best players, but just picking the best player in each position doesn't always work.

"Alf knew that. He built a team. Take big Jack [Charlton]. He was picked quite late in his career and later confronted Alf. Why had he picked him then, at 30 years old? But Alf said he wasn't interested in who was the best centre-half, he was only interested in who worked best alongside Bobby [Moore]. Jack proved that it was him."

When the word 'camaraderie' comes up in conversation, Hurst is onto it with all the eagerness that he used to greet inviting ▶

"RON WAS ALL ABOUT ATTACK AND MAYBE THAT COST US IN TERMS OF THE CONSISTENCY WE NEEDED TO WIN THE TITLE"

through-balls. "You can write 'camaraderie' 10 times," Hurst says. "That's what it was all about. We were such a tight group. Alf would use club relationships on the pitch, but he made sure that there were no cliques – not like more recent England squads when some players wouldn't mix. Our spirit was our big strength… and we'd need it."

Soon, with the group stage successfully manoeuvred after wins over Mexico and whipping boys France, Ramsey would also need his squad. During the final group game against Les Bleus, Greaves had his shin raked by the studs of midfielder Joseph Bonnel, opening it up "like a red rose towards the end of its bloom," as the late striker would write. Despite a goalless start for Greaves, England were loath to lose the man whose boots were supposed to fire them to victory – he'd miss at least two matches.

"That squad had five world-class players," Hurst says. "The spine of the team: Gordon Banks, Bobby Moore, Bobby Charlton, Jimmy Greaves – and I'd add Ray Wilson to that at left-back. The rest of us were all hard-nosed professionals, tough and picked to fit in."

Hurst would do just that. While Greaves's ability to snaffle opportunities couldn't be bettered, the partnership between Hunt and Hurst offered England what Ramsey cherished most: industry. Both accomplished finishers themselves, it was their readiness to stretch defences which created space for Bobby Charlton, as his two goals in the semi-finals against Portugal aptly proved.

The quarter-final had been won against a robust Argentina, in a tight and infamously dirty game – but crucially, one settled by a Hurst goal sculptured at West Ham. With the skilful but ill-disciplined Argentines down to 10 men after the dismissal of their skipper Antonio Rattin, England's breakthrough came when Peters took possession on the left wing, looked up and spotted Hurst's run

to the near post. With the South Americans flat-footed, Hurst expertly glanced Peters' cross into the net.

Greaves admitted that he knew Ramsey couldn't change a winning team for the final, and as calmly as Hurst had taken to missing out at the start of the tournament, he was just as unruffled when picked.

"That's football and Jimmy understood that," Hurst says. "I couldn't dwell on it. Chances come along and you have to be ready to take them. Injuries are part and parcel of the game, and there was never an issue between me and Jimmy. We never discussed it. I couldn't even tell you if he was fit enough to play in the final. You move on."

SAY A LITTLE PRAYER

July 30, 1966 was the day that football *did* come home. With Baddiel and Skinner still wearing short trousers, there was no aching soundtrack; no more years of hurt. No need for dreaming.

It's the day everyone thinks of when they see Hurst – the day he's had to talk about more than any other for over 56 years. To a hurting nation, it has become an occasion of near-mythical importance, but listening to Hurst, there's a simplicity about that World Cup final that ultimately won it for England.

"It was business as usual," he says. "Ron had drilled into us at West Ham to prepare for a big game like it was any other. I had an appetite: we ate eggs on toast, some fish maybe, and then just relaxed. I know that Nobby [Stiles] went to find a Catholic church in Golders Green, which is a very Jewish area. He made a prayer somewhere. But other than that, it was business as usual."

And that was key. Hurst clattered West Germany keeper Hans Tilkowski early doors, but when the visitors sought revenge by going 1-0 up inside only 12 minutes, there

was no panic. Six minutes later, England were level through another goal perfected at West Ham: Greenwood's love of a quick free-kick caught the Germans flat, as Moore's deep delivery was met by Hurst's head.

That's how the score remained until late on. It took until the 78th minute for Peters to nab England's second goal, after latching on to a scrappy deflection from Hurst's shot outside the box – but what looked to have been the winning goal was then cruelly cancelled out by Wolfgang Weber's bundled equaliser with only a minute left. That might have flattened lesser teams – instead, going into extra time, England simply went again.

"We were so strong," Hurst recalls. "They were two very hard hours, but it came back to our preparation. We'd worked so hard with 28 players, before getting the squad down to 22. Even a workhorse like Nobby Stiles talked about how physically tough and aggressive training was. We played friendlies against each other and it was tough – I mean, it got physical. People were trying to impress, trying to get noticed, trying to get picked for a World Cup squad, so no prisoners were taken. I think that kind of mentality proved vital for the final itself."

Socks rolled around cramped calves, but England pinned the Germans back before the perpetual Alan Ball fed Hurst. You know what happened next: his right-footed shot struck the crossbar and cannoned down, supposedly behind the goal-line. "Goal!" screamed the onrushing Hunt.

"Of course, it was controversial, but Roger's response and his instinct was enough for me," Hurst shrugs. "I've spoken to Franz Beckenbauer since and he acknowledges that we were the better team on the day.

"We also proved that this was no flash in the pan – even four years later in Mexico, we were the team to beat. Had Gordon played in goal against Germany, I think we would have

Below Hurst took his chance with a glancing header against Argentina

reached the final and given Brazil another close game. That said, I was pleased to score the fourth goal, just to settle it..."

That strike today is as much a part of the nation's psyche as a Shakespearean speech, or the bongs of Big Ben: the commentary of Kenneth Wolstenholme, that red ball striking the white net. *It is now.* For Hurst, though, his golden moment stemmed from a rather less romantic place.

"As I received the ball, I saw the whistle was in the ref's mouth and knew the game was close to ending," he says. "So I thought, 'Just hit it hard, and if it misses then that's just more time wasted'.

"What's funny about it, though, is that Bobby [Moore] had no such thoughts when he coolly made that goal. Last minute, one goal in it, and Bobby chests the ball in his own box, plays a pass in his defensive third – which at that point is criminal – gets it back, dribbles and then plays the perfect ball to me. Now, I was used to that, but you should have heard Jack screaming, 'F**KING CLEAR IT!' Bobby didn't ever just clear it."

Above Did it cross the line? "Roger [Hunt]'s response was enough for me," says Sir Geoff

With a combination of finesse and hard graft, English football had its day – and Hurst's life would never be the same again. He continued to score goals regularly at West Ham (so much that Matt Busby at Manchester United offered Greenwood £200,000 for his services, only to receive a telegram that simply read, "No thanks"), before leaving in 1972 for Stoke, where he continued to find the net.

His life after playing began in the dugout. When talk turns to just how close he came to winning promotion for Chelsea in 1980, in Hurst's first year in charge, you sense an itch that was never fully scratched.

"Oh, don't!" he laughs. "The club was in difficulty when I took over, but without any money we almost got up. Mike Fillery at Swansea, he shaved the post with a header that would have clinched it. Astonishing."

Hurst was sacked the year after, and apart from a brief spell managing in the Middle East, he began to enjoy life outside of the game that had consumed him for 25 years – even if his next move seems hard to fathom.

"I realised I could make as much money away from the game, so eventually got into insurance – although learning to sell had its challenges," Hurst remembers. "One of my first lessons involved opening the phonebook and randomly cold calling a number, trying to sell them the product. This woman answered the phone and I said my bit: 'My name is Geoff Hurst...' She explained that her husband dealt with those things and put him on the phone. 'I gather you say you're Geoff Hurst,' he said. 'That's correct,' I said. 'If you're Geoff Hurst, I'm bloody Marilyn Monroe' – and then he put the phone down."

Over five and a half decades have passed since Hurst scored his fabled treble, but he and his team-mates that day (of which only two more of the 11, George Cohen and Sir Bobby Charlton, sadly remain) continue to offer English football its greatest moment.

While those of a certain vintage purred over Marilyn Monroe's peroxide blonde locks and red lips, football fans of that era instead hold Bobby's combover, Nobby's toothless smile and Hurst's hat-trick in a very similar reverence. Three of the best from England's only man. ⊙

'Eighty at Eighty: An A to Z of Masters from Ali to Zidane', by Sir Geoff Hurst with Norman Giller, is out now via Pitch Publishing (£19.99)

MORE ON FOURFOURTWO.COM

• Was England's 1966 winning XI destiny, fate, or a chance affair? *(by Paul Simpson)*

• The 1966 World Cup was fixed... and 27 other bonkers football conspiracy theories (by Greg Lea)

• The best footballers in the world... in 1966. Who comes top? *(by Paul Simpson)*

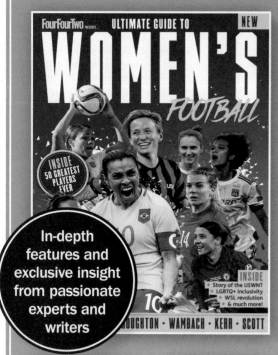

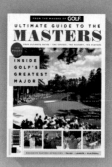

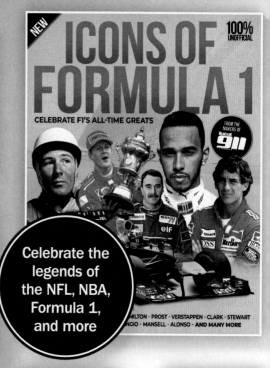

Get great savings when you buy direct from us

1000s of great titles, many not available anywhere else

World-wide delivery and super-safe ordering

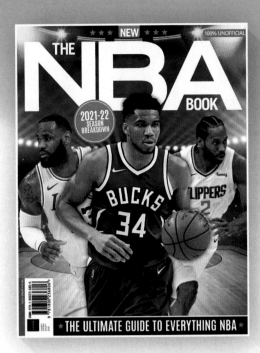

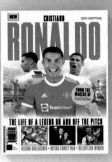

SUBSCRIBE & SAVE UP TO 61%

Delivered direct to your door or straight to your device

Choose from over 80 magazines and make great savings off the store price!

Binders, books and back issues also available

Simply visit www.magazinesdirect.com

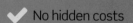 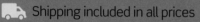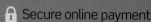